Japan – Change and Continuity

Japan is currently undergoing many interesting changes, which the Japanese government trumpets as fundamental reform, but which some observers suspect will turn out to be superficial, part of a long sequence of changes which have been much less far-reaching than at first anticipated. This book provides a survey of the many changes currently in progress in Japan, including political reform, economic deregulation and liberalisation, and reforms to environmental policy, science and technology, education and immigration policy. The chapters in this volume explore the reform process in Japan overall, and provide a thorough overview of major current developments in Japan.

Contents

CONTINUITY AND CHANGE IN JAPAN
Rethinking reform in Japan

POLITICS AND DIPLOMACY
Japanese politics: reforming the rule makers
The changing role and status of the SDF

BEYOND THE ECONOMIC CRISIS
The changing patterns of corporate governance and rationalisation
Reforming Japanese banks and the financial system
Japanese science and technology policies

JAPANESE SOCIETY AND CULTURE
Reforms in the education sector
Immigration policies and citizenship

Javed Maswood is an Associate Professor in the School of International Business and Asian Studies, Griffith University in Brisbane, Australia. He is the author of several books on Japanese politics and political economy. **Jeffrey Graham** is a Lecturer in the School of International Business and Asian Studies, Griffith University. **Hideaki Miyajima** is a Professor in the School of Commerce at Waseda University, Japan. He is also a Director of the Institute of Financial Studies at Waseda University and a Special Research Fellow at the Policy Research Institute at the Japanese Ministry of Finance. He has written several books about the Japanese economy.

Japan – Change and Continuity

Edited by
Javed Maswood, Jeffrey Graham
and Hideaki Miyajima

First published 2002
by RoutledgeCurzon
11 New Fetter Lane, London EC4P 4EE

Simultaneously published in the USA and Canada
by RoutledgeCurzon
29 West 35th Street, New York, NY 10001

RoutledgeCurzon is an imprint of the Taylor & Francis Group

© 2002 Javed Maswood, Jeffrey Graham and Hideaki Miyajima;
individual contributors, their contribution

Typeset in 10/12 Times New Roman by
Newgen Imaging Systems (P) Ltd, Chennai, India
Printed and bound in Great Britain by
Antony Rowe Ltd, Chippenham, Wiltshire

All rights reserved. No part of this book may be reprinted or
reproduced or utilised in any form or by any electronic,
mechanical, or other means, now known or hereafter
invented, including photocopying and recording, or in any
information storage or retrieval system, without permission in
writing from the publishers.

British Library Cataloguing in Publication Data
A catalogue record for this book is available from the British Library

Library of Congress Cataloging in Publication Data
A catalogue record for this book has been requested

ISBN 0–7007–1644–0

Contents

List of figures vii
List of tables viii
List of contributors ix

1 **Introduction** 1
   JAVED MASWOOD

2 **Much ado about nothing? The limited scope of political reform in Japan** 9
   PURNENDRA JAIN

3 **Regulatory reforms in Japan: issues and prospects** 30
   JAVED MASWOOD

4 **Reforming Japanese banks and the financial system** 54
   JENNIFER AMYX

5 **Changes in the J-type firm: from bank-centred governance to internal governance** 72
   HIDEAKI MIYAJIMA AND HIDETAKA AOKI

6 **Continuity and change in Japanese human capital formation** 106
   CHRISTOPHER POKARIER

7 **Changing environmental policy agendas: Japan's approach to international environmental problems** 125
   JEFFREY GRAHAM

8	**Crusaders of the lost archipelago: the changing relationships between environmental NGOs and government in Japan** MIKE DANAHER	148
9	**Immigration and citizenship in contemporary Japan** TESSA MORRIS-SUZUKI	163
10	**The reformatting of Japan for the people: science, technology and the new economy** MORRIS LOW	179
11	**Japanese 'Education Reform': the plan for the twenty-first century** SHOKO YONEYAMA	192
12	**Conclusion** JEFFREY GRAHAM	214
	Index	219

Figures

5.1	Dispatching directors and improvement of firm performance	77
5.2	Presidential turnovers	80
5.3	(a) ROA (3 periods moving average) and (b) Diversification	81
5.4	Succession from enlarged candidates pool (3 periods moving average)	83
5.5	The concept of logit model I	85
5.6	Concept of logit model II (interaction term)	93

Tables

5.1	Issued financial instruments by large Japanese manufacturing firms (1,000 million yen)	74
5.2	Main-bank relationship and ownership structure	76
5.3	Insider succession type	82
5.4	Base regression (each period)	87
5.5	Business risk and diversification (1990–8)	89
5.6	Base regression for sub-samples	90
5.7	Effect of governance structure (MB, portfolio investor)	94
5.8	Effect of employees (insider succession)	98
7.1	Environmental policy and administrative reform in the context of Japan's ODA	140
8.1	Cross-national membership of environmental NGOs	150
9.1	Registered foreigners in Japan by nationality 1980–99	168

Contributors

Jennifer Amyx is Assistant Professor, Department of Political Science, University of Pennsylvania, USA.

Hidetaka Aoki is Assistant Professor, Chiba University of Commerce, Japan.

Mike Danaher is Lecturer, Faculty of Arts, Health and Sciences, Central Queensland University, Australia.

Jeffrey Graham is Lecturer, School of Asian and International Studies, Griffith University, Australia.

Purnendra Jain is Professor, Centre for Asian Studies, Adelaide University, Australia.

Morris Low is Senior Lecturer, University of Queensland, Australia.

Javed Maswood is Associate Professor, School of International Business and Asian Studies, Griffith University, Australia.

Hideaki Miyajima is Professor, School of Commerce, Waseda University, Japan.

Tessa Morris-Suzuki is Professor, Pacific and Asian History, Australian National University, Australia.

Christopher Pokarier is Senior Lecturer, School of International Business, Queensland University of Technology, Australia.

Shoko Yoneyama is Senior Lecturer, Centre for Asian Studies, Adelaide University, Australia.

1 Introduction

Javed Maswood

Until the 1990s, speculation of a coming Pacific Century, dominated by Japan, did not seem altogether unreasonable. The Japanese and many East Asian economies were experiencing rapid economic growth and there was nothing uncommon about the coming shift in the center of economic gravity. Hegemonic transitions are a historically recurrent pattern. If, however, the idea of a Pacific Century was at all unpalatable it was because Japan and East Asian economies represented a significantly different model of domestic and international political economy, with an extensive role for governments in industrial policy and trade development. The role of governments in East Asia extended well beyond simple counter-cyclical economic interventions. Japan's postwar economic success is often attributed to successful state intervention in industrial development and this was a model that was emulated by many East Asian countries in replicating the Japanese growth experience. The developmental state model was a contrast to the largely market dominant Anglo-American model. The West seemed unable to keep up with competition from Japan and East Asia. Yet, just as the long run of economic growth and prosperity was remarkable, so too was the quick descent into economic stagnation. Few had anticipated that the trend lines would fall away so suddenly.

In the 1990s, as Japan and East Asian countries were beset by economic and financial crises, the Pacific Century was no longer a credible reality. For Japan, the final decade of the twentieth century was one of lost opportunities, as the economy remained mired in a Great Stagnation. Successive governments poured enormous amounts of monies into large infrastructure projects in an attempt to generate growth but these efforts produced few positive results and only worsened the fiscal crisis of the state. As the financial and economic crisis lingered, Japan was no longer seen as a model to be emulated, but rather as a model that had run its course and was now unable to provide answers to new challenges on the horizon. The developmental states are now expected to converge on the western model of market discipline and incentives. Yet, convergence may be as much of a wishful thinking as was the notion of a Pacific Century.

The decade of the 1990s was also a period of political instability in Japan. The 1955 system of conservative governments and a socialist opposition fell apart in the mid-1990s and this was followed by a period of enormous fluidity, as political parties formed, merged and disappeared in a manner that was in sharp contrast to the stability of the 1955 system. Political instability perhaps delayed effective responses to the lingering economic crisis, which many argued could only be resolved through an extensive overhaul of economic and corporate structures.

We cannot deny, however, that the winds of change are blowing across Japan and implicate not just political and economic structures, but many facets of Japanese society. Economic and political crises are not the only sources of change in Japan but demographic shifts, globalisation and demands of an information technology (IT) based economy are also fomenting change in human resource management strategies, education and immigration policies. Growing domestic and international environmental sensitivities have also strained existing parameters of environmental policy making in Japan. The record of environmental management in Japan is both exemplary and disappointing. Following a spate of environmental disasters in the early postwar period, the Japanese government introduced new environmental legislations and these contributed to environmental outcomes that exceeded international standards. Yet, Japan's voracious appetite for natural resources to power its industrial economy casts a large ecological and environmental shadow over its region, and there is increased pressure to contribute more to protect regional and global ecology and toward nature conservation in Japan and elsewhere. In the West, the environmental movement has been supported by well-organised non-governmental organisations (NGOs) and green political parties, but these have not played a prominent role in Japanese politics. There have been some significant changes however, and it is important to consider and review Japanese efforts at environmental management.

Although interest in reform and change has been stimulated by persisting economic crises in the 1990s, the agenda of reforms in Japan, particularly political and administrative reform, emerged in the 1980s. Japan began to debate reforms at around the same time as other western countries were implementing reforms, typical of the slow pace of the policy machinery in Japan. Interest in political reform was a result of the spread of money politics and gerrymander and it was high on the domestic political agenda, if not for the ruling Liberal Democratic Party at least opposition parties. Reform became inevitable in the mid-1990s as the ruling political party became embroiled in a succession of financial scandals that heightened public disenchantment with the way political processes had become distant from shifting electoral dynamics and become a captive of money politics. The scandals implicated politicians and senior bureaucrats, the latter groups suffering further loss of prestige as a result of continuing economic malaise and policy failures.

In this volume, we survey the process of reform to highlight the elements of continuity and change in Japanese political economy. To say that the process of change has been slow and cautious is both true for specific cases and misleading as a broad generalisation. The pace of reform and the mix of continuity and change varies considerably across issue areas. The papers that have been collected here do not necessarily provide a consistent view of reforms, or of change and continuity and that is a simple reflection of diversity in the field of Japan studies.

All but one of the papers collected in the volume were first presented at a workshop in Brisbane in January 2001. The papers have been revised to incorporate discussion and comments at the workshop. The papers cover a range of issue areas and if there is a central message it is that the record of achievements is varied and has to be carefully assessed for individual areas. Japan is slow to change but change does occur. The focus has been on analysing the process of change in the 1990s, over a range of themes, including politics, economics and society. Reform of course is socially and economically painful to the disaffected, a message that was highlighted by Prime Minister Koizumi in his first major policy speech in early May 2001. He asserted, nonetheless, that reforms were essential even if it meant some pain and suffering in the short term.

The chapter on political and electoral reforms by Purnendra Jain provides a background to the reforms that were implemented in the mid-1990s. Pressure for reform had been building for a long time but came to a head in early 1990s as a result of a succession of political crises and corruption scandals. Japan's politics had become dominated by money politics and elections had degenerated to crass money politics rather than policy contests. Jain outlines the nature of reforms and probable future developments. He also looks at other issues of political reform, including administrative reform and reforms to the centre–periphery balance. In Japan, political power is concentrated in the capital of Tokyo and there is a continuing movement to devolve some of the power and authority to local governments as a way of ensuring better representation of community interests in policies.

The chapter by Maswood on regulatory reforms begins with the assumption that regulatory reforms are essential not only because of the demands of economic globalisation and international competitiveness, but also as a strategy for sustainable growth and development. The Japanese economy is highly regulated relative to other western countries and while the reformist debate has waxed and waned since the early 1980s, progress has been slow and measured. The main obstacle to reform is not simply an entrenched bureaucracy but also the nature of party politics, which have failed to provide voters with alternative policy choices or even to fully reflect constituency interests.

It is inevitable that vested interests will obstruct reform and change and, not surprisingly, bureaucratic obstructionism was one factor in delaying regulatory reform in Japan. Similarly, Chris Pokarier argues that reform in the corporate sector has been obstructed by senior management. Pokarier emphatically argues that corporate reform and restructuring is essential to future competitiveness of Japanese industry. Instead, management has continued to emphasise long-term employment contracts and remuneration based on seniority, rather than merit and competence. He cogently argues that this has important consequences. First, it is a practice that will leave Japanese firms vulnerable and exposed by being unable to respond to pressures of IT, since corporate staffing has a commitment to long term employment. This has prevented the entry of new blood and led to a retention of older employees who may be inadequate in responding to future needs of global competition and IT. Second, he also argues that while the persistence of earlier patterns of human resource management have prevented a blowout in the overall levels of unemployment, this has come at the expense of high unemployment among the young Japanese, who are unable to find employment opportunities because of corporate commitment to current employees. Retention of high-cost older employees, despite worsening business conditions, may have mitigated some of the potential social dislocations of planned lay-offs and redundancies, this same practice has exacerbated the 'freeter' phenomenon, of young Japanese in casual or part-time employment. In Japan, social commentators have focused on the alleged lack of discipline among the freeters, implying that faults lie within them as individuals instead of the fact that the freeter phenomenon may largely be a creation of inappropriate human resource strategies of Japanese companies. Thus, Pokarier asserts that aversion to reforms not only has had considerable socio-economic costs so far but will also have negative consequences in future, by making it harder for Japanese companies to compete in a global economy.

Nonetheless, we cannot be dismissive about Japan's capacity to rebound from present difficulties. The Japanese economy has demonstrated its capacity to overcome crises in the past and the Japanese people and government have shown similar determination to overcome obstacles. It is true that the present economic crises has extended to more than a decade but it would be premature to write off Japan as having lost the competition between the old economy and the new economy. Morris Low, for example, points out that while Japan may be lagging in the development of e-commerce, it is competitive in a number of other technology indicators. The takeup of new technology is very high in Japan, especially cell phone and mobile communications, and research and development expenditure has been maintained at a high level, despite prolonged economic stagnation. To survive in the frontiers of modern technology, many scholars have emphasised the importance of education reform to encourage innovation and creativity rather than discipline and uniformity. The issue of educational reform is one of the most important challenges confronting the Japanese political economy and it is explored at length by Yoneyama Shoko. She looks at recent proposals for reform and is disturbed by the emphasis on morals and nationalism, as well as the likely stratification of education into an elite stream, with its focus on creativity and excellence and a mass stream focused on discipline and uniformity. One of the key features of the Japanese political economy is the practice of *amakudari* (descent from heaven), whereby senior bureaucrats parachute into plum private sector positions following retirement. Yoneyama finds that a similar practice might be emerging in the education sector to allow redundant and retrenched corporate executives find suitable positions within the schools system as, for example, principals. Yoneyama argues that this pattern is part of the corporatisation of education and designed to create an industrial workforce that is imbued with an appropriate corporate culture and work ethics. Her analysis suggests that the proposed reforms are designed more to reflect the conservative and nationalistic values of the Liberal Democratic Party than the requirements of a global economy. According to her, the reform proposals do not even address some of the critical problems in the education sector, such as bullying.

Reform and change is an uncertain process, at least to the extent that there is no certainty about the final configuration. This uncertainty has generated debate and disagreement as to whether the process of change in Japan will result in a convergence on the Anglo-American models of corporate and economic governance. This is an issue taken up by Miyajima and Aoki, who argue that the emerging corporate governance structure in Japan is a combination of internal governance mechanism (indigenous Japanese) and market based (Anglo-American). The governance issues are important considering that sustained economic failure can be partly attributed to poor governance and regulatory controls. Miyajima and Aoki test a number of hypotheses and demonstrate that internal governance structures are strong, such that presidential turnover and appointment is not unrelated to corporate performance and profitability.

Jennifer Amyx looks at the banking crisis in Japan and the unresolved problem of non-performing loans. The financial crisis is at the heart of Japan's contemporary economic malaise and Amyx suggests that information asymmetry was an important factor in the failure to deal effectively with the crisis. The Ministry of Finance (MOF) had ultimate regulatory authority over banks and financial institutions in Japan and the basic regulatory principle was the convoy approach, which carried implicit guarantees that no bank would be allowed to fail. The convoy approach offered banks the security of knowing that the MOF would engineer a 'rescue merger' under dire circumstances. This approach broke down in the late 1990s and in the ensuring reforms, the MOF was stripped of its regulatory authority, which was now vested in an independent Financial Supervisory Agency. New regulatory controls have been put in place to ensure transparency and consistency with international practices, such as in the definition of non-performing loans. As a result of regulatory and structural changes, information dynamics have been significantly improved and this has made financial policy making more transparent and enhanced the role of markets in exercising discipline and due diligence. There remains the problem of non-performing loans and Jennifer looks at three solutions to deal with this remaining problem: debt discounting, debt forgiveness and strict market discipline. In the end, it appears likely that the government will opt for a solution that shares the responsibility and burden between banks and the borrowing institutions.

Global environmental issues continue to attract considerable interest and there are expectations that Japan will play a constructive role in global environmental management. Japan's own experience with environmental management is mixed. It has been particularly successful in resolving issues of environmental pollution and damage, to the extent that it moved from being one of the most polluted countries to a relative clean environment. However, its record on nature conservation is less exemplary and Mike Danaher probes this interesting paradox. He looks in particular at the role of NGOs in Japan and traces their evolution from being marginal players in policy processes to being more involved within a corporatist structure, with relatively close links between some of the larger environmental NGOs and government agencies. Nonetheless, the conclusion is that the influence of NGOs is very limited and this can be attributed partly to their incapacity to raise their domestic profile because of organisational and financial obstacles. Jeff Graham looks at the evolution of Japan's environmental policies and says that while the challenge of policy reform had become evident at least three decades earlier, it has only been in recent years that we can see genuine policy movement. For example, it was in 1997 that Japan legislated the Environmental Impact Assessment Law and was one of the last OECD countries to do so. Japan's environmental aid to other countries also, until recently, included no requirement for environmental impact assessment whereas countries like the US had introduced such requirements in the late 1970s. Graham observes that many of the reforms can be classified as superficial, involving no more than a simple rebadging of existing programmes as 'Green Aid' or 'Initiatives for Sustainable Development' to give a impression of environmental sensitivity and concern. Yet, at the same time, we can also notice policy innovation and leadership in initiatives to promote regional environmental protection. These initiatives include mechanisms for acid deposition monitoring. While these are worthy developments, there remains some uncertainty about ultimate objectives of these monitoring mechanism, whether these are envisaged are preliminary to legally binding agreements at a later date. Graham suggests that likely outcome will be a continuation of 'old diplomacy' and emphasis on consensus building rather than preparedness to assume a leadership role in multilateral agreements.

Most of the chapters deal with reform and changes in postwar structures that have underpinned Japanese political economy. Morris-Suzuki's Chapter 9 on nationality and immigration, however, is an analysis of the '1899 system' regulating immigration and citizenship policies. The first Nationality Law was passed in 1899 and the principles established therein have continued to find expression in the revisions since then. She argues that the 1899 system is being challenged from a number of sources, including an international human rights regime which questions, for instance, the patriarchal assumption behind existing nationality legislation, from domestic indigenous rights advocates and from demographic shifts. While there has been little evidence of policy shifts, the reality on the ground is changing rapidly as a result of inflow of foreign labour. Rather than real policy responses to reflect these changes, what has emerged, according to Morris-Suzuki is 'cosmetic multiculturalism'. This may yet be a significant move from 'ethnic homogeneity' and Morris-Suzuki also suggests that the government, apart from being cautious in its own rights is also constrained by broad societal forces, which reflect a complex and intricate mixture of xenophobia and xenophilia.

Acknowledgements

Finally, we should acknowledge our thanks to a number of individuals who contributed to the workshop, in particular Hayden Lesbirel, Peter Ross and Donna Weeks. We would also like to thank all the individual authors who were prompt in delivering their revised manuscript, which has allowed us to put this volume together without undue delay. Our thanks also to the

8 *Javed Maswood*

Japanese Consul General in Brisbane, Mr Kai Korenari, who attended all the proceedings and participated actively in the debate and discussion. Robyn White cheerfully prepared the manuscript for publication and we owe her a big vote of thanks. The workshop was sponsored by the Griffith Asia Pacific Council, with additional funding provided by School of International Business and Asian Studies, Griffith University.

2 Much ado about nothing? The limited scope of political reform in Japan

Purnendra Jain

Seiji kaikaku (political reform) has appeared in patches on Japan's political landscape for decades, largely as rhetoric. In the 1990s, political reform took on ever more life – in the machinations of political parties, in parliamentary debate and eventually as legislated change to the political system. Reform implies a problem (e.g. corruption) to be corrected or improved. Throughout postwar, those with political and moral authority to cast the national debate on political reform have set its margins narrowly around the electoral system. Their claim has been to clean up money politics that has seen the nation's political life run less on ideology or policy pursuing the national interest than on brokered deals driven by vast amounts of money, favour and obligation – a well-fed political pork barrel. Since the Japanese political system is fuelled by money, the economic recession of the 1990s added a new imperative to the political reform agenda. The need for financial prudence sparked calls for greater political efficiency and effectiveness, and strengthened the position of those pushing for substantive political reform rather than superficial fiddling on the margins.

It may be inevitable that political reform is the product of power struggles among the nation's political elites. As a term, '*seiji kaikaku*' is a valuable vote-winning tool that most political aspirants espouse energetically at election time. But those with power in the nation's political system fear that systemic reform will harm their position. They have continued to actively buck real political transformation, limiting actual reforms to those that merely tinker at the edges of the electoral system. This is neither surprising, nor atypical in national politics. Those who have the most political clout are part of a political elite that has come to power and retained it through this very system, one that they have mastered and that has rewarded them well. True reform of the political system threatens to unseat this elite from power by eroding the structures that undergird their hold on government. However, it is also true that as those who helped to consolidate these political structures vacate the system through age or death, or as in 1993 through loss of power in a national election, there is more space for real reform voices to register.

Given these circumstances, if we are to consider political reform as a vehicle for change in Japanese politics we must acknowledge not just what has been cast as '*seiji kaikaku*' by the politicians and media that popularise this term. We need to look also at other areas of the political system where reform – correction or improvement – is an issue. In this chapter I focus on the three major areas of governance and public administration in Japan where, for the complex reasons mentioned above, reform has become an ever more salient issue since the 1990s. First is electoral reform, which in the 1990s was taken beyond tinkering to induce more substantive structural change in the political system. The second and third areas of reform are not recognised as '*seiji kaikaku*', instead labelled as '*gyosei kaikaku*' or administrative reform. This is despite the unambiguously political nature of both, involving redistribution of power (not just administrative responsibility) across the nation's political institutions.

The second involves adjustment of the roles played by elected representatives and bureaucrats. Here the problem is seen as the strong influence of bureaucrats *vis-à-vis* the relative weakness of elected representatives in matters of public policy. Reform is to produce a more democratic, less venal system of government where politicians are responsive to and representative of the electorate. The third reform involves territorial redistribution of power between the national and sub-national levels of government. Over-concentration of power in the central government has restricted both policy and financial autonomy of local governments and produced administrative delays, inefficiency and corruption. Decentralisation of power and resources may reduce the potential for corruption and enable more efficient and effective delivery of services across all levels of public administration.

As we see in this examination, limited headway has been made in all three areas of political reform in Japan since the 1990s, particularly in electoral reform. Ouster of the Liberal Democractic Party (LDP) in 1993, departure of some of the conservative old guard, through death and retirement, budget constraints and public exposure of systemic corruption shifted the power relationships between the main political players and lubricated the pro-reform wheels. Yet as I argue in this chapter, within Japan's well-entrenched power structures, change born of political reform comes slowly. However, inevitable reform may appear, the limits upon it remain formidable.

Electoral reform

A new electoral system was officially introduced in Japan in 1994. Two general elections – in 1996 and 2000 – have been held under the new system. The old system had been in place since 1947 when the government returned to the one adopted in 1925 after a brief early postwar flirtation with a new electoral system (Kohno, 1997: 30). Elections to the Lower House (House of Representatives) of the national parliament were based on single non-transferable votes (SNTV) in medium-sized multi-member districts (MMDs).[1] The nature of this electoral system has been long seen as the root of money-for-power politics (*kinken seiji*), widespread corruption and unfair electoral representation (Jain, 1995: 404–7), that is the reasons for electoral reform. As Stockwin (2000: 1.11) observed, 'The advertised purposes of abandoning SNTV in multi-member constituencies (MMCs) and moving to a new system were to get rid of money politics, shift the emphasis of electoral campaigning from personality-based appeals to appeals based on policy choices, and create a politics that should be genuinely competitive between parties'.

The problem of multi-member districts

Until 1994, most electoral districts returned three, four or five members who were the top vote winners, although some districts had one, two or six members. In theory, the number of seats in any given electoral districts was based on the number of voters but, in practice, urbanisation and gerrymander distorted true representation. With members of the same party competing against each other in the same district (since more than one candidate from the same party could be elected), politics was centred on a candidate's individual style rather than party platform, policy stance or ideological leaning. Blatantly, money bought votes. Thus, the need for money to sustain expensive vote buying virtually assured widespread money-for-favours corruption by self-interested politicians.

Attempts to reform multi-member districts

The propensity of the MMD electoral system to stimulate political corruption was recognised soon after the system was reintroduced early postwar. For the next four decades reform advocates made numerous attempts, some at the highest level of politics, to shift to a system of single-member districts (SMDs) with proportional representation that reformists hoped would end or at least reduce the role of money in politics. However prevailing MMD arrangements favoured the ruling LDP and party leaders not only resisted reform moves but worked actively to further entrench the electoral structures that magnified their access to power. Interestingly, not all LDP politicians were anti-reform and not all non-LDP politicians were pro-reform. The reform advocates in the LDP recognised the electoral popularity of a pro-reform stance but they were not united in the type of reform they favoured, even though an SMD system was popular among them (Wada, 2000: 183–217). We see that the resilience of the reform opponents owes much to the disunity among the reform advocates.

In 1956 Prime Minister Hatoyama Ichiro proposed an SMD system that would give the LDP a two-thirds majority in the Lower House. His proposal met widespread opposition inside the party and could not proceed (Kataoka, 1992: 12–13 and 164–5). In 1973 an attempt by Prime Minister Tanaka Kakuei to replace MMDs with SMDs, with 40 per cent of members elected through proportional representation, met a fate similar to that of Hatoyama's proposal. New leaders favouring reform emerged from time to time within the LDP but in the absence of consensus, fundamental reform was deferred. Many outside the LDP believed that proposals put by LDP politicians to reform the electoral system would benefit the ruling party and seriously disadvantage opposition parties. With the LDP's continued hold on government, the electoral debate remained low key.

Through the 1960s to the late 1980s before reform gained real momentum, reform-minded politicians in both the opposition parties and the ruling LDP were generally young and ardent in their reformist beliefs. In 1986 about ten first-time LDP parliamentarians established the Utopia Politics Study Group. In December 1988 this group submitted a list of reform proposals and called for a new electoral system with single-member electoral districts and proportional representation (PR). At this time the LDP formed its own political reform committee and six months later the party's committee recommended a set of political reforms that closely resembled the Utopia Group's recommendations.

In early 1990 the Eighth Election System Council recommended sweeping changes to the existing election system. These involved a reduction in the number of Lower House members from 512 to 501, with 301 members from SMDs and the remaining 200 from eleven regional blocs on the basis of PR. Immobilised by conflicting views between and within the ruling and opposition parties, the Kaifu government (1989–91) was unable to present a reform bill in the Diet.

Minor electoral reforms

Some piecemeal reforms were introduced during the long period of LDP rule. Significantly, these had nothing to do with replacement of the MMD electoral system. For example, electoral boundaries were readjusted from time to time to reduce disparity in the value of votes between rural and urban electoral districts. In 1992 ten seats were cut in rural districts and nine added in urban districts. In 1974 following exposure of Prime Minister

Tanaka Kakuei's role in the infamous Lockheed scandal that forced him from office in disgrace, his successor Miki Takeo introduced a number of reforms to the political donations law.

These changes might suggest that the LDP was translating its rhetoric into reality. However the nature and timing of these changes make it clear that the purpose was primarily to clean up the LDP's tarnished image rather than clean up the money-driven, gerrymandered electoral system. Politicians, especially from the LDP, were quick to discover loopholes in new laws to clean up electoral practice, and money politics flourished unabated. Indeed, it was public exposure of widespread corruption from the late 1980s that helped to unseat the LDP from government and created the political climate in which reformists from various political parties could also dislodge the MMD electoral system.

Political corruption as stimulus to reform

Voters are naturally angered to learn that their elected representatives have abused positions of political power for personal gain. Yet a system of money politics leaves politicians highly vulnerable to corruption. When public exposure of corruption by senior LDP politicians rocked the nation at various times through the almost four decades of LDP rule, the party responded with various reform proposals to create at least the appearance of electoral reform, as noted above.

However, from the late 1980s exposure of apparently endemic corruption in the LDP so aggrieved the Japanese public that the LDP could not simply paper over with the appearance of reform. The unrepentant involvement of many senior LDP politicians in the Recruit shares-for-favour scandal of the late 1980s was followed, in the early 1990s, by revelations of the Sagawa Kyubin scandal involving bribery of LDP heavyweight Kanemaru Shin and other LDP top brass. Here were some of the nation's most senior political figures mired in corruption. The magnitude and ignominy of these 'scandals' not only changed the mood of the electorate dramatically; they also raised the expectation of pro-reform politicians that they could now move seriously on electoral reform.

Momentum for reform

The scope for electoral reform was shaped very much by the electoral fortunes of the LDP. Hence it took more than simply public exposure of corruption to sustain the newly gained momentum. For the LDP reform advocates, achieving their reform goals eventually meant leaving the party. They did so in 1976 (formation of the New Liberal Club, which reunited with the LDP in 1986) and again in 1993 after their efforts to reform from within the party were continually frustrated. Here was the lesson for the LDP reformers: reform of the electoral system could come only with the LDP ousted from office, with them outside the party to help in the ouster and take up influential positions in a replacement government.

In the backdrop of public hostility over the Recruit scandal, the LDP in 1989 lost control of the Upper House for the first time since the party was formed in 1955. This was fuel for the reformists. But when the party won the 1990 Lower House election under Kaifu Toshiki, momentum temporarily slowed. Even so the complacency of senior party colleagues did not dampen the enthusiasm of the LDP reformists – the Utopia Group, the Young Diet Members for Political Reform (formed in 1991) and others – who kept the pressure on but achieved very little.

In response to the Miyazawa government's failure to introduce a political reform bill, three groups of LDP reformers saw no alternative but to split from the LDP to form new parties.[2] Within months the LDP lost government in a national election for the first time since 1955, and eight opposition parties that included the three LDP breakaways formed the first non-LDP coalition government. Enacting political reform legislation became a central concern of the coalition government, reflected in the new cabinet position: a special minister for political reform.

The ex-LDP reformists

The three groups that broke from the LDP played a crucial role in maintaining the momentum for electoral reform and moving it into legislation. First to leave the LDP was a group that formed the Japan New Party (JNP) headed by Hosokawa Morihiro who became the first non-LDP Prime Minister in the new coalition. Second were those in the Utopia Group who formed the Sakigake (Harbinger Party) under Takemura Masayoshi (Otake, 1996: 269). Ozawa Ichiro led the third group that formed the Shinseito (Renewal Party). During the early 1990s, Ozawa took the centre stage of the political reform movement. Ozawa's approach to reform was similar to that of former prime minister Nakasone Yasuhiro, advocating reform of the neo-liberal economic system and a more active role for Japan in international affairs (Otake, 1996: 284; Ozawa, 1994). He articulated his reform ideas brilliantly in his 1994 book, *Blueprint for a New Japan: The Rethinking of a Nation*.

The overwhelming majority of the new Sakigake Party were *nisei* (second-generation) Diet members. As Otake (1996: 277) explained, the young *nisei* were more inclined to take the political risk of decamping as they had much less at stake than their first-generation cohort. Their electoral support bases were strong and they could be elected under any party banner. Even if they were defeated, most could still live very well on immense inherited wealth. Important allies of the young reformers were in a group of elder party politicians who, close to retirement, also had less at stake than others and so could consider the future of Japanese party politics from a less self-interested position. These elders included well-known politicians Gotoda Masaharu and Ito Masayoshi. Otake (1996: 279–80) concluded that 'It was this coalition of old and young 'idealists' who were the driving force in pushing political reform to the top of the political agenda' (see Johnson, 1995: 220–4).

Like electoral reform advocates outside the LDP, reformers inside the LDP saw the MMD electoral system as the root of money politics and widespread corruption. They argued that an SMD system was essential for shifting the focus of Japanese politics to parties and policy. Their views opposed those of the many LDP politicians who were apprehensive about the single-seat system advantaging incumbents and making entry into the Diet difficult for all but *nisei* politicians who usually come into the system loaded with electoral support. In government as elected members of the ruling coalition, the reformers were very quick to act on reform legislation.

Electoral changes introduced in 1994

Under Hosokawa's leadership, the Lower House passed a reform package consisting of four bills in November 1993. The bills locked in four major changes: (1) reduction in the number of Lower House members from 511 to 500 (274 from SMDs and 226 through PR); (2) establishment of a neutral group to draw up single-seat districts; (3) a ban on corporate donations to individual politicians, but with corporate donations to political parties and political groups still allowed; (4) establishment of a system of state subsidies to political parties. Although the bills were passed by the Lower House, they were rejected in the Upper House where the Socialist Party had enough votes to defeat the bill. The Socialists particularly opposed the abolition of multi-member electoral districts, concerned this would bring the slow death of smaller parties and the emergence of mega parties.

Meanwhile, deals were struck (foreshadowing the style of 'reform' that would follow) between ex-LDP strongman Ozawa (in the ruling coalition) and LDP Secretary General Mori Yoshiro (in opposition). They produced a compromise plan that closely resembled the 1990 proposals of the Eighth Election System Council (see Jain, 1995: 413–16). The Lower House would comprise 500 members: 300 elected through SMD and 200 through PR from eleven regional blocs. Restrictions were imposed on individual politicians fund-raising from corporations.[3] Most importantly, the reform

16 *Purnendra Jain*

package introduced a state subsidy system that would make available to political parties from state coffers about 31 billion yen annually for parties' political activities.

An aspect of the reforms that later drew criticism was the 'dual candidacy' arrangement, where a candidate in a single-seat district could also be on the PR constituency list. Known as 'second chance winners', 83 were elected to the parliament in 1996 (Hrebenar, 2000a: 50). Dual candidacy provided the perfect means for influential politicians who were unpopular with their electorate to stay in the Diet legitimately through 'backdoor' entry. But as I discuss later in this chapter, the dual candidacy reform was itself soon 'reformed'.

The effect of electoral reforms: real change?

For all the struggle to institutionalise electoral reforms, has the business of politics really changed? Have the stated purposes of these reforms been achieved to clean up the conduct of political life in Japan? A simple answer to both questions is no. Some may claim that it is still too early to judge; deep reform does not take root over night. Others may claim that with little on show that bespeaks a cleaner, more democratic electoral system, the reform is much ado about nothing, or at least very little. I will look at three benchmarks to inform this appraisal.

(i) Establishment of a competitive two-party system: The expectation that the new electoral system would pave the way for a two-party system to emerge has not yet been realised. The hybrid of PR with SMD allows minor parties to win seats via the PR districts in regional blocs. Instead of a two-party system, a string of coalitions has emerged with participation by all parties, except the Communists, and led by a new party, the socialists or the LDP.[4] The defining principles of these coalition arrangements are not policy or ideological similarities but mutually agreed political deals made behind the scenes. Many would assess this as politics as usual!

The new arrangement is likely to keep advantaging the LDP, although in the June 2000 general election the LDP lost many of its seats in metropolitan areas, including all its seats in Tokyo. As the principal coalition partner with the power to dole out huge funding for public works and other services, the LDP has satisfied its coalition partners by allocating funds and favours as these partners have requested. In return, the partners have guaranteed the LDP parliamentary support for its bills in the Diet. This has enabled the party to ram through contentious legislation such as on the national flag and the national anthem with little debate or public knowledge. Opposition parties remain as fragmented as before. Under the 1955 system, leftist political parties acted as a significant break on the ruling party sponsored bills and policies. Now the influence of these parties has waned, especially with the withering of the Socialist Party, which is to some extent part of an international trend.

(ii) Rural–urban imbalance: Imbalance between the weight of votes in rural and urban Japan continues. In mid-2000 the ratio between urban Kanagawa Prefecture's seventh district and rural Shimane Prefecture's third district was 2.49 : 1. The number of small districts where the value of a vote is twice that of the most densely populated districts increases as people continue to desert small towns. The problem of imbalance is intensified by the way the new electoral system allocates one seat to each prefecture (47), with allocation of the remaining 253 seats based on population (www.asahi.com, 17 August 2000). A new law requires that the ratio of vote value be less than two to one. But re-districting to keep vote values under this ratio involves breaking up a politician's home turf and since it is invariably an LDP politician who is affected by the redrawing, this is usually a difficult process.

(iii) Ethical standards: Political corruption continues to make headlines in Japan, and LDP politicians still keep close ties with business and other interest groups. Some politicians resign when questioned about their political impropriety in the public arena; others simply disregard such calls. Newspapers report these cases frequently. During the government of Obuchi Keizo, news broke of serious scandals involving police and the Defence Agency, and one of the Prime Minister's personal aides was reported to be involved in shady share deals. Prime Minister Mori took up office with a past tainted by influence pedalling in both the Recruit Cosmos and Sagawa Kyubin scandals. A senior LDP Upper House member and Mori confidant Murakami Masakuni was arrested in March 2001 on suspicion of accepting bribes from the KSD foundation while serving as Labour Minister from 1996 to 1998.

Assessment

The evidence suggests that money – and all that goes with it – still drives politics, that even the legislated reforms are merely pussyfooting around the edges. Observers across the board have given the electoral reforms a very poor report card, pointing to continuity much more than change. Eminent Japanese political scientist Otake Hideo (1998: xxviii) claimed the electoral reform programme had shown 'only little success'. Yamaguchi Jiro (1997: 36,23) shared this view, explaining that 'most politicians had acted in their self-interest rather than in the interest of robust party politics in Japan'.

Among outside observers, Stockwin defined the new system as fundamentally the product of compromise that 'turned out to be far less radical in its impact than some reformers expected and hoped' (Stockwin, 2000: 1.10). Seligmann is similarly critical: 'On balance, it is difficult to discern any major influence that the new electoral system has had thus far on the political scene. There was also far less to the new electoral law than may have met the eye, many of its features favouring the status quo' (Seligmann, 1997: 428).

The issue of intent is important here. Many observers consider that how the 'reformed' system operates is far removed from the original intention of electoral reform: to make the nation's political life run less on deals driven by money and favour than on policy pursuing the national interest. Many who saw the MMD system as the source of the money-politics problem claimed the SMD/PR system and its adjunct reforms would deliver more representative, 'cleaner' politics. Yet policy is still not important in this picture, and money most certainly is. Neither the LDP and its coalition partners nor the parties in opposition stand on clear, well-devised policies that could revive voters' interest in politics and end their disillusion. The new system's structural disincentives to corruption such as state support for campaigning appear to miss their mark. The imperatives to raise vast amounts of money to feed political life continue almost unabated. The LDP was returned to government within eighteen months of its 1993 ouster, but observers agree the LDP will need to embark on a mad grab for support while its rural voter base dwindles and urban voters are rejecting the party (Kabashima, 2000). Thus for the LDP, and for the nation's political life, it appears to be business as usual.

Continued reform

In response to widespread criticism (and to accommodate demands of its coalition partners), the LDP agreed to change some of the earlier controversial arrangements. Under pressure from Ozawa whose Liberal Party joined the Obuchi coalition government, legislation was passed in February 2000 to reduce the number of Lower House seats from 500 to 480, with twenty cut from the PR seats. In May 2000, the Diet passed two major changes related to dual candidacy. First, if a candidate loses in an SMD, this candidate is ineligible for re-election through PR if s/he receives less than 10 per cent of votes. Second, members of parliament who vacate their seat to run in a local election and lose are ineligible to run in a by-election to retake the seat they vacated at national level.

In November 2000, an anti-graft law was passed banning politicians from profiting in return for mediating between business, individuals and public officials.[5] Politicians are forbidden from such mediation even if the other side requests and the politician does not profit from the mediation. This law applies to heads of local governments, Diet and local assembly members and their publicly hired secretaries, but it excludes privately hired secretaries. Hatoyama Yukio as leader of the largest opposition party, the Democratic Party of Japan, slammed the new law as 'defective legislation with many loopholes' (*The Daily Yomiuri*, 24 November 2000).

Again, loopholes are set to save the reform resisters, who usually have been involved in diluting the reform to create the loophole. We are reminded here of how well the power structures within the Japanese political system are entrenched. Thus, even with reforms to the reforms, it is likely to be business as usual for the politicians. We see that in the brief life of electoral reform, even when it is institutionalised, reform may produce very little intended improvement and very little change at all.

Shifting power from bureaucrats to politicians

For the past few decades there has been concern in Japan over who wields influence in policy and other political decision-making. At its core is the distribution of power between the two arms of government: politicians and bureaucrats. Scholars presents a diverse range of opinion about who really calls the policy shots. For example, for Johnson (1982, 1995) and Ikuta (2000) bureaucrats wield much greater power than politicians; for Muramatsu and Krauss (1984) politicians play a key role despite influential bureaucrats; for Ramseyer and Rosenbluth (1993) and Muramatsu (2001) bureaucrats are essentially subservient to their political masters. While opinion is divided on precisely the type and degree of bureaucrats' power, Japanese bureaucrats are known to play a major role in the nation's political decision process.

Problems of the politicians/bureaucrats power distribution

Extensive bureaucratic influence raises concerns about the undemocratic nature of a political system whose appointed staff (bureaucracy) predominate over the people's elected representatives (governing party/ies) in policy decisions. However political life in the 1990s extended this debate beyond the issue of being 'undemocratic'. Newspaper headlines highlighted to the public two other issues that indicated major problems with the power divide between politicians and bureaucrats. These too underscored the need for systemic remedy – the stuff of political reform.

One issue is institutional inertia. The political system, or more accurately the people in it, failed to respond effectively to a series of national emergencies that needed fast and effective response: the Korean peninsula crisis in 1994, the Great Hanshin earthquake and Aum Shinrikyo subway gas attack in 1995, and the Peru hostage crisis in 1997. These crises made it clear that the circuitous process of decision-making – effectively the politician's lack of both power and will to use it when truly needed – had dire consequences for the Japanese people.

The second issue is the corruptibility of hitherto revered bureaucrats. Public exposure of scandal and dubious practices within the bureaucracy in downtown Kasumigaseki where government ministries are concentrated set alarm bells ringing among the public.[6] Even the most hallowed Ministry of Finance (MOF) came under the spotlight in 1998 when two senior officials were arrested on charges of accepting bribes from banks and the Minister of Finance resigned. More cases of bribery were revealed with many more banks implicated. In the public eye, corruption was no longer the preserve of the party politicians; it had intruded into the bureaucracy.

These circumstances helped to build a public consensus on the need to make elected politicians more proactive in the policy arena, with bureaucrats in a less influential support role. But blatant transfer of power and influence is clearly problematical when power relations are entrenched in the political structures. The notion of 'shifting' power from bureaucrats to politicians assumes that this power is fungible and that the players will not resist. The redistribution of political power did proceed, but subject to considerable political brokerage in the face of bureaucratic resistance.

New legislation

In March 1998 the Diet passed the Basic Law for the Reform of Central Government and Ministries and Agencies. The new system became effective in January 2001. Its intention was to reduce the influence of bureaucrats in public policy in favour of elected representatives and to increase the efficiency and effectiveness of the decision-making process. It aimed to make political processes more dynamic and pluralistic to address the inertia mentioned above and improve cost effectiveness in economically recessed times. It was also to signal to a disenchanted electorate that the government was responding to electoral grievances.

The new structure attempts to streamline responsibility as well as redistribute power. To strengthen the power and administrative leadership of the Prime Minister and Cabinet it has made the Cabinet Office the centre of policy formulation with a comprehensive coordination role. It gives greater control and political support to ministers and their deputies with 60 new political positions: 12 state ministers, 22 deputy ministers and 26 state affairs officers. As one way to regulate industry access to the power centres, the Cabinet office is to have more than 100 private-sector personnel (about 10 per cent of the total staff) though most of these will be part-time advisers. To reduce the power of bureaucrats it reduced the number of ministries and agencies (from 22 to 12) and increased the number of political supervisors of these ministries. Plans are to reduce the number of national bureaucrats by 25 per cent over a decade.

This is the first comprehensive overhaul of the administrative structure since new structures were put in place following First World War. The comments of several observers pointed to the democratic issue behind the move. Eda Kenji[7] claimed that it was meant to be 'a shift from government of the bureaucrats, by the bureaucrats, for the bureaucrats to government of the people, by the people, for the people' (*Asahi Evening News*, 5 December 2000; Look Japan, 2001). The Asahi Newspaper noted its primary purpose 'to transfer leadership from bureaucrats to the cabinet, which represents voters' (*Asahi Evening News*, 5 December 2000). Yet this popular daily was not optimistic about the effectiveness of the new structure, claiming it was unlikely that policy content would change in any significant way ('Shocho saihen nan no tame', *Asahi Shinbun*, 6 December 2000).

The Asahi assessment prompts us to again question whether the new system will induce real change in policy formation and decision making or whether this legislation, like the '*seiji kaikaku*' to clean up money politics, is more concerned with the appearance of change. Power inside the nation's political institutions cannot be simply 'shifted' without widespread consensus, support and cooperation of those who will win and loose from the redistribution. The goals of the new system are grand and laudable but the prospects of achieving them are slim. As with the reform moves discussed in the first section above, those who are set to lose in the power shuffle – this time the bureaucrats – were involved heavily in reshaping the system and are unlikely to have power stripped from them without considerable resistance.

Reforming the centre–local relationship: power to the periphery?

Some degree of decentralisation has been intrinsic to calls for political reform. The core of this issue is essentially the same as in both cases discussed above – the redistribution of political power. So the parallels are considerable. The imperatives for decentralisation are similar: public anger at media exposure of corruption through *kan kan settai* (local officials entertaining central bureaucrats) and *kara shutcho* (paper business trips by local officials), and the need for greater efficiency and effectiveness in administering public policy during financially tighter times. Democracy is to some extent an issue here too, around gaining political space for local voices in the policy system. And again, it was only after the formation of the non-LDP government in 1993 that the decentralisation movement gained some momentum. The crucial issue of what is to be decentralised still remains contentious, with those in the centre skilfully manipulating the issue to frustrate any attempts to take away their power.

Although legislation was introduced from the mid-1990s to transfer some central government functions to local government, central ministries and agencies have continued to ensure that transfer of authority to local governments has not matched the legislation's original intent and has instead swung to their favour. The result has been transfer of administrative burden without transfer of control. Yet despite the centre's feet-dragging, political and economic imperatives for reform have enabled local governments to gain some responsibility for managing local issues and have forced many local chief executives to act with more transparency and accountability. Local governments are nevertheless still hamstrung, particularly by tight central control over local government finances.

Legislative changes

In June 1993 both houses of the National Diet passed a joint resolution on decentralisation with support from all political parties. Under the Hosokawa and Hata cabinets (July 1993 to June 1994) the issue of decentralisation was included in the broader agenda of political and administrative reform, which created the political space for concrete institutionalising moves to begin. Yet the weakness of the legislation virtually ensured it would be toothless.

In May 1995, the Law to Promote Decentralisation (*Chiho bunken suishinho*) was passed with a validity period of five years. It did not spell out the specific details of decentralisation, and simply empowered the seven-member Committee to Promote Decentralisation (*chiho bunken suishin iinkai*)[8] to make recommendations to the Prime Minister. The Committee consulted widely, including meetings with local leaders nationwide.[9] It produced an interim report and five other reports. The interim report set out a number of possible changes that included clearly demarcating responsibilities between the national and local governments, abolishing agency-assigned (*kikan inin jimu*) functions (discussed below) and establishing new rules for consultation and coordination between the national and local governments.

To the great disappointment of many local advocates, the recommendations in the five reports were simply watered-down versions of the Interim Report. Many derided the Committee for buckling under pressures from the central bureaucrats. Critics argued that the real issue of local autonomy was hijacked by the central government's ploy to reduce its own administrative burdens. It transferred the centre's administrative functions, but not its responsibilities, to local governments. This would create for the central government the economic efficiency that is a main plank of its administrative reform agenda (Shiratori, 1998: 3). But the move would not invigorate the system by giving responsibility for local matters to local political leaders. It would instead ensure that the entrenched power relations this highly centralised system sustains would not be disrupted and that local governments would be stretched, perhaps weakened, even further.

Agency-assigned functions

The most significant achievement of this phase of local reform was the legislative changes to the system of agency-assigned functions. In the Japanese system the central government is free to assign functions to local governments, which must carry out the centre's commands without assuming legal authority for what they do. The changes are, ironically, a form of decentralisation: one that devolves work but not power. The centre has continued to resort to this system to relieve its own administrative load. By the mid-1990s assigned functions had been increased fivefold through postwar so that local governments performed about 80 per cent of prefectural and 40 per cent of municipal services in this capacity. The central government offers national equality as justification, claiming the assigned functions system helps to standardise the quality of government programmes nation-wide (Nakamura, 1999: 129).

The decentralisation advisory committee indicated initially that it would recommend abolishing this system. But it retreated under pressure from the central government. The new law is a compromise and divides the assigned functions into two categories: *jichijimu* (local functions) and *hotei jutaku jimu* (entrusted functions). Local functions are those that need to take account of local needs so local governments must perform them, for example city planning, school education and some welfare policies. Entrusted functions serve the nation but for administrative efficiency they are to be carried out by local governments, such as maintenance of family registers, census and administration of national elections. Under the new law just over half the former agency-assigned functions come under the category of local functions and the rest are entrusted functions.

Central financial control

Crucial to the centre's tight administrative control is its tight financial hold on local governments (Jain, 1989). Some observers recognise this financial arrangement as the source of the system's shortcomings: political corruption and administrative inefficiency. Those who agree advocate greater financial autonomy as essential to reforming local government. The absence in the Committee's reports of any recommendations to change the deliberately constraining financial dependence shocked and deeply disappointed many. Retaining the financial status quo has fundamentally compromised local government autonomy.

Indeed, retaining the financial status quo as part of reform measures presents an obvious paradox. The centre's tight financial hold over local governments has provided the structure that is largely responsible for the corruption that 'reform' measures are, at least rhetorically, to clean out. This system's central subsidy for local projects and its central control over issuing local bonds to raise local government finances are recognised to have fostered *kan kan settai* entertaining and *kara shutcho* business trips. These two methods for financial control are the most hotly debated issues since the Shoup Mission in 1949 recommended that local governments be provided with their own tax sources. Yet, here both remain untouched.

Transferring administrative functions to local governments without adequate resources or independence to generate them will intensify the difficulties that many local administrations already face. Smaller administrations with weak financial bases are particularly vulnerable. The burden of extra unfunded tasks from the centre will force many of the smaller local governments to seek strategic alliances or amalgamation with other local governments so they can deliver services most efficiently to their residents. Implementing the nursing care insurance system for the elderly from April 2000 will be a test case for many of Japan's municipalities, since it requires them to provide an important service for local residents while virtually completely dependent on the central government to finance the scheme (Yamasaki, 1999: 17–21).

Indeed, a number of contentious issues such as the transfer of national personnel to local governments remain beyond this round of decentralisation recommendations. Their absence highlights the polemic that surrounds government decentralisation and the extent to which the centre's entrenched interests make the present system resistant to any reforms that seek to download the centre's power.

The LDP's fall from government, at least temporarily, and other economic and political imperatives drove many local governments to initiate reforms from below aimed at providing efficient and effective government in response to citizens' needs and free of corruption. Some local governments continued to resist reform but others took initiatives to ensure that reforms would deliver efficient, transparent and representative government. Local ordinances for freedom of information and adoption of business accounting practices are examples of reforms that local leaders have taken up to help improve local political practices.

Centre–local conflict of policy interests

Because local and national priorities sometimes differ, the interests of local and central governments are sometimes irreconcilable. The centre claims that because local administrations seek to address narrow local issues, local administrations do not know the national context of their actions and neither recognise nor appreciate national interests. As the centre sees it, only when the centre holds the bulk of responsibility can the interests of the nation be served best; local priorities can sometimes satisfy local constituencies at the expense of the nation. The refusal of the Okinawa prefectural government to renew land leases for the US military and Tokyo Metropolitan Governor Ishihara Shintaro's electoral pledge to seek the return of the US Air Base in Yokota to Japan or at least to secure joint Japan–US use of the base with the aim of making it a third airport for Tokyo indicate conflict of interest over important foreign policy issues for the nation and important domestic concerns for the relatively few in the region. Other polemical issues such as movements against construction of a nuclear plant in Maki Town in Niigata, a dam in Tokushima and industrial waste-disposal facilities in Mitake Town in Gifu have highlighted domestic policy tensions between what the centre identifies as the national interest on the one hand, and what local citizens identify as their safety and well-being on the other (Jain, 2000: 551–70).

As with the two reform areas discussed above, the absence of consensus even among those who share some vested interests helps to shape the course of decentralisation. It disables the development and pursuit of clear policy direction and consequently of real reform. Competing views tug at the principal questions of reform – why, into what, and how – making the reform agenda up for constant grab. The range of answers to these three questions shows up the irreconcilable conflict between the centre's struggle to retain power and the local administrations' struggle to attain greater independence.

Reform advocates have been unable to moderate their views to form a united front, so the centre has effectively held sway. The new rules governing centre–local distribution of functions have pushed decentralisation beyond debate into policy implementation. This is change, but it is not political reform. Initiatives from the local administrations and their supporters have added momentum to the decentralisation movement. However, progress cannot but be incremental. Japan has a labyrinthine, centre-heavy political system with a long history of centralism. Neither are about to yield.

Conclusion

We have seen in this examination of three areas of political reform that each confronts the hugely difficult task of relocating entrenched power – from politicians whose power is based largely on money to politicians who play clean, from kasumigaseki bureaucrats to elected political representatives, and from the central government to local governments. Here we have three different but inextricably linked parts of a national political system whose adhesion comes from the interweaving of shared interests, personal connections, favours and obligation, as well as – perhaps more than – formal institutional structures. Inevitably the three areas share much when it comes to reform. '*Seiji kaikaku*' is a certain type of political reform.

The LDP's temporary loss of government is a crucial backdrop to the recent reform developments since it created the space for reform advocates to gain some sway. Under thirty-eight continuous years of the LDP regime there had been debate and piecemeal change, but mostly a reasonably united front that frustrated any attempts to induce 'reform', which could unseat LDP power-mongers from office. Ironically, the LDP downfall was triggered by revolt within the party ranks, as reformist groups split to form their own parties. In turn the LDP downfall fed further into the confluence of circumstances that produced it, dislodging the power of the conservative old guard enough to enable reformist voices to finally register on the nation's political landscape.

In all three areas reformists pushed through legislation under coalition governments. This is certainly change. But it is questionable reform, as in cleanup or improvement. We see surface change – in what things are called and the legal means through which politics is played out literally on centre stage. But, still literally, we do not see it in the deals that run politics from behind the scenes through convenient legislative loopholes. This is more appearance than actual reform. Who wields power, how they do it and what is the outcome are largely as they were under the well-embedded money-politics regime that gave rise to the reform movement and, as we should not overlook, helped in Japan's postwar rise to economic pre-eminence and international standing. Today the political system is not visibly cleaner, or more effective and efficient in delivering service to the people.

Hrebener's critical assessment surely goes to the heart of this matter: 'Reform in *seiji kenkin* can be undertaken only as part of a sweeping reform – a reform that alters the very foundation of Japanese politics. Anything short of such a 'revolution' is likely to produce only variations on the present theme' (Hrebenar, 2000b: 82). That is precisely what we see. Very limited political will cannot engineer reform of an entire political system, which is made all the more inflexible by a firmly embedded power regime that came into power under the money politics that still sustains this system. This tradition applies not just to the LDP, but to all political players who must play by its rules if they are to survive, let alone thrive.

Thus some of the features of the reform movement are inevitable. Absence of consensus, both between and within the divided political ranks, slows the process and creates the divisions into which resistance feeds. Because deal-making is still the way of political life, outcomes of the reform legislation are far removed from the stated intentions that motivated it.

It is useful to remember that while the discussion above looks at each area of political reform separately, the players and structures in each area are the same, across the central government politicians, the bureaucrats and the local governments. Furthermore, these developments take place concurrently and feed between each area into the brokerage of favours and money-wielding, the factional divides, personal alliances and legislative loopholes that are ironically instrumental in all three areas of political 'reform'. Thus, deals as usual have meant that legislation in all three areas is the product of severe compromise that is significantly different from original stated intent.

Similar forces have driven all three reform areas. The need for financial stringency as the national economy slowed forced more attention to performance issues – effectiveness and efficiency of all levels of government. The departure of the political old guard cleared the way for younger reformist blood. Finally, popular media exposed to the electorate a clearer picture of the severity of the nation's political corruption. These are the forces driving serious reform, and the public surely has reason to push its political representatives ever harder to deliver it. Such is the way of power and politics in many national political systems.

Notes

1 I focus here on the Lower House electoral system as this house is substantially more powerful than the Upper House (House of Councillors) of the Diet.
2 For background information leading to the formation of these parties, see Jain (1997: 19–24).
3 The original bill had proposed a total ban on corporate donations to individual politicians, but this was unacceptable to the LDP and the compromise plan allowed corporations to donate up to 500,000 yen annually to individual politicians.
4 Since 1993, six Prime Ministers (Hosokawa, Hata, Murayama, Hashimoto, Obuchi and Mori) have headed one or the other type of coalition governments.
5 Many cases of mediation by politicians between businesses and public officials surfaced in the past. For example, in mid-2000 Yamazaki Tai, a Tokyo Metropolitan Assembly member was arrested after overcharging small businesses in return for pressing the Tokyo Credit Guarantee Corporation to extend loans to the businesses in violation of an investment and interest control law. Similarly in 1994, former Construction Minister Nakamura Kishiro was indicted after he allegedly imposed inappropriate pressure on the Fair Trade Commission at the request of a major construction company. Nakamura was charged on suspicion of receiving

bribes from the company in exchange for his mediation. At the time of writing this case was still being tried at the Tokyo High court.
6 Inoguchi (1997), for example, critically surveys the extent of scandal and dubious practices within the bureaucracy.
7 Eda worked as secretary to Hashimoto Ryutaro who was Prime Minister when this reform was legislated.
8 The committee was chaired by a business leader (Moroi Ken of Taiheiyo Cement) who has been on numerous central government advisory committees. The six other members were three academics (Horie Fukashi of Kyorin University, Nishio Masaru of International Christian University and Higuchi Keiko of Tokyo Kasei University) and three local leaders (Nagasu Kazuji, former governor of Kanagawa Prefecture, Kuwahara Keichi, former mayor of Fukuoka City and Yamamoto Soichiro, former governor of Miyagi Prefecture).
9 Seminars, symposiums and workshops at local centres were organised throughout Japan to discuss issues around decentralisation. Published reports on some of these meetings include: 'Chiho bunken fuoramu '96 in Aomori', 'Chiho bunken fuoramu '97 in Iwate', 'Chiho bunken fuoramu '98 in Tokushima', all sponsored by the Nippon Foundation and proceedings published by Jichi Sogo Center, Tokyo.

References

Hrebenar, R. J. (2000a), 'Rules of the game: the impact of the electoral system on political parties', in Ronald J. Hrebenar *et al.* (ed.), *Japan's New Party System*, Westview, Boulder.

Hrebenar, R. J. (2000b), 'The money base of Japanese politics', in Ronald J. Hrebenar *et al.* (ed.), *Japan's New Party System*, Westview, Boulder.

Ikuta, T. (2000), *Kanryo: Japan's Hidden Government*, ICG Muse. Inc., New York.

Inoguchi, T. (1997), 'Japanese bureaucracy: coping with new challenges', in Purnendra Jain and Takashi Inoguchi (eds), *Japanese Politics Today: Beyond Karaoke Democracy*, Macmillan, Melbourne.

Jain, P. (1989), *Local Politics and Policymaking in Japan*, Commonwealth Publishers, New Delhi.

Jain, P. (1995), 'Electoral reform in Japan: its process and implications for party politics', *The Journal of East Asian Affairs* (Seoul), 9(2), 402–27, Summer/Fall.

Jain, P. (1997), 'Party politics at the crossroads', in Purnendra Jain and Takashi Inoguchi (eds), *Japanese Politics Today: Beyond Karaoke Democracy?*, Macmillan, Melbourne.

Jain, P. (2000), 'The people have spoken: *Jumin Tohyo* and the Tokushima anti-dam movement in Japan', *Asian Survey*, XL(4), 551–70, July–August.

Johnson, C. (1982), *MITI and the Japanese Miracle: The Growth of Industrial Policy, 1925–1975*, Stanford University Press, Stanford.

Johnson, C. (1995), *Japan: Who Governs? The Rise of the Developmental State*, W. W. Norton and Company, New York.

Kabashima, I. (2000), 'Chiho no 'okoku' to toshi no hanran', *Chuo Koron*, September, pp. 130–43. (For a summary of his main points, see David Fouse's posting on the SSJ-Forum 28 August 2000 <ssj-forum@iss.u-tokyo.ac.jp> accessed 3 January 2001.)

Kataoka, T. (1992), *Creating a Single Party Democracy*, Hoover Institution Press, Stanford.
Kohno, M. (1997), *Japan's Postwar Party System*, Princeton University Press, Princeton.
Look Japan (2001), Interview with Koike Tadao, January.
Muramatsu, M. and Ellis S. Krauss (1984), 'Bureaucrats and politicians in policy-making: the case of Japan', *American Political Science Review*, 78(1), 126–48, March.
Muramatsu, M. (2001), 'A bureaucrat's burden', *Look Japan*, January.
Nakamura, A. (1999), 'Reforming government and changing styles of Japanese governance: public administration at the crossroads', in Hoi-kwok Wong and Hon Chan S. (eds), *Handbook of Comparative Public Administration in the Asia-Pacific Basin*, Marcel Dekker Inc., New York.
Otake, H. (1996), 'Forces for political reform: the liberal democratic party's young reformers and Ozawa Ichiro', *Journal of Japanese Studies*, 22(2), 269–94, Summer.
Otake, H. (1998), 'Overview', in Otake Hideo (ed.), *How Electoral Reform Boomeranged: Continuity in Japanese Campaigning Style*, Japan Centre for International Exchange, Tokyo, 1998.
Ozawa, I. (1994), *Blueprint for a New Japan: The Rethinking of a Nation*, Kodansha, Tokyo.
Ramseyer, J. Mark and Frances McCall Rosenbluth (1993), *Japan's Political Marketplace*, Harvard University Press, Cambridge.
Seligmann, Albert L. (1997), 'Japan's new electoral system: has anything changed?' *Asian Survey*, 37(5), 409–28, May.
Shiratori R. (1998), 'Naze ima chihojichi o ronjirunoka' (Why debate local autonomy now?), in Nihon Chiho Jichi Kenkyu Gakkai (ed.), *Chiho jichi no sentan riron*, Keiso Shobo, Tokyo.
Stockwin, J. A. A. (2000), 'Electoral pressures for change: the effect of political reform', in Australia-Japan Research Centre, *Toward Reform and Transparency in Japanese Policymaking Process*, Pacific Economic Paper, AJRC, Canberra, no 301, March.
Wada S. (2000), 'Generational change and political upheaval', in Otake Hideo (ed.) *Power Shuffles and Policy Processes*, Japan Center for International Exchange, Tokyo.
Yamaguchi J. (1997), *Nihon seiji no kadai*, Iwanami Shinsho, Tokyo.
Yamasaki Y. (1999), 'Toward the Adoption of Nursing Care Insurance in Japan', *NIRA Review*, 6(4), Autumn. (http://www.nira.go.jp/publ/review/99autumn/yamasaki.html)

3 Regulatory reforms in Japan
Issues and prospects

Javed Maswood

Beginning in the late 1970s but more so in the 1980s and 1990s, governments in western industrial countries began an ambitious programme of regulatory reforms and deregulation. In the US, regulatory reforms began in the late 1970s and examples include the Airline Deregulation Act (1978), Natural Gas Policy Act (1978), Motor Carrier Reform Act (1980), the Cable Television Deregulation Act (1984) and the Telecommunications Act (1996) (Lincoln, 1998: 56). Apart from an ideological commitment to small governments and market forces, these reform measures were spurred along by imperatives of national competition in an emerging environment of economic globalisation. Globalisation, a product of progressive trade and financial liberalisation in the postwar period and of revolutionary advances in communication and information technology (IT) has rendered national economies more porous and susceptible to global market forces. It also highlighted a need for domestic structural reforms in order to enhance the resilience of national economies to global pressures and to boost national competitive advantage.

Structural adjustment is socially painful and costly but countries that introduced reforms have performed better, as measured by aggregate economic indicators, compared to countries that held reformist pressures largely at bay. Reform has been debated in Japan since the early 1980s and the reform agenda included electoral and political reform, administrative reform, education reform, regulatory reform, constitutional reform and corporate reform and rationalisation. Following extensive political turmoil, the Japanese government, in 1993, overhauled the electoral process and replaced multi-member electoral constituencies with a combination of single-member districts (SMDs) and proportional representation (PR).[1]

In this chapter, I will focus on regulatory reform and deregulation as an important component of a strategy to reverse persisting economic stagnation. Until the late 1990s, however, deregulatory commitments were more rhetorical than real. Instead, to resolve a festering banking crisis, the government encouraged banks to consolidate their financial position by generating revenue and profits through offshore activities, mainly in Asia. The expectation was that banks would use externally generated profits to dispose the high proportion of non-performing loans that had been leftover following the collapse of the Japanese bubble economy in the early 1990s. And to generate economic growth and recovery, the ruling party adopted a strategy of massive public works programme rather than remove regulatory inefficiencies and impediments to growth. Regulatory reform and restructuring did not figure prominently, despite rhetorical assertions, until after the 1997 Asian financial crisis. Even then, the pace and extent of reform was tortured and slow compared to western countries.

One explanation for this could be obstructionism by the many vested interests in society that benefit from existing regulatory structures and processes. However, this ignores that there are also many powerful interests, including big business, advocating reforms and deregulation. Another explanation could be bureaucratic resistance since deregulation can be expected to curtail the influence of the powerful ministries. There is some truth to this notwithstanding the substantial diminution of bureaucratic influence and prestige in the 1990s, as a result of economic policy errors, corruption and incompetence. In this paper, I will combine the bureaucratic politics model with the argument that regulatory reforms have suffered because of the nature of party politics and the absence of policy competition between the main political parties.

I will begin with a general discussion of reforms in a historical and comparative context. The urgency of reforms was evident in official policy rhetoric but continuities, rather than sharp breaks, continue to define the main characteristics of Japanese politics. I have structured the paper in three main sections. The first section includes a general discussion of reform and change in Japan to place the current reform agenda in an historical context. The following section looks at the rationale and necessity of reforms in Japan. While emphasising the imperative of reform, it should be pointed out that there are many who reject the reformist push, in the belief that reforms will undermine some of the positive features of Japanese political economy, such as income equality and egalitarianism, and cooperative labour–management relations. In the third section, I will look at regulatory reforms and explain how its progress has been affected by party politics in Japan. I will also consider future prospects in light of electoral reforms and changes in the party structure and party politics.

Continuity, change and reform

Change, to use a well-worn phrase, is a constant and can either be adaptive or transformative. Adaptive change is gradual and evolutionary whereas transformative change usually follows a breakdown, partial or total, in the process of adaptive adjustment. Systemic transformation, however, is not easy because it entails a zero-sum redistribution of costs and benefits. The changes advantage and disadvantage different sections of the community and this asymmetric distribution of costs and benefits makes significant reform difficult, because those who are adversely affected will invariably seek to obstruct the reform process.

Still, despite impediments, reforms do happen and one of the main stimuli for reform and transformation, in the contemporary period, has been international trade. Exposure to international competition forces states to adjust to shifts in competition and demands. This adjustment can be gradual and managed but when demand conditions change rapidly or when a new competitor enters the global marketplace, the first temptation usually is to protect industries facing economic decline. National policy makers often use trade restrictive practices as a way of avoiding structural adjustment. As with structural adjustment, protectionism too, is a costly process because import restrictions redistribute incomes from consumers to 'uncompetitive' producers. Still protection is relatively easy, compared to structural adjustment, not only because it can be justified as being in the national interest but also because consumers are poorly organised to advocate freer trade policies and producers, being fewer in numbers, are better organised and more influential. In democracies, political processes are more responsive to the needs of organised interests groups. Because beneficiaries of protection are concentrated (small number of manufacturers) and losers diffuse (large number of consumers), it is easy to see why interest of a numerically smaller group, being better organised and more influential, are often translated into policy decisions.

Protectionism can be averted through specific programmes to encourage and facilitate industrial relocation from internationally uncompetitive to competitive sectors. Depending on the effectiveness of such strategies, it may be possible to reduce protectionist pressures emanating from industries threatened by international competition. With this in mind and in the interest of securing a domestic consensus on liberal trade policies, the US government, at the start of the Kennedy Round of trade liberalisation talks, promised to introduce specific trade-related structural adjustment programmes to facilitate retraining and the movement of workers from depressed to emergent industries. The implementation of this programme was essential to securing Congressional support for further trade liberalisation. In practice, however, structural adjustment programmes became simply another measure to support unemployed workers rather than a specific programme for retraining workers displaced by foreign competition and imports. The flawed implementation of this programme was a factor behind protectionist sentiments in the late 1960s and 1970s.

Since the early 1980s, multilateral agencies, such as the International Monetary Fund (IMF), have been involved in promoting structural adjustment in countries that experience financial and economic difficulties. Again, the experience with IMF structural adjustment programmes stands testimony to the difficulties of transformative change. The IMF, as the lender of last resort for many countries in Latin America, Eastern Europe and East Asia, required borrowing countries to introduce structural adjustments to ensure long-term economic viability and ability to service foreign debt. Few countries, however, were able to faithfully implement programmes designed by the IMF. Structural adjustment programmes required countries to dismantle costly subsidy schemes, withdraw support from uncompetitive industries, etc. and these ultimately led to loss of political support for governments. For governments it created a dilemma of choosing between structural adjustment and political instability.

Reforms do happen but often as a last resort when the easy options have been exhausted. Social and political revolutions are one way of overhauling inefficient and decrepit structures but this route to reform involves considerable violence and destruction. Ideally, reforms are best carried out through existing political processes without undue violence and turmoil. Political dictatorships are able to transform structures through a top-down process of reforms in the absence of open political participation. In democracies, by contrast, successful reform requires the consent of the electorate. This can be achieved in the context of a competitive party structure, in which one or another political party offers a rationale and logic of reforms. Reform, as purposive political action, is more likely when there exists a clear champion of reform.

The process of step level changes in democratic political systems is well-exemplified by swings in American foreign policy between isolationism and internationalism. Similarly, electoral politics, in the US and elsewhere, provides periodic examples of normalcy interrupted by critical elections that alter basic policy directions. New Deal economic policies in the US became a reality following the electoral triumph of the Democratic Party and more recently, economic policies in US, UK and several western countries marked a significant departure from Keynesian liberalism toward conservative supply-side economics, involving privatisation, corporate rationalisation and regulatory liberalisation. Such drastic economic policy changes were possible only after majority support for the reform agenda of the relevant political party. In Britain and in the US, the Conservatives and the Republicans, respectively, claimed to have a popular mandate for reform to make the respective national economies more competitive internationally.

Economic globalisation, as indicated above, is a product of progressive trade and financial liberalisation in the postwar period and a revolution in communications and IT. The industrial revolution laid the basis for a particular type of social formation and the IT revolution is in the process of instigating a similar societal and structural transformation. In Britain and America, the focus of new administrations was to position the economy to meet the challenge of new technology and a global economy. This meant rationalisation of industry structures to make them to more competitive and deregulation to encourage private sector creativity, entrepreneurship, and instil a more competitive ethos into both government and the private sector. The microeconomic policies of the British government was to create an 'enterprise culture' which involved mainly negative policies, including 'tax reductions, eliminating Government controls, breaking up monopolies and restrictive practices and freeing the labour market' (Harris, 1988: 123). The social costs, in terms of unemployment and economic stagnation, were considerable but, in Britain, Prime Minister Thatcher refused to give in to growing demands to reflate the economy, abandon the determined attack on social welfarism, or to veer away from rigid monetarist dogma.

The long sweep of Japanese history is punctuated by only a few major shifts from existing social, political and economic structures. The pattern of historical progression has typically involved short periods of foreign borrowing followed by a lengthy process of adaptation and indigenisation. For example, following the introduction of Chinese scripts at an early period of Japanese history, the Taika reforms of the seventh–eighth century introduced many of the administrative, legal, taxation, land tenure and town-planning models that had been perfected in China during the Tang dynasty. The borrowed institutions were gradually adapted to suit indigenous culture and social practices. The long period of evolutionary change was disrupted again during the Meiji period. In the latter half of the nineteenth century, Japan, threatened by western technological superiority tried to quickly overcome its economic and military vulnerability by introducing western technology, administrative and legal practices. This period of foreign borrowing instigated by the Meiji government was motivated by a determination both to renegotiate the 'unequal treaties' imposed on Japan, and to restore national dignity. Another radical transformation of Japan occurred at the end of the Second World War. This time, a foreign occupying force initiated political, economic and social reforms to prevent a future return to militarism and to democratise and liberalise the economy. Not all the reforms survived the end of Japan's occupation. For example, the anti-monopoly legislation and the Fair Trade Commission were pared back to strengthen bureaucratic capacity for industrial targeting and guidance.

Transformative changes have been few and far between and instigated either by an acute sense of vulnerability (the Taika and Meiji Reforms) or by a foreign occupying force. The weight of scholarly opinion is that Japan changes only slowly, through an adaptive process, and that it is a poor reformer of existing constructions. Against this historical background, questions of reforming the Japanese politics (electoral and party reforms, constitutional reforms, administrative reforms) and the Japanese economy (administrative and deregulatory reforms, banking reforms, corporate reform and rationalisation) have resurfaced in the contemporary period and been the subject of debate within and outside Japan. Actual achievements have been modest however.

The contemporary reform debate in Japan: rationale and resistance

The contemporary reform agenda cannot be classed in the same category as those in the nineteenth century and in the postwar period. Each of the earlier two periods was characterised by an acute sense of national crisis in which there was wholesale questioning of existing structure that had brought the country to its crisis. This also opened up possibility of extensive reforms. The 1980s and 1990s have also been infused by a sense of crisis, but of an entirely different magnitude. There is neither a consensus on the extent of necessary reforms, nor even a pervasive sense of crisis. The Japanese economy has been mired in a 'Great Stagnation' but this has not contributed to a pervasive sense of gloom. There may be some concerns about future employment prospects, leading to a decline in consumption demand, but there is no immediate, or pervasive, sense of deteriorating living standards or prosperity. It is worth emphasising as well that there are no suggestions that the reform agenda must replicate the British or the American experience of the early 1980s (see Chapter 5 in this volume). Even if there is some convergence, we should not expect homogenisation. Indeed, as I shall explain further below, the debate on reform in Japan is substantively different to the processes that led to deregulation and rationalisation in the west. In the end, Japan will retain distinctive features although the broad thrust of regulatory reform and deregulation must be at the centre of reform efforts.

To add perspective to the contemporary debate on Japanese reforms, it should be mentioned that reforming Japan has been an American objective since at least the 1970s. Successive American administrations have attempted to transform Japanese economy to ensure fair trade practices, and broadly complete the reform that were initiated after the Second World War but reversed by the onset of the Cold War. One of the objectives of American occupation forces was to restructure the Japanese economy away from monopolistic structures to more competitive market processes but this objective was set aside as priority shifted to rebuilding Japanese economy and recruiting Japan as an ally in the strategy of containment. The new priorities helped shape Japan's economic resurgence but ever since the first trade conflicts, American strategy has been to force Japan to reform and abandon 'unfair' trade and economic practices. The partial success of American policies gave rise to an extensive literature on the effectiveness of foreign pressure, *gaiatsu*, in reforming Japanese political economy.

The many existing case studies of gaiatsu and its effectiveness point to a conclusion that gaiatsu is most likely to succeed when there are strong and powerful domestic lobby groups to resonate foreign demands and pressure. By that logic, a combination of domestic support and foreign pressure for change should have produced extensive changes to postwar economic structures but, as ever, reforms have been measured and slow, and produced a sense of frustration, both within and outside Japan. The western, more particularly American, 'frustration of rising expectations'[2] is understandable considering the long-standing expectation that Japan will adhere to transparent and liberal economic practices or, maybe, even converge on the western models of economic liberalism. Within Japan there is frustration that successive political leaders have failed to grapple with the hard choices confronting the country to ensure future economic success. One reason for the halting process of reform might be the absence of consensus around the nature of reforms, as well as basic disagreement on the need for change.

The contemporary reform agenda is being driven largely by on-going economic crises but it should be emphasised that there is as yet no overwhelming consensus on need for extensive reforms. There are many groups that are overtly hostile to reforms and even some of the potential beneficiaries, such as consumers, are ambivalent about reforms. Still, reform is an imperative of economic globalisation to ensure Japan's competitiveness in a global economy. Other reform agenda in Japan include political reforms to reduce the prevalence of money politics and corruption, as well as Constitutional reform. The Japanese Constitution was written by the occupation forces and arguably constrains Japan's capacity to engage on the international stage as a 'normal' country. Proponents of Constitutional reform are insistent that the fundamental law of the country be a product primarily of Japanese interests and reflect Japanese cultural and historical values. Reflecting the interest in constitutional reform *The Daily Yomiuri*, in November 1994, published a draft of possible revisions to the Japanese Constitution with the objective of generating debate and public approval for reforms. Constitutional reform had previously been a taboo subject but is now a legitimate topic for discussion and debate.

As far as economic and regulatory reforms are concerned, supporters insist that globalisation and demands of national competitiveness require radical overhaul of economic practices. They maintain that regulatory reform is essential to overcome the economic malaise that has continued since the collapse of the bubble economy in the early 1990s. Through the decade, the Japanese economy has performed markedly poorly, in comparison to its main economic competitors. The miracle economy that recorded double-digit growth in the 1960s, a higher than average economic growth rates in the 1970s and 1980s has practically marked timed while the US and other western countries have marched ahead. Large infusions of public funds also failed to generate sustainable economic growth and, inevitably, expert opinion began to emphasise structural reform in order to overcome contemporary economic difficulties. Within Japan, there are increasingly loud voices, especially from within the business community and independently of foreign expectations, in support of economic and regulatory reforms.

During the growth phase of the Japanese economy, several features unique to the Japanese political economy were lauded for their contributory role, such as state activism, industrial targeting and regulation of investment activity. In addition, a particular style of industrial management that emphasised long-term market share rather than short-term profitability, enterprise unionism, seniority-based wage structure, and lifetime employment was credited with contributing to Japanese economic success.

Increasingly, however, there is concern that the old structures have ossified the capacity of the economy to respond to global market forces, resulting in a loss of competitiveness and inability to meet the technological challenges of the future. Nakatani Iwao says that Japanese economic stagnation is a result of 'institutional fatigue' and that the new requirements are a more competitive industrial structure, a better structure of corporate governance to replace the main bank system, and elimination of close government–business relationship to liberate private entrepreneurship and initiative (Nakatani, 1997: 399–400). He argues that economic globalisation makes it imperative for Japan to undertake major deregulation of its economy, without which private sector innovation and creativity is impossible. Proponents of deregulation argue that Britain and the US, in the 1980s, successfully reformed their economies to increase the importance of market forces and withdraw the state from established roles in regulating private activities and providing so-called public goods. The corollary to this is the argument that Japan must follow in their steps, unleash private sector creativity by winding back the public sector, in order to remain internationally competitive. Japan has a highly regulated economy. As a result of deregulation in the US during the 1980s, for example, the percentage of GDP in the regulated sector of the economy declined from 28.9 to 23.3 per cent between 1980 and 1992 (MacAvoy, 1995: 5). By comparison, Miyauchi Yoshihiko, Chairman of the Regulatory Reform Committee estimated the percentage of Japanese industry affected by regulatory controls to be 42.3 per cent in the late 1990s (Miyauchi, 2000).

Sceptics, however, dismiss any need for major reforms. The President of Toyota Motor Corporation, Okuda Hiroshi, cautioned against excessive reformist zeal. He expressed concerns that western-style rationalisation of industrial production would rebound to corporate disadvantage making it difficult for companies to retain and recruit new workers in future when Japan was likely to have labour shortage (Okuda, 1999). Ronald Dore, similarly, has argued that reforms along western lines are unnecessary and carry the danger of undermining the functional and desirable features of the Japanese system, such as equity and cooperative labour–management relations (Dore, 1999). But, according to Nakatani, the emphasis on equality and egalitarianism has robbed the Japanese economic system of a necessary competitive edge and is at odds with efficiency needs. There is sufficient acknowledgement of the reality that past models (involving regulation, state intervention and guidance, labour–management relations) might not be adequate to meet the challenges of a global economy dominated by rapid changes in technology.

However, even if key groups agreed on reforms they seemed motivated by different objectives. This is most clearly highlighted by Carlile (1998) who points out that reforms have been debated since the early 1980s but that the main actors had different motivations. He argues that the reformist debate has passed through three separate phases. The first phase, early 1980s to 1985, saw the establishment of a reform commission to present options to the government. In the second period, 1985–93, the reform debate was in abeyance as the bubble economy growth pushed the need for reform to the backburner. In the third phase, from 1993 to 1997, reforms were taken up again in the context of a stagnant economy. These shifts in the reform debate suggest that as far as the government and elected politicians were concerned, administrative and regulatory reforms were seen mainly as a solution to a worsening fiscal crisis of the state. In the second period, the urgency disappeared because good economic growth appeared to restore state capacity to continue to fund pork-barrel *zoku* politics. If the government was concerned with a looming fiscal crisis, business organisation, like Keidanren, were more intent on reforms to reposition Japan as a competitive player in the new and challenging world of economic globalisation. Thus, business groups and the government approached the issue of reforms from different perspectives. That was true at least until the Asian crisis, which finally produced a consensus, however weak, that global pressures required an overhaul of state–society relations and hence of administrative and regulatory structures. The Asian crisis has been termed the first crisis of economic globalisation and it demonstrated the consequences of ignoring the imperatives of global market forces. As such, we can argue that since the Asian crisis the reformist debate has entered a fourth phase, marked by some progress and some unity of purpose.

Following the Asian crisis, new measures were introduced to reform and strengthen the banking and financial sector and hasten economic recovery. These reforms had a learning effect on the private sector and led to some rationalisation of production to enhance international competitiveness. The measures so far employed represent a tentative first step if Japanese industries are to recapture lost ground.

In terms of regulatory reforms, it should be noted that Japan was the first developmental state and its political economy was characterised by high levels of state interventionism that led to a close working relationship between the administrative arm of government and the private sector. This structure was designed to facilitate recovery and catch-up development without wastage of scarce resources through duplication or investment in relatively unproductive activities. The catch-up phase of economic development had been realised by the 1970s following rapid growth in the 1960s. Thereafter, under American pressure, the Japanese government progressively liberalised its economy and relaxed overt controls on private sector activities. Still, the regulatory framework remained both extensive and intrusive, with the objective of creating an ordered market rather than competitive markets that were seen as chaotic and undesirable. The penchant for orderly transaction is evident, for example, in regulation governing location of liquor stores so that each 'would have a fixed territory, thereby minimising direct competition among them (Lincoln, 1998)'. Competition, however, is increasingly the essence of the modern market economy and Japanese regulatory structures have the effect of impeding its progress.

In the 1980s, many western governments engaged in large-scale deregulation of their economies but this movement completely by-passed Japan. The bureaucracy, committed to ordered rather than competitive markets, continues to jealously guard its regulatory prerogatives. The divergent growth outcomes of the 1990s have been attributed to this fundamental fact. Where western deregulation sparked private sector creativity and entrepreneurship, Japanese industries remained sluggish and slow to take advantage of emerging opportunities.

Reform has been recognised as important within Japan but it is important also to differentiate between the rhetoric and reality of reform. Successive governments emphasised their commitment to a reform agenda. Former Prime Minister Hashimoto's reformist rhetoric was particularly impressive, promising in 1996 to introduce a series of reform measures, conveniently labelled the Big Bang Reformation Plan. Likewise, Prime Minister Mori also emphasises reform, insisting that Japan can only resolve its difficulties by creating an 'IT society'. He likened 'IT' to a 'divine wind' (*kamikaze*) which required as a precondition regulatory openness and liberalisation (*Bungeishunju*, 2000: 171). Even though reform is openly acknowledged as necessary, the reality is that the government has held on to slender and false hopes that persisting economic and banking crises can somehow be overcome through normal and gradual recovery processes without extensive reform and restructuring. It was only in the period after the Asian financial crisis, and even then after the installation of the Obuchi government in 1998, that reforms began to be implemented. This phase of reform however was short-lived as Prime Minister Mori, his successor, failed to sustain the momentum that had been generated.

The objectives of the 'Big Bang' Reformation Plan were to introduce and create free markets; fair trade practices; and global standards of accounting, legal and supervision systems. Implementation of the Big Bang began with the enactment of Laws for Financial System Reformation (LFSR) and establishment of Financial Supervisory Agency (FSA) in June 1998. Among some of the measures dealt with by the LFSR, the government made it easier for small- and medium-sized enterprises (SMEs), previously reliant on bank finance, to secure capital from non-bank finance companies. The objective was to make it easier for SMEs to secure venture capital for risky projects that banks might not be willing to support. The FSA had surveillance authority to monitor the financial sector and entailed a weakening of the powerful Ministry of Finance (MOF), which previously had performed the dual function of surveillance, as well as with budgetary and taxation matters (Horiuchi, 2000). The Obuchi government also, in the end, decided to use public funds to restructure and bail out the financial system. This had long been argued as imperative to crisis resolution but the preferred government strategy was to shelter the financial institutions for a lengthy enough period for them to overcome the problem of non-performing loans through regular operating profits.

With the implementation of Big Bang reforms, Hoshi Takeo and Hugh Patrick confidently affirmed that the economic crisis was over and that it was now only a matter of time for recovery to kick in. The Big Bang reform, they claimed was an important step toward economic resurgence (Hoshi and Patrick, 2000: 1). The completion of Big Bang reforms in 2001 may be an important step in resolving Japan's economic crisis since the early 1990s but sceptics, including the Chairperson of the Regulatory Reform Committee, Miyauchi Yoshihiko, maintain that real Big Bang financial reform is unlikely unless the government relinquishes control of the postal savings system, which has deposits amounting to approximately 20 per cent of total private financial assets (Miyauchi, 2000). Thus, deregulation to place Japan on a sustainable growth trajectory and prepare for technological innovation remains an important on-going task for the government. In addition, privatisation of state owned enterprises is still to be completed. The Japanese government began privatising the railways in 1993 but it still maintains a significant stake in several regional rail networks.

Excessive regulatory intervention inhibits risk-taking behaviour and drive and adds to compliance costs for business, causing a loss of international competitiveness. Two points need to be stressed here. Firstly, innovation and entrepreneurial spirit were not absent even at the height of strong state period. There were examples of new and innovative enterprises, like Honda and Sony, which successfully carved out their own niche within a highly regulated economic structure. The point however is that entrepreneurship needs to be facilitated rather than obstructed as was the case in the past, when the government tried to make things difficult for 'upstarts'. Second, pursuing deregulation in order to catch up to the west for a third time in its history does not imply equi-finality, or convergence. As mentioned above, Japan's earlier borrowing had not led to convergence and there is no reason to assume either a different outcome in the contemporary period or that a global economy demands an end to differentiation.

Prime Minister Hashimoto also emphasised administrative reforms, not only to restructure and scale down bureaucratic institutions but also reduce the outreach of the bureaucracy and diminish its policy-making role. Bureaucratic influence is based on its role in introducing and implementing policies as well as informal administrative guidance. Although Mikiso Hane painted a picture of Japanese bureaucracy as the *key* to understanding trade and economic policies, as well as domestic politics (Hane, 1996: 71), the role of Japan's elite bureaucracy has undergone considerable change since the 1970s, partly as a result of liberalisation and internationalisation of the economy. Further shifts in the balance of power between elected politicians and bureaucrats occurred with the emergence of policy-savvy *zoku* politicians.

The changing dynamics of political and bureaucratic influence in policy-making was evident in the process leading to formulation of the Big Bang Plan. But the timing was opportune also because bureaucratic prestige and infallibility had been dented by a series of policy blunders (e.g. use of tainted blood in transfusions and chaotic response to the Kobe earthquake of 1995) and failures in economic management. Prior to the 1990s, the bureaucracy was perceived as the backbone of economic and political stability but was now recast as capable of nothing more than confused activism and engaged in the same corrupt practices that one expected to find only among the elected politicians. The reforms weakened the MOF, the most powerful bureaucratic agency in Japan, by removing the surveillance function of the MOF and vesting it in a newly established FSA. The reformed MOF, renamed the Treasury Ministry, now has jurisdiction over only taxation and budgetary issues. This could not have been in the interests of the MOF but continuing economic mismanagement and corruption scandals had weakened its bargaining position and influence. The Big Bang Plan was based on reports by various *shingikai*, or consultative committees, attached to the MOF but the agenda was set not by the Ministry but by the Deregulation Subcommittee of the Administrative Reform Committee. The demands of the latter forced the MOF to concede to 'positive deregulation' (Horiuchi, 2000: 238). Still, it is important not to overplay the rise of elected politicians in policy-making processes because established bureaucracies retain considerable residual influence.

The politics of regulatory reform in Japan

At the outset, it should be pointed out that there are important differences between Japanese and western perceptions of regulatory reform. In the West the process of deregulation abolished or phased out controls and restrictions in many areas of private sector activity. In Japanese, the corresponding term for deregulation is *kisei kanwa*, which implies not abolition of controls but rather a relaxation of regulations. The business community, in Japan, may be in favour of deregulation but policy makers have avoided the western route, which is seen as having contributed to a collapse of social morals and national cohesiveness. As mentioned above, the task of reform was recognised in the 1980s and the government established, in 1995, a Deregulation Subcommittee under the broader umbrella of the Administrative Reform Commission. The Subcommittee was enhanced to the status of Deregulation Committee in January 1998 but in April 1999 was renamed the Regulatory Reform Committee. This name change was perhaps intended to dampen western expectations that Japan would emulate the West, which would then only heighten frustration with the seeming lack of progress toward deregulation.

The Regulatory Reform Committee, under the Cabinet Headquarters for Promoting Administrative Reform, is chaired by Miyauchi Yoshihiko Chairman and CEO of ORIX Corporation, Director of Keidanren and Vice Chairman of Keizai Doyukai. Keidanren and Keizai Doyukai are representative industry bodies and Keidanren, in particular, has actively promoted the principle of reform and deregulation. According to Lonny Carlile, Keidanren leaders have tended to view deregulation as the solution to Japan's economic malaise, trade frictions, yen appreciation and technological challenges. Carlile writes that Keidanren official began in the mid-1980s, 'a campaign to foster a proderegulation, anti-bureaucratic climate among its membership' (Carlile, 1998: 89).

The reform agenda extends beyond economic and administrative issue areas and progress will depend, to a considerable extent, on political activism and leadership. There are two issues that need to be emphasised. First, it is obvious that administrators and bureaucrats are wary of a process that must ultimately erode their influence. Regulatory reforms imply a basic redefinition of state–society relations and a diminution of bureaucratic influence and for that reason the Japanese bureaucracy has not embraced reforms with any enthusiasm.

Second, quite apart from lingering bureaucratic obstructionism, there are additional problems within Japan's party structures. The politically dominant Liberal Democratic Party (LDP) abnegated its policy responsibility and allowed instead a separation between LDP rule and bureaucratic reign – a pattern that is replicated throughout Japanese history,[3] as during the Tokugawa period when formal political authority resided in the Emperor but the Shogun governed the country. For meaningful regulatory reform, policy leadership is essential and this, in turn, requires a revitalisation of party structures and electoral politics, to transform political parties into policy organisations.

To preserve the integrity of reforms, the task must be the responsibility of political leaders. Of course, political leaders in Japan are not entirely without influence or dependent on the bureaucracy. Moreover, they have progressively enhanced their policy-making capacity relative to the bureaucracy. Thus, as noted above, political leaders were largely responsible for outlining the parameters of Big Bang reforms. However, given continued and residual bureaucratic influence, the reforms delivered much less than promised by way of administrative and bureaucratic reforms. Administrative reforms that have been approved are largely superficial rather than substantive.

The LDP monopolised government for much of the postwar period and while some individual zoku politicians used professional longevity to good use, the party, as an institution, did not distinguish itself as a policy organisation or as an organisation capable of introducing fundamental reforms. Instead, the LDP relied on 'reformist' and 'dynamic' politicians to translate reform objectives to policy instruments. Responsibilities were derogated to key individual and we had examples of this in the current Mori administration, which included two politicians, Hashimoto and Yanagisawa, who supposedly possessed the requisite reform credentials and capacity. This same logic was apparent in the challenge to Prime Minister Mori's by Kato Koichi in November 2000. Kato legitimised his challenge on the basis of his superior reform capabilities and considering that Prime Minister Mori's first cabinet seemed to have stalled on reforms introduced by his predecessor, Prime Minister Obuchi.

LDP's policy abnegation was not an electoral disadvantage given the fragmented and weak opposition parties. The main opposition party, the Japan Socialist Party (JSP) had been weakened by a split in 1960, by its own ideological rigidity and by the emergence of minor political parties competing for the opposition votes. The post-split JSP remained the largest opposition party until the mid-1990s but had little prospect of ever winning government. The longer it stayed in opposition, the more irresponsible it was in formulating an alternative policy platform. With policy vacuum among the opposition political parties, there was little incentive for the LDP to be more policy assertive. The LDP, by contrast, found strength by deliberately eschewing policy principles and by broadening its appeal beyond its traditional support base in the countryside. The party re-invented itself as a 'catch-all' or a 'catch-almost-all' political party. For example, it would have been logical for the JSP to try and incorporate the emerging environmental movement of the late 1960s, but it was actually the LDP that responded to these growing concerns by legislating tough environmental measures in the 1970s. For successful reforms political leadership is fundamental and I will in the remainder of this section, look at the prospects for policy activism among Japan's political parties following the electoral reforms of 1994.

The JSP, relegated to the political backwaters for much of the postwar period, became even more anachronistic and irrelevant to the political future of Japan following the collapse of socialism globally in the 1990s. This probably contributed to the decision by Ozawa Ichiro, Hata Tsutomu and others, in 1993, to defect from the LDP and create, what they hoped, would be a viable and an alternative conservative political party, in opposition to the LDP. This course of action was less fraught with danger because of the weakened opposition political parties.[4] In 1994, they formed the Shinshinto (New Frontier Party, NFP) and held out the prospect, at least initially, of a competitive two party political system. Ozawa intended his actions and that of his group to become the basis for a competitive party structure in which politicians bore the responsibility for policy formation and which gave the voting population real choices about Japan's political development. The risks were minimal because the ideological divide in Japanese party politics had practically disappeared and there was no chance that the LDP split would in any way benefit the socialists.

The formation of a non-LDP coalition government following elections in 1994, and for the first time since 1955, did produce an important breakthrough in electoral reforms. The maladies of a multi-member electoral system, money politics and political corruption, had sparked the crisis in Japan and in its place the government of Hosokawa Morihiro brought in a combination of 300 SMD and 200 PR seats. Similar reforms in France, following political turbulence in the 1950s, had ushered in an ideological 'bipolar quadrille' (Grunberg, 1985) but Ozawa's actions were motivated by a desire to create a non-ideological bipolar party structure or coalition of political parties. Theoretically, single member districts are productive of a stable two party political system theory but a combination of SMD and PR led to a period of extreme fluidity and uncertainty. It was difficult not only to predict the possible coalitions but even whether individual parties would survive, merge or disappear entirely. Political parties emerged, merged, or re-emerged with considerable frequency but by 2001 some semblance of stability appeared to have replaced extreme volatility, with a three party governing coalition led by the LDP on the one hand, and an opposition block led by the Democratic Party of Japan (DPJ), on the other. Ozawa's own reconstituted Liberal Party has been reduced to the role of a minor party in the opposition camp. If Ozawa had hopes of heading an alternate government, that no longer appears to be a realistic ambition.

There are a number of reasons to be optimistic about a shift toward policy oriented politics over the medium term. In this emerging structure of Japanese politics, however, the LDP is unlikely to be the reform party despite individual attempts to swing the party hierarchy around to a reformist position. Within the LDP, Kato Koichi, had been vocal in advocating reforms and envisioned himself, like Margaret Thatcher in Britain, as helping to reshape the structure of the Japanese economy. It meant wresting control of the party from a leadership that had failed to meet the necessary requisites. This set the scene for a clash within the party between a group of reformers led by Kato and another group of traditionalists led by Mori. The outcome of a leadership challenge appeared to favour Kato because he had a popular approval rating of 54 per cent compared to just above 12 per cent for Mori, seen as inept. Mori's sins of omissions and commissions had also lowered his stock within the party. Even the leader of his own faction, Koizumi, criticised his performance as party leader and Prime Minister. Koizumi insisted that the government had to press ahead with administrative and structural reforms, even at the risk of negative economic growth for a few years, in order to revitalise the country for the longer term. In Mori's defence, it should be noted that it would be inordinately bold for any prime minister to risk the fledgling economic recovery that had just become discernible. Indeed, a longer-term perspective would have convinced any political leader that reform could only be deferred, not avoided, and that it made more sense to act decisively than vacillate. If resistance to reform is not entirely attributable to concerns for economic recovery, then it is more likely that the LDP, as a political party, was not the party to introduce major reforms. Kato was brought down by this fundamental contradiction between his advocacy of reforms and the party's unwillingness to embrace reforms.

Kato threatened a no-confidence motion in order to depose the incumbent but was also determined to work within the party rather than defect. Past defections had done little to change the internal workings of the LDP. But when it looked like his no-confidence motion might not succeed, he quietly decided to withdraw his challenge. Unlike Ozawa, he had decided that it was better to work within the party to bring in reforms rather than defect and risk failure like others before him. Yet, the abortive challenge also has, according to some observers, sealed the fate for Kato and made it near impossible for him to ever achieve leadership of the Party when before it was seen as one for his taking. Critical of Mori for lacking vision and conviction, Kato demonstrated his own weaknesses and poor judgement.

In April 2001, Koizumi won the LDP presidency based on his campaign pledge to reform Japanese politics. His victory was achieved not as a result of traditional backroom deals and factional alignment but as a result of strong support from the rank and file membership of the LDP. Popular support forced party bosses to throw their weight behind him, despite a reputation for being a loose cannon and a maverick. Whether Koizumi is able to deliver on his campaign pledge will depend on the ability to carry the parliamentary wing of the LDP, which remained doubtful since his legitimacy was based on rank and file support rather than support within the parliamentary party. However, if the LDP, under Koizumi, is able to return better than expected results in the July 2001 Upper House elections, that may strengthen his position within the parliamentary wing and facilitate the task of reform.

Even if the Koizumi administration ends in failure, there are reasons to be optimistic that policy competition between the two coalitions will lead to conditions favourable to regulatory reform, including electoral contestation based on policy issues.

First, responsible politics and a move away from money politics is premised, partly, on new legislation to provide political parties with public funds for campaign finance purposes. As recipients of tax-payer monies, political parties will inevitably be obliged to justify their expenses by putting forward responsible policy alternatives. That would be a logical outcome of the new arrangements but of course consumers and tax-payers everywhere, more so in Japan, are poorly organised to articulate their demands.

Second, the two dominant political parties, the LDP and DPJ, derive their electoral support from distinct communities. The support base of the LDP is in rural districts and a rough analysis of the representative base of the DPJ reveals its strength to be in the urban districts, much like the disbanded Shinshinto. This distinctiveness can be expected to have significant policy implications. It is worth noting that the demographics of the DPJ are similar to that of the NFP and it is in a position to campaign for regulatory reform, either through political pressure while in opposition or as the party in power. At the time when NFP appeared to be positioning itself as a leading political party, a poll of party members revealed that they were more substantially inclined towards aggressive deregulation than LDP politicians (Vogel, 1999: 11–12).

Japan's urban consumers have, and continue to suffer in silence with the LDP looking after mainly agriculture and producer interests. Big business in Japan is supportive of deregulation and regulatory reform while consumer groups remain unconvinced of the potential benefits, despite estimates that regulatory relaxation in the period 1990 and 1997 had resulted in a net benefit to consumers of Yen 6.6 trillion a year. In this same period, the total benefit to producers was estimated to be Yen 8.2 trillion a year (*Nihon joho kyoiku kenkyukai*, 2000: 104). Consumer apathy and antipathy towards reform is not unique to Japan and there are global examples of consumer preferences for trade protectionism and regulation despite demonstrable benefits of trade liberalisation and deregulation. This emphasises the importance of education and explanation of different arguments.

If the DPJ consolidates its position in urban centres, it could eventually pave the way for policy oriented electoral contestation. The crucial question is whether the party will remain a unitary political party at all or go the way of the NFP. A fractured opposition handed easy victories to the LDP through much of the postwar period and more so in the period following electoral reforms in 1994. The obvious lesson for aspiring opposition political party is to maintain party unity. Leadership contests within the DPJ brought the party to near collapse in 2000 but it managed to weather the storm. Whether it will build on that to strengthen unity of purpose remains still to be seen. As an urban-based political party, the DPJ can be expected to advocate liberalisation and deregulation to reduce the cost of living for Japanese consumers and workers. This strategy will also benefit the export sector and lower wages pressure within the economy. Liberalisation and deregulation are economic imperatives from a globalist perspective and have been advocated by Keidanren, the peak business group in Japan. It is also a policy position that should also appeal to Ozawa's Liberal Party.

Third, policy oriented politics assumes that the LDP will abandon both its strategy of representing a diverse set of electoral interests and its attempt to be a 'catch-all' political party. T. J. Pempel argues that the LDP will be forced to abandon its inclusionary, all embracing and unprincipled political stand, as a result of the negative fallout following liberalisation of the agriculture sector in the 1980s, which alienated core electoral supporters of the LDP. Moreover, in late 1988 a government advisory committee proposed changes to laws that had long provided protection to small shopkeepers, and in 1989 the government introduced a consumption tax, which added to the burden of small business and shopkeepers. The cumulative effect of these policies was to erode LDP's electoral strength and, according to Pempel, reversing the backslide in electoral fortunes will require the party to re-discover its primary roots and cultivate support more actively in its traditional support base, especially among the rural community (Pempel, 1999). The catch-all electoral strategy emerged at a time when the JSP played the role of the leading opposition political party. The JSP was formed in 1955 but expectations that it would be one of the poles of a bipolar party system were quickly proved false. In 1960, the moderate wing of the JSP broke away to form the Democratic Socialist Party (DSP) and in the decade of the 1960s, a number of smaller centrist political parties emerged to erode the support base of the JSP. By the late 1960s, the JSP was already a party in secular electoral decline and in the 1970s, when LDP began to reposition itself as a catch all political party, it was to be the final nail in the coffin of the JSP. A common assumption about competitive two party political systems is that there is an inevitable race to capture the middle ground, or become a catch all political party. This had been observed in Britain, Germany and several European countries but in Japan, it was only the LDP that was successful in broadening its support base to what might be considered non-traditional conservative voters. While it became a catch all political party, the LDP did not turn away from its traditional supporters in the rural districts and maintained protection for the farm industry until forced to bring in liberalisation under pressure from its trading partners. The JSP, by contrast, was prevented from adopting a more moderate line by it association with the radical left wing labour unions and by the emergence of moderate, left of centre political parties, such as the DSP and the Komeito. JSP derived its core support from the members of the Sohyo affiliated labour unions and the militancy of Sohyo prevented it from reaching out to the growing middle class or to non-unionised labour. In the party structure, the centrist political parties became the spoilers of a two-party political system. These were, at the same time, too small to capitalise on emerging social forces and interests, such as environmental and welfare concerns. The success of the LDP strategy effectively marginalised the JSP and ensured long-term conservative rule in Japan. And as LDP support declined, these smaller parties became logical alliance partners, resulting in a transition from a catch all political party to a catch all coalitional alliance.

The role of the leading opposition party has now devolved to the DPJ – a conservative political party formed around a core of former LDP politicians. Its former leader and currently Chair of the Policy Research Committee,

Kan Naoto, was a Health Minister in the Hashimoto government and distinguished himself by taking on the health bureaucracy to expose bureaucratic corruption. Despite his reformist credentials, the path to reforms lies in initiatives by the ruling LDP that clears the path for a competitive bipolar party structure. In a conservatively oriented, non-ideological party structure, as exists at the moment, there may still be some incentive to appeal to a wider section of the community but there can be no advantage in alienating core party supporters.

It is clear that neither the LDP nor the DPJ can expect to secure parliamentary majorities by relying sole on core supporters but there are no clear advantages of a shift to the middle ground if such a strategy also alienates core supporters. A successful electoral strategy must involve coalitional arrangements where centrist political parties, like the Liberal Party or the New Komeito, are genuine keepers of a balance of power, rather than spoilers of the ideologically based party structure of the period before the 1990s. To the extent that this becomes a political reality, we can expect the LDP and the DPJ to consolidate their specific electoral roots and rely on successful coalition strategies to win government. This will also be conducive of policy-based electoral competition. The LDP may, therefore, become more principled and less catch all but it is not the party that can be expected to lead with regulatory reforms. There are reform-minded individuals within the party, obviously Kato and Koizumi, but the party hierarchy is more likely to be suspicious of radical change. There are however, two factors that might force a shift in LDP stance toward reform. First, is the potential electoral and political pressure from the DPJ as it begins to gather support among the urban electorates and big businesses. The second factor is the question of survival itself. If the LDP drifts increasingly toward a position favoured by the farm community and other protectionist interests, it may find itself in a minority status, unable to compete with the DPJ.

Conclusion

Opponents of the regulatory agenda argue that the central problem plaguing the Japanese economy is insufficient demand, rather than supply side bottleneck. Thus Krugman and others argue that it is much more important to create the basis for demand expansion, even if through induced inflation. Japan has been in a period of deflation that has depressed consumption demand and from this perspective, it may indeed be the case that other measures, apart from deregulation, may hold the key to the present crisis. Nonetheless, deregulation and regulatory reforms are essential to the long-term competitiveness of Japanese industries and overall economic prosperity and this is the main crux of arguments by Takeo Hoshi and Hugh Patrick.

Regulatory controls are an impost on business but the costs of regulatory compliance are ultimately passed on to consumers. Deregulation, as such, can be expected to provide benefits to consumers in terms of lower costs and this has been demonstrated to be the case in many industries in the US, for example. According to Paul MacAvoy, the contrast between regulated and deregulated industries is striking. He writes that in the US, 'The four deregulated industries – rail, trucking, airline and petroleum products – experienced price declines of the order of 26–50 per cent after controls were ended. The three regulated industries – natural gas, electricity and telephone – continued to experience price increases except in markets specifically subject to decontrol' (MacAvoy, 1995: 8–9). Japanese experiences with regulatory reform have produced similar benefits to both consumers and producers. A government White Paper on regulatory Reform estimated that between fiscal years 1990 and 1997, the benefit to consumers and producers from regulatory reform amounted to an annual average of ¥6.6 trillion and ¥8.3 trillion, respectively (*Nihon joho kyoiku kenkyukai*, 2000: 104).[5] It is interesting, nonetheless, that consumers in Japan have not embraced regulatory reform as wholehearted as might be expected. There remain lingering doubts that reform will weaken standards on health and safety and that the welfare gains may be offset by negative externalities.

Consumer ambivalence might be attributed to the way political parties in Japan have played out their electoral contestation and, in this paper, I have argued that this policy aversion on the part of political parties may change as a result of electoral reforms. The electoral bases of the LDP and the DPJ may have a powerful effect in forcing the competing coalitions to clearly articulate policy preferences and win consumer/voter support for their respective positions. Enhancing the role of political parties is roughly equivalent to a diminution of bureaucratic influences in policy-making, and it is clear that the bureaucracy has been an impediment to regulatory reform.

Breaking the policy role of the bureaucracy also requires an understanding that a practical reason for bureaucratic involvement in policy-making is to ensure suitable *Amakudari* options for retired bureaucrats. Senior bureaucrats retire early in Japan and begin a new career in private sector and this transition is sustained only be the fact that the bureaucracy has a policy-making function and for firms and corporations, having retired bureaucrats on corporate payroll is an easy way of gaining access to the bureaucracy. The bureaucracy needs its policy-making role in order to sustain the Amakudari practice and if this is to be altered, it will be necessary to retain senior bureaucrats within government ministries longer. This, of course, will have implications both for government budgets and promotion prospects within ministries and agencies.

Notes

1 Electoral reform can be enormously beneficial to ruling parties but reforms are rare. In France, the socialist government moved to a system of proportional representation in 1985 in order to minimise potential electoral losses in the 1986 elections and retain government. The reforms did cushion the socialist losses but not enough to prevent the conservatives from winning government. And once in power, the conservatives quickly repealed electoral changes brought in by their predecessors (see Reeve and Ware, 1992: 10). Electoral reform has rarely been successfully manipulated by ruling democratic governments and one of the latest example of lasting electoral reform in a democratic country is, again, France. In 1958, the Fifth Republic abandoned proportional representation in favour of a two-ballot majority voting system. This was not an opportunistic power play but rather a genuine attempt to restructure a chaotic party system portrayed in a depiction of France as containing ' … two fundamental temperaments – that of the left and that of the right … three principal tendencies, if one adds the centre; six spiritual families; ten parties, large or small, traversed by multiple currents; fourteen parliamentary groups without much discipline; and forty million opinions' (see Lewis-Beck, 1984: 426). The electoral reforms effectively created a bipolar party/parties structure, dominated by the ideological left and the right, but at the same time, more pragmatic, more national, and more 'catch-all'.

2 Based on his study of the French Revolution, Alexis de Tocqueville made the counter-intuitive observation that revolutions are more likely in societies that have experienced economic improvement rather than stagnation, suggesting that it revolutions occur when expectations exceed the pace of improvement and lead to rising frustration (see Johnson, 1982: 63–4). In the context of US–Japan relations, a similar approach was taken by John Haley (1987) who argued that misguided assumptions of bureaucratic powers had frustrated American expectations of speedy dispute resolution.

3 The separation between nominal and real power centres was a necessity based on the principle of 'mandate of heaven'. In the Japanese understanding of this principle, since the Imperial lineage was absolute, the ruling Emperor had to be insulated from worldly policy failures, such that failures could be blamed on others, whether the Tokugawa shogunate before the Meiji Restoration or the ruling *genro* (elder statesmen from the four southern provinces who inspired the Meiji Restoration) during the Meiji period. By contrast, in the Chinese understanding of this same principle, Imperial authority was not an absolute and so the ruler could reign supreme. Instead, Emperors could be held accountable for policy failures and a ruling monarch could thereby forfeit the mandate of heaven and replaced by another dynasty. As such, Chinese history provides evidence of many dynastic transitions whereas the Japanese are proud of an unbroken line of Emperors. There are some very rare exceptions in Japan, as when the ruling Emperor in the eighth century accepted blame for a series of natural disasters and attributed them to heavenly displeasure at his lack of virtue. Imperial infallibility, however, is the rule that has been adhered to in Japan (see Sansom, 1958: 75).

4 Ozawa, Hata and others were following an earlier example of LDP politicians who, in the mid-1970s, defected to set up the New Liberal Club (NLC). The NLC had very small beginning, with only four politicians, and was unable to boost its numbers to pose any serious threat to LDP longevity. In the end, after about a decade of inconsequential existence the NLC returned to the fold of the LDP.

The difference in 1993 was that many more politicians were involved in the defection, encouraged in the knowledge that JSP was too weak to exploit any short term divisions in the ranks of conservative politicians.

5 See *Nihon no Hakusho: Waga Kuni no Genjyo to Kadai*, Nihon Joho Kyoiku Kenkyu Kai, Seibun sha, Tokyo, 2000, p. 104.

References

Bungeishunju (2000), 'Sori to iu no wa fujiyu na mon da: Mori Yoshiro sori tandoku interview', October.

Carlile, L.C. (1998), 'The politics of administrative reforms', in Lonny E. Carlile and Mark C. Tilton (eds), *Is Japan Really Changing its Ways? Regulatory Reform and the Japanese Economy*, Brookings Institution Press, Washington DC.

Dore, R. (1999), ' Japan's reform debate: patriotic concern or class interest? Or both?', *Journal of Japanese Studies*, 25(1), 65–89, Winter.

Grunberg, G. (1985), 'France', in Crewe, I. and David Denver (eds), *Electoral Change in Western Democracies*, Croom Helm, London and Sydney.

Haley, John O. (1987), 'Governance by negotiation: A reappraisal of bureaucratic power in Japan', *Journal of Japanese Studies*, 13(2), 343–57.

Hane, M. (1996), *Eastern Phoenix: Japan Since 1945*, Westview Press, Boulder, Colorado.

Harris, K. (1988), *Thatcher*, Weidenfeld and Nicolson Ltd., London.

Horiuchi, A. (2000), 'The Big Bang: idea and reality', in Hoshi, T. and Hugh Patrick (eds), *Crisis and Change in the Japanese Financial System*, Kluwer Academic Publishers, Boston.

Hoshi, T. and Hugh Patrick (2000), 'The Japanese financial system: an introductory overview', in Hoshi and Patrick (eds), *Crisis and Change in the Japanese Financial System*, Kluwer Academic Publishers, Boston.

Johnson, C. (1982), *Revolutionary Change*, Stanford University Press, CA.

Lewis-Beck, M.S. (1984), 'The stalled electorate', in Dalton, R.J., Scott Flanagan and Paul Allen Beck (eds), *Electoral Change in Advanced Industrial Democracies: Realignment or Dealignment?* Princeton University Press, Princeton.

Lincoln, E. (1998), 'Deregulation in Japan and the United States: a study in contrasts', in Gibney, F. (ed.), *Unlocking the Bureaucrat's Kingdom: Deregulation and the Japanese Economy*, Brookings Institution Press, Washington, DC.

MacAvoy, P.W. (1995), 'Twenty years of deregulation', in Paul W. MacAvoy (ed.), *Deregulation and Privatization in the United States*, Hume Papers on Public Policy, 3(3), Edinburgh University Press, Autumn.

Miyauchi, Y. (2000), Speech at the Foreign Correspondents Club of Japan, 26 May. (http: //www.somucho.go.jp/gyoukan/kanri/speech.htm).

Nakatani, I. (1997), 'A design for transforming the Japanese economy', *Journal of Japanese Studies*, 23(2), 399–417, Summer.

Nihon joho kyoiku kenkyukai (2000), *Nihon no hakusho: Waga kuni no genjyo to kadai*, Tokyo.

Pempel, T.J. (1999), 'Structural *gaiatsu*: international finance and political change in Japan', *Comparative Political Studies*, 32(8), 907–32, December.
Reeve, A. and Alan Ware (1992), *Electoral Systems: A Comparative and Theoretical Introduction*, Routledge, London.
Sansom, G. (1958), *A History of Japan to 1334*, The Cresset Press, London.
Vogel, K. (1999), 'Can Japan disengage? Winners and losers in Japan's political economy, and the ties that bind them', *Social Science Japan Journal*, 2(1), April.

4 Reforming Japanese banks and the financial system

Jennifer Amyx

Introduction

Unprecedented policy breakdown characterised Japanese finance in the 1990s. The failure of government authorities to aggressively tackle a serious non-performing loan problem in the nation's banking sector combined with macroeconomic policy mistakes to sink the economy into prolonged recession and set the stage for national financial crisis. Out of this large-scale policy breakdown emerged a new legal framework for dealing with ailing banks. The regulatory breakdown also spurred multiple reorganisations of Japan's institutions of financial governance. In June 1998, authority over financial supervision was transferred from the Ministry of Finance (MOF) to a new and independent Financial Supervisory Agency (FSA) and in April 1998, greater independence was granted to the Bank of Japan (BOJ). Then, in December 1998, the Financial Reconstruction Commission (FRC) was established to oversee the FSA and in July 2000, the MOF's Financial System Planning Bureau was merged with the FSA to form a new Financial Services Agency (FSA). Finally, in January 2001, the Financial Reconstruction Commission was dissolved and its functions assumed by the FSA.

Despite the introduction of a new legal and institutional framework for financial regulation, however, many of Japan's financial and economic indices looked even bleaker in the year 2001 than in any of the eleven years since the collapse of the nation's speculative asset bubble. Japanese banks held unprecedented amounts of non-performing loans, unemployment stood at a postwar high, the economy was in deflation, growth remained largely stagnant, the Nikkei Stock Index hit a sixteen-year low and mounting national debt – at approximately 130 per cent of annual gross domestic product (GDP) – led Japan's own Finance Minister to describe government finances as 'nearly catastrophic'. Upon this backdrop, one might suspect that legal and institutional changes implemented since 1997 have failed miserably to bring about any meaningful change in Japanese banks or the financial system.

This chapter argues, however, that truly significant changes have occurred in recent years in the regulation of Japanese financial institutions – despite the outcomes cited above – and locates this noteworthy change in the nature of information dynamics surrounding financial policy-making and regulation. The chapter contends that changes in the legal framework and regulatory structures from late 1998 on began to alter these dynamics by undermining the bureaucracy's capacity to strategically monopolise or manipulate information to influence financial policy-making. The result has been the elevation of the bad debt problem to the top of the political agenda and an end to the MOF's policy of regulatory forbearance towards banks. Banks are no longer permitted to delay the realisation of true portfolio values and circumvent regulations in the hopes that they will eventually regain their health.

Yet, while a necessary step towards reforming Japanese banks and the financial system, this change in information dynamics surrounding the non-performing loan problem is alone insufficient for achieving the reform of Japanese banks and the financial system. Delinquent borrowers – the source of the banks' bad debt – must now be dealt with aggressively if the non-performing loan problem is to be resolved once and for all. Whether and how this next step is carried out will determine not only the course of reform in Japanese banks and the financial system, but also whether or not the Japanese economy will be revived or simply muddle through with near-stagnant growth for another decade. The chapter identifies the political impediments to dealing with delinquent borrowers in a way that promotes structural transformation in the economy and the restoration of banks to health, arguing that most of these impediments derive from the Liberal Democratic Party (LDP)'s attempts to protect key support constituencies. The findings suggest that only a drastic transformation in the party or the emergence of powerful non-LDP forces will produce the political leadership necessary to resolve Japan's financial and economic woes, the ultimate reform objectives.

Inter-governmental relations and financial regulation

Understanding the magnitude and salience of recent change in Japanese financial regulation first requires an understanding of the critical characteristics of the pre-1998 system that produced delay rather than action in dealing with the non-performing loan problem. Prior to 1998, distinctive features of Japanese political, economic and administrative institutions produced incentives for passive Diet behaviour in the area of financial regulation, while also providing the bureaucracy with an informational advantage over the Diet. These information dynamics meant the absence of a market for policy-relevant information. The dysfunctional nature of the market surrounding information relevant to the policy-making and regulation of banks, in turn, enabled banks to serve as a buffer between the collapse of the speculative bubble and the real economy and permitted the Finance Ministry to postpone aggressive action on the bad debt problem. The non-performing loan problem was like a ticking time bomb, however, and with economic recession and a continued decline in asset prices, this time bomb eventually exploded in the form of acute crisis in late 1997.

A passive Diet

While Diet approval of legislation related to private sector finance was always necessary, the structure of the Japanese electoral system and paucity of legislative staff long gave politicians incentives to focus their political resources on more locally based niches of the economy.[1] Accordingly, Japanese private sector finance was governed by very few pieces of legislation until the mid-1990s and the MOF had a high degree of discretion in filling in the details of these broad and vaguely worded laws through cabinet ordinances, ministerial regulations and administrative notices.[2] Furthermore, few procedural controls were in place to detail the manner in which the MOF was to conduct its administrative guidance to industry.[3] Much of policy-making thus circumvented the Diet and the ministry played an important role in policy formulation, as well as implementation. Notably, in the early postwar period, the LDP's refrain from vocal articulation of policy positions on particular financial regulations worked in favour of national economic reconstruction. By keeping private sector financial issues largely outside of Diet debate, the LDP provided the opposition with little opportunity to challenge the government's low interest rate ceiling on bank deposits or unfavourable terms of consumer credit – policies that contributed to economic growth in that period (Mabuchi, 1997: 159).

The concentration of responsibility for financial regulation in a single government agency and this agency's organisational continuity relative to the Diet also meant that the MOF (more so than the Diet) was able to make credible commitments to industry (Vogel, 1994).[4] Industry actors, therefore, faced incentives to focus lobbying efforts on the bureaucracy.[5] On rare occasions when the MOF miscalculated the strength of *industry-wide* opposition to policy reforms and tried to move forward without first reconciling relevant interests, the bureaucratic-led bargain appeared to be temporarily displaced by interest group dominance. At such times, the industry's lobbying of LDP leaders prevented the ministry's reform initiatives from being incorporated into legislative proposals (Rosenbluth, 1989).[6] Turning to politicians for policy favours invited political interference in lending decisions, however.[7]

Furthermore, the highly compartmentalised nature of the financial sector meant significant divergence of interest across industry association membership. Thus, industry-wide consensus was possible only on a relatively small number of issues.

The regulatory principle underlying the MOF's supervision of the sector was the so-called 'convoy approach' (*goso sendan hoshiki*), which ensured that no financial sector actor was left behind and no actor moved forward so fast as to endanger the viability of others. This approach complemented statutory provisions that explicitly minimised competition in the sector and served a multiplicity of interests. Through supporting banks in this way, the government cushioned the impact of economic shocks on borrowers, including politically important locally based firms. At the same time, the *amakudari* practice of MOF officials retiring into positions in private sector financial firms meant that this principle was a reflection of self-interested ministry behaviour as well: Any bank that went under would be one fewer potential depository for officials retiring from the ministry. As long as the convoy principle was upheld – as it was until 1995 – politicians had no need to worry about banks in their constituencies failing.[8] In these ways, then, incentives of legislators, bankers and MOF bureaucrats were aligned in support of a passive Diet role on issues of financial regulation and supervision.

'Private' bureaucratic information

The MOF never monopolised policy-relevant information in the literal sense. Banks always knew more about their own operations than did MOF bureaucrats and, as time progressed, the ministry relied increasingly on the financial sector for both technical knowledge and information about the actual state of affairs in the industry. Yet, for all practical purposes, the MOF monopolised information on the state of the financial sector in intergovernmental relations. Private sector financial institutions cooperated in sharing information through informal liaison channels with the ministry because doing so helped officials ensure that no financial institution fell through the cracks and worked to support the maintenance of a cartel-like industry arrangement benefiting all members. If a financial firm fell into difficulty, the MOF arranged for a 'rescue merger' (*kyusai gappei*) behind the scenes, thereby pre-empting depositor or market panic. And, with its unblemished track record through the mid-1990s in guaranteeing banks, the ministry faced little pressure to disclose its privately held information to the Diet or public.[9] Demand for information from bank shareholders was likewise weak. The price of bank shares varied little across the industry and major shareholders were typically loan customers or related financial institutions holding shares as a sign of commitment rather than for profit-making purposes. Investor relations specialists were thus notably absent from Japanese firms and financial institutions.

In contrast to the perceived benefits to the financial industry of sharing information with the MOF's Banking and Securities Bureaus, there was little perceived benefit to sharing information with politicians. In fact, doing so potentially incurred significant costs. LDP leaders were staunch supporters of the government-subsidised postal savings system, which competed with private sector banks for deposits.[10] Furthermore, information 'leaks' were more likely in the political world.[11] Career-long employment systems and incentive structures in the bureaucracy and private sector financial firms, in contrast, placed a priority on organisational loyalty, therefore minimising the leakage of 'private' information that might otherwise occur with a more fluid labour market for bankers and bureaucrats.[12]

The rarity of outside directors or auditors in Japanese corporations further limited the access of the public to information concerning the financial soundness of banks and their borrowers. Until September 1996, a 'settlement of accounts approval system' (*kessan shonin seido*) was used for distressed banks, whereby the MOF guided and approved the settlement of accounts for these institutions, thereby alleviating auditing firms of responsibility (Karube and Nishino, 1999: 15). Information disclosure requirements for financial institutions and their borrowers prior to 1998 were also minimal and far below international standards. Without consolidated accounting, market value accounting or the inclusion of unfunded pension liabilities on corporate financial statements, the true health of financiers and their customers was difficult to discern. Vague asset assessment criteria further compounded the opacity both of corporate balance sheets and the little data that was made public. Moreover, the government's implicit guarantee of banks lowered incentives depositors might otherwise have had to monitor the health of particular financial institutions, given the insufficiently funded deposit insurance system.[13] For all these reasons, then, the gap between information available to financial authorities and the public concerning the state of the Japanese financial sector was distinctively large.

Ministry officials aspiring to enter politics might have been expected to be viable information sources for Diet members on matters relevant to financial supervision. Almost without exception, however, ex-MOF officials serving in the Diet spent the majority of their careers in the ministry's Tax or Budget Bureaus.[14] And, the MOF's lack of intra-ministerial coordination due to its extremely expansive range of authority and highly compartmentalised organisational design was infamous, long summed up in the phrases, 'a collection of bureaus rather than a ministry' (*kyoku atte, sho nashi*) and 'bureaucracy within a bureaucracy' (*kancho no naka no kancho*). With little information flowing across bureaus, the MOF not only monopolised information concerning the state of the financial sector *vis-à-vis* the Diet, but particular bureaus within the MOF also enjoyed informational advantages over others (Karube and Nishino, 1999; Author interviews with MOF officials, 1998–2000).[15] The MOF's jurisdictional monopoly on financial regulation furthermore meant little likelihood of bureaucratic turf wars uncovering otherwise hidden information.[16]

An enduring shift in information dynamics

Once the MOF became unable to effectively execute rescue mergers and protect the 'convoy' of domestic financial institutions from the impact of market forces after the bursting of the bubble, the supply of information from non-bureaucratic sources increased. The MOF's Banking Bureau encountered its first outright failure to arrange a rescue merger in 1995 but was still able to arrange for the disposal of failed institutions through non-legislative means in this year. Nonetheless, these failures attracted the attention of domestic and international market players alike and the MOF's regulation of the sector drew more scrutiny.

In 1996, public funds were used for the first time to dispose of seven housing and loan corporations called *jusen* and a prerequisite for gaining public support for the resolution scheme was more open disclosure of the real magnitude of financial sector problems. Yet, the passage of the legislation to dispose of the *jusen* was virtually impossible politically without the promise that public funds would not again be necessary. As a result, the use of public funds was ruled out thereafter as a policy option. With the collapse in November 1997 of the nation's tenth largest bank and fourth largest securities firm, however, the severity of the non-performing loan problem was no longer open to question. Nonetheless, LDP leaders assumed that the standard operating procedure of the rescue merger could continue to function and remained less costly than the alternative of using public funds to directly recapitalise banks and establish an infrastructure for dealing with failing banks. Thus, while the *supply* of policy-relevant information had expanded considerably by 1997, the *demand* for policy-relevant information from non-bureaucratic sources remained weak.

After an abysmal showing in the 1998 Upper House elections, however, the LDP no longer had the numbers to pass legislation on its own. The opposition parties seized this opportunity to put forward an alternative legislative proposal for how the Government should deal with the financial crisis. Drawing on information provided by foreign financial institutions and other non-bureaucratic actors, the Opposition was able to succeed in the passage of legislation to establish a safety net to deal with financial institution failures. This was the biggest reform issue of the 1990s and the new legal and institutional arrangements ushered in by the Financial Revitalisation Law (FRL) and related bills had significant implications for the flow of information into the public domain. Combined with the changes in accounting rules and competitive pressures introduced by the ongoing 'Big Bang' financial reforms, the October 1998 laws drastically narrowed the scope of potentially 'private' information and brought financial policy-making more out into the open.

Information disclosure pressures on private sector actors

By establishing a credibly funded infrastructure for dealing with insolvent financial institutions and granting the Financial Supervisory Agency (FSA) greater independence,[17] the FRL legislation made it possible for the agency to proceed simultaneously with the introduction of wider definitions for non-performing assets, stricter capital ratio requirements and heightened disclosure rules. The widened definition of bad debt used by regulators after 1998 is often overlooked when comparing bad debt levels in this period with amounts held by banks in the past. Until the latter 1990s, the definition of a non-performing loan was more restrictive in Japan than in other advanced industrial countries. Before fiscal year 1994, for example, loans to borrowers in legal bankruptcy or considerably past due were categorised as non-performing loans but restructured loans were not. From fiscal year 1995 on, however, regulatory authorities progressively widened the definition. Today, definitions of bad debt in Japan fall in line with globally accepted standards. Thus, while a rise in figures given for bad debt in the banking system since 1998 indicates that problems of a large magnitude remain, these figures also reflect more transparent standards.

Today when a financial institution's capital base falls dangerously low, the FSA also issues a prompt corrective action (PCA) order to the institution, requiring it to raise additional capital and take steps to address management failures or face the possibility of closure. Because this order is made public, depositors and investors are alerted of problems in particular banks, brokerages and insurance firms before these institutions reach the stage of insolvency. This procedure contrasts starkly with past attempts by the government to arrange rescue mergers behind the scenes for financial institutions under distress. The injection of public funds into banks since the passage of legislation in October 1998 has also been accompanied by the disclosure of the particular conditions attached to those funds for each bank. This greater transparency has the effect of bringing the public in as an additional monitor of compliance.

Stricter accounting standards also require banks and their borrowers to disclose more and realise the true value of their loan portfolios, making it increasingly difficult for financial institutions to hide problems. In the past, ailing financial institutions often tidied up balance sheets by transferring non-performing assets to affiliates. With the introduction of consolidated accounting, such practices no longer serve to hide problems. The new requirements to disclose unfunded pension liabilities and assess at market value further serve to clarify the financial soundness of financial firms and their customers.[18] The rapid unwinding of cross-held shares by Japanese banks in 2001 was one indicator that banks are at last feeling pressure from these new accounting rules that require the realisation of latent losses. Responsibility for the auditing and settlement of accounts now also falls squarely on the shoulders of external auditors rather than being implicitly borne by regulators. As a result, certified public accountants face legal penalties for affirming dubious accounting practices of firms.

As consolidation and restructuring of the financial sector move ahead, some semblance of competitive disclosure has emerged among financial institutions – that is, the disclosure of more information than legally required is now being used as a means for boosting credibility in the market. Management now has incentives to disclose negative information as quickly as possible so that market concerns can be addressed proactively rather than defensively. Pre-emptive disclosure also defends against lawsuits brought by shareholders against imprudent management. And, such lawsuits have not only risen in number since 1998 but many have also proven successful.[19]

Economic downturn and regulatory breakdown has furthermore effected a change in employment patterns and injected more fluidity into both the private sector and government labour markets. In the bureaucracy, too, rising numbers of officials – even those destined for the very top positions – opt to leave the civil service mid-career to pursue second careers in the private sector. As a result, neither Japanese firms nor Japanese government agencies retain the same extraordinary capacity to hide organisational secrets that they did in the past.

The different role of political vice-ministers today also suggests greater transparency in financial policy-making. In the past, politically appointed vice-ministers of finance often never even visited the MOF. Today, however, these individuals are integrated into the policy-making process, testify in the Diet concerning developments in the financial sector, and attend international meetings on financial issues. Moreover, in the past, the MOF's legislative proposals proceeded from the Director-General of the Banking Bureau to the MOF's Administrative Vice-Minister, and then to the Finance Minister, leaving the parliamentary vice-ministers entirely out of the loop.

Now, however, any proposal from the MOF or FSA must be presented to the two politically appointed vice-ministers as well. While this change does not guarantee substantive participation in policy decisions by these political appointees, it does ensure that they are informed and included in the policy-making process.

Increased competition for role of credible information provider

The discrediting of the MOF due to massive policy failures and scandals has given rise as well to greater scrutiny of data emerging from the government and the introduction of new legal requirements for information disclosure by the bureaucracy to the Diet and general public.[20] The outcome is a narrowing of bureaucratic discretion over when and where information sharing takes place. And, within this new context, the bureaucracy must actively seek to regain – and then retain – credibility as the main provider of technocratic policy-relevant information to the Diet.[21]

Some major political parties have moved to establish think tanks while others have increased their reliance on existing independent think tanks as alternative sources of policy information. Information contestation has also emerged from *within* the government. In the year 2000, for example, the Ministry of International Trade and Industry (MITT) and the Economic Planning Agency (EPA) requested that the MOF provide more detailed data on public works investment because such data is a prerequisite for more accurate calculations of GDP estimates. In the meantime, the growing presence of foreign actors in the Japanese financial sector and the increasing divergence in interests *among* Japanese industry actors mean that the number of entities with incentives to provide alternative views and supply information in support of those views will only proliferate.[22]

The fragmentation of financial authorities brought about by the FRL and the revision of the Bank of Japan Law, also implemented in 1998, has furthermore led to the generation of more information through inter-agency negotiation and debate. The MOF no longer enjoys exclusive jurisdiction over finance, as the FSA operates as an independent regulatory agency while the BOJ oversees monetary policy. MOF and FSA officials have engaged in open debate over a number of issues such as a change in the capital gains withholding tax, with each agency marshalling data to support its stance. The open and transparent debate over the BOJ's zero interest rate policy also contrasted sharply with past patterns of opaque decision-making related to monetary policy.[23]

The stark contrast between the MOF's propping up of the stock market in 1993 and the Government's response to the plunge in the stock market in 2001 is further illustrative of the greater transparency of government actions today. In 1993, amid concerns about continued declines in the Nikkei and the effect of those declines on bank assets, the MOF funnelled billions of dollars of pension funds overseen by its Trust Fund Bureau into the market. In fact, the Government carried out one-third of all purchases on the Tokyo Stock Exchange in that year (Tabb, 1995: 220). In contrast, when the market plunged in 2001, open debate was carried out concerning appropriate measures to support the stock market. This debate took place among members of the coalition government, between the coalition government, the MOF and the FSA, and between the Japan Bankers' Federation and the FSA. Although some of the proposals put forward by political leaders resemble the MOF's so-called 'price keeping operations' of 1993, these proposals remain the subject of intense debate, as of March 2001.[24]

Clearly, the bureaucracy's capacity to monopolise and manipulate policy-relevant information has decreased significantly. Moreover, the previous system of opaque informal relations-based regulation of financial institutions has been replaced with a more transparent arms' length rules-based system of regulation. As a result, the severity of problems in the financial sector is now exposed for the public to see in a way that they never were in the past. And, the exposure of these problems has raised the attention accorded these problems in the political arena.

Unfinished business: dealing with delinquent borrowers

Clearly, however, the change in information dynamics surrounding the bad debt problem and the clamping down on banks by a more independent regulator are alone insufficient for resolving Japan's financial sector problems. Translating these changes into far-reaching reforms of Japanese banks, the financial sector now requires the political will to deal with delinquent borrowers.

Since the bursting of the bubble, banks have dealt with bad debt primarily through indirect means, by holding onto this debt and provisioning for future losses. With the decline in business conditions and asset prices, however, these amounts of bad debt inflated considerably over time. At the same time, the decline in the stock market squeezed the unrealised profits on banks' portfolios, the main source of funds used to cover bad debt write-offs.[25]

When the Obuchi Administration initiated aggressive measures in the fall of 1998 to deal with banking sector problems, the political decision was made to tackle banking sector problems first and then address problems in corporate Japan once the financial sector was stabilised (Author interview with Deputy Commissioner of the Financial Services Agency, Hamanaka

Hideichiro, December 2000). It was for this reason that the FRC temporarily nationalised large financial institutions such as the Long-term Credit Bank of Japan (LTCB) and the Nippon Credit Bank (NCB) but refrained from clearing all of the bad debt from their balance sheets before their resale. Political leaders feared that the simultaneous emergence of *de facto* bankruptcies of large-scale financial institutions and large-scale lenders might throw the nation into panic. Initially, the market reacted favourably to the new infrastructure put in place to deal with failing banks and applauded the injection of public funds. Stock prices rose, relieving some of the pressure on banks and their borrowers, and some signs emerged that the economy might be on the upswing.

Bad loans amassed far more quickly than banks were able to write them off from 1999–2000, however. It became clear that the economy was not set for a quick rebound and the introduction of new accounting rules placed greater pressure on banks to unwind their cross-held shares. Following a drop of over 4,500 point in the Nikkei Index between September 2000 and March 2001 and the announcement that amounts of non-performing loans held by leading banks had increased for two consecutive years, the failure of the indirect method of dealing with bad debt could no longer be denied. Clearly, more direct methods of disposal were required if the bad debt was to be cleared once and for all from balance sheets. As long as the bad debt remained on the books of banks, it tied up capital that might otherwise be loaned for more productive investments and hampered the profit-making capacity of banks. And, with their survival no longer guaranteed, banks now had to pay more attention to profits. The Government, too, had an interest in seeing the profit-making capacity of banks enhanced due to the large amount of public funds injected into the banking system in 1998 and 1999.

Yet, the process of direct bad debt disposal has attracted significant political debate and faced significant obstacles because the direct disposal of bad debt naturally brings more pressures to bear on delinquent corporate borrowers. While such pressure ought to be welcomed as a means to force inefficient and unsound companies out of the market and facilitate structural reform of the economy, this increased pressure has raised serious concerns among politicians who fear that such business failures will undermine key electoral constituencies. Indeed, while a number of alternative routes for bad debt disposal exist, each is accompanied by political impediments to implementation.

The sale of non-performing debt

The first means of direct bad debt disposal, the sale of bad debt, is a method widely used across the globe for cleaning up banking systems plagued by large amounts of non-performing loans. A state-backed debt collection is typically established to purchase loans from banks through the buying of collateral at a discounted rate. The agency then attempts to collect on the debt.

Due to the emphasis on long-term relationships within the main bank system and the MOF's implicit guarantee of banks throughout most of the postwar period, however, a legal framework for a secondary debt market was slow to develop in Japan. When a corporate borrower became financially distressed in earlier periods, debt claims were often renegotiated and the main bank often dispatched individuals from the bank to attempt a management turnaround. In general, banks worked with their borrowers to help them cope through hard times.

Although a state-backed Resolution and Collection Corporation (RCC) was established in Japan in 1998 to purchase debt from banks, the RCC faced many obstacles to operating effectively. In particular, the business and economic conditions after the bursting of the bubble impeded the liquidity of the asset market, making it difficult to collect on collateral. Whereas the sale of assets of failed institutions was facilitated in the US following the US Savings and Loan crisis by an upturn in the economy and a rise in asset prices, economic stagnation and a sustained decline in asset prices characterised the environment in which Japan's RCC operated. The nation experienced ten consecutive years of falling land prices, meaning that banks experienced sharp declines in the value of their loan collateral. In fact, the RCC pays less than 10 per cent of the principal when purchasing most non-performing assets from financial institutions. The selling of bad debt to a state-backed debt recovery firm thus incurs large losses for banks.

Recent developments related to the securitisation of real estate holdings have facilitated the development of a secondary debt market and the purchase and sale of debt among private financial institutions. In November 2000, the government lifted a ban on real estate investment trusts (REIT) and the introduction of these instruments represents a step forward in stimulating the real estate market. Further legislative changes – such as amendments to tenancy laws – are needed to complement this development and make the real estate market more liquid, however. A market with greater liquidity would, in turn, enhance the capacity to sell assets of failed firms. A more liquid real estate market would also give a boost to the Japan Syndication and Loan-trading Association (JSLA), a privately initiated association trading in the secondary debt market since early 2001.

Following the February 2001 meeting of the Group of Seven industrialised nations, Japan's State Minister for Financial Affairs, Yanagisawa Hakuo, called on banks to rid their balance sheets of bad debt by selling off the collateral and cutting off ties with weak borrowers. Notably, however, Yanagisawa was censured within the party for his encouragement of this means of bad debt disposal, and became markedly more quiet on the issue thereafter. This means of debt disposal clearly posed a threat to too many LDP support groups such as the construction and retailing industry. As noted earlier, the sale of bad debt means the severing of long-established ties between banks and particular borrowers and therefore sparks fears among borrowers and their political backers that they will be left without a credit line. The sale of non-performing debt by a borrower's main bank, in particular, tends to trigger a domino effect wherein all financiers refuse to extend further assistance to a particular borrower, thereby leaving the borrower facing possible bankruptcy.

Liquidation of the borrower

The direct disposal of bad debt may also be facilitated by the invocation of bankruptcy procedures. The implementation of the Civil Rehabilitation Law in April 2000 has facilitated a more orderly restructuring of corporate Japan through the introduction of new bankruptcy proceedings. This law made it easier for small and midsize companies to declare bankruptcy and began to speed up the corporate rehabilitation process. The new law led to a surge in bankruptcy applications and has been utilised not only by the targeted small and midsize companies but also by large corporations such as Sogo Department Store.

Although the Opposition has argued that bad debt disposal should be carried out along with the legal liquidation of ailing firms, the LDP-led coalition has opposed resort to such a legal framework, arguing that further bankruptcies threaten to destabilise not only the economy but also Japanese society. Notably, however, the coalition has failed to pass numerous pieces of legislation that would alleviate some of the inevitable anxiety produced by large numbers of bankruptcies. One example is the coalition's repeated postponement of introducing legislation in the Diet to legalise a 401 k-style portable pension system so that workers can become more mobile in changing jobs. With a portable pension system, bankruptcies and the lay-offs that inevitably follow liquidation would not generate the same level of distress as at present. The reasons for postponement of this system's introduction have, predictably, been political. Its introduction was initially slated for April 2000, a date that coincided with the maturation of long-term deposits in postal savings. Expectations were high that these maturing funds would flow out of postal savings and into the 401 k-style mutual funds. This development, in turn, would not have curried the LDP favour with the private organisation of postal workers, an important support group of the party. Other examples abound of legislative measures that might have been taken to facilitate the use of bankruptcy proceedings as a means of bad debt disposal but have not.

Loan forgiveness

Finally, banks may simply forgive or waive delinquent loans. With loan forgiveness, banks typically forgive a large portion of debt in the hopes that the remaining outstanding debt will be recoverable once the borrower restructures. Officials in the LDP have understandably favoured this means of direct disposal of debt because it precludes the failure of key electoral constituencies. Throughout most of the post-bubble period, the party has kept its key constituencies such as the construction sector alive through massive amounts of public works spending. In fact, despite the harsh economic environment and the world-renowned inefficiencies and over capacity of Japan's construction industry, the number of construction companies in Japan grew in the 1990s and now numbers approximately 600,000. With such government support, the companies have had little incentive to restructure or merge. Similarly, the government also adopted a special 30 trillion yen loan guarantee programme for small and medium-sized enterprises in 1998 to support this key constituency. Despite these efforts to prop up weak companies, however, thousands of firms taking out loans ended up insolvent and increasing numbers of construction companies have proven unable to survive despite the fiscal stimulus packages. Thus, pressuring banks to forgive loans has become a primary focus of the coalition and it appears that this will be the most probable route of direct debt disposal aggressively pursued – to the likely detriment of deep-seated reform.

While debt waivers theoretically may encourage corporate rehabilitation, the obvious danger is that loan forgiveness will simply be a means to guarantee the survival of weak and undeserving firms. And, in guaranteeing their survival, such support would not only suggest the likely emergence of more bad debt from these same companies in the future but would pose an obstacle in the needed structural transformation of the economy. Without the exit of actors using resources inefficiently, the reallocation of resources so as to promote the entry of new actors into new and more promising areas of the economy is hampered. Sensitive to such criticisms, LDP leaders proposed in March 2001 the introduction of a framework under which relevant government agencies evaluate the restructuring plans of debt-ridden firms and then press for debt forgiveness by financial institutions if these restructuring plans are judged viable. Many remain sceptical that such a framework would provide the tough debt waiver standards needed to ensure corporate restructuring plans are properly screened. After all, many of the relevant government agencies have vested interests in preventing the failure of large numbers of their regulatory constituencies.

Conclusion

Significant change has occurred in Japanese financial regulation – most notably in the information dynamics surrounding policy-making in this sector. The past system of bank regulation was one in which the MOF enjoyed a significant information advantage over the Diet. The breadth of 'private' bureaucratic information enjoyed by the ministry derived from its reliance on informal relations-based regulation rather than arms' length rules-based regulation and long distinguished the process of financial regulation in Japan from more legislature-centred processes in Western democracies. Since October 1998, we have seen a critical shift away from relations-based regulation to rules-based regulation of financial institutions and a more Diet-centred financial policy-making process. The Government's simple acknowledgement of the magnitude of financial sector problems today is reflective of this change in information dynamics.

Nonetheless, the positive changes that have taken place since 1998 represent only the first step in a larger process of reform necessary to truly resolve the nation's financial sector woes. Today the political stand-off surrounding reform of Japanese banks and the financial system does not centre on whether or not bad loans must be disposed of, but rather, how this disposal should take place. And, the primary source of policy inertia comes from within the governing coalition – and the LDP, in particular – rather than within the MOF. While a financial safety net effectively precludes a meltdown of the financial sector, the political concern today is the collapse of many politically powerful corporate borrowers. These corporate borrowers need to be dealt with in a way that facilitates the needed structural transformation of the economy. Yet, doing so requires repealing the long-practised protection of many of the sectors that came to provide a key support base for the LDP and facing some economic pain in the short term in the form of further increases in numbers of bankruptcies and unemployment rates. Political leadership is a prerequisite for moving forward with such measures. However, its emergence is difficult to envision in the absence of drastic reform in the LDP's support base. Without the party's transformation, the comprehensive and lasting reform of Japanese banks, the financial system, and the greater economy is likely to remain out of grasp for some time to come.

Notes

1 For more on the nature of incentives that Japanese politicians face due to electoral system attributes, see Ramseyer and Rosenbluth (1997).
2 Although a powerful 'finance tribe' (*okura zoku*) operated within the LDP and finance committees met regularly in the LDP and the Diet, these individuals and committees focused on the budget-making process rather than on issues related to private sector financial regulation or supervision.
3 The Administrative Procedures Law went into effect in October 1994, helping to clarify the boundaries of bureaucratic discretion. Prior to this date, however, explicit procedural controls were absent.
4 In the US, for example, authority for financial regulation is split among multiple government agencies, thereby making it a more pluralistic process.
5 This is not to deny that select banks maintained close ties with particular politicians or to suggest that the MOF was able to carry out reforms without being mindful of the links between particular segments of the financial industry and the flow of political funds. However, the relationship most central to working out policies prior to the bursting of the bubble was that between the MOF and financial industry actors.
6 In the events leading up to the 1981 Banking Law Revision, for example, more rigorous disclosure requirements planned by the MOF were vetoed by the LDP's Policy Affairs Research Council (PARC), thus pre-empting the inclusion of these provisions in legislative proposals. The industry's recourse to LDP officials was a major loss of face for the MOF, however, signalling a breakdown in the ministry's ability to skilfully work out bargains with industry actors. The lasting impact of this incident on strategies employed by the MOF thereafter serves as a testimony to the way in which the bureaucratic-led bargain was perceived to be a part of the ministry's mandate. Ministry officials in the Banking and Securities Bureaus began thereafter to more actively utilise daily face-to-face interaction with financial institution employees – the MOF liaisons (*MOF-tan*) to gain a better sense of industry positions on reform prior to presenting proposals to the LDP (author interviews with MOF officials, 1999). As a result of this change, the MOF was able to avoid a repeat of the outright LDP veto observed in 1981.
7 Although top contributors to the LDP for most of the postwar period, Japanese banks funnelled political donations primarily through a Keidanren-managed 'Peoples' Association Fund' to the party until 1994 rather than directly to the party or individual politicians. The banking sector's contributions to the LDP were viewed as a kind of insurance premium paid to guard against electoral advances by the Japan Socialist Party, the main opposition party for most of the postwar period. In 1994, Keidanren discontinued its role as political funds mediator.
8 Although Diet members occasionally made requests to the Banking Bureau to apply pressure to particular banks to extend credit to ailing firms seen to be politically important, these requests were typically ignored (author interview with former Banking Bureau Director-General Yoshimasa Nishimura, 1999).
9 One sign of this lack of demand was the absence of a public relations office within the ministry until the later 1990s.
10 The support of LDP politicians for the postal savings system derives from the role played by the over 3,000 post offices scattered throughout Japan in mobilising votes at election time.

11 Japan's 1927 banking crisis, for example, was triggered by an ill-advised remark made by the Finance Minister disclosing 'private' but out-dated information about a particular bank's financial unsoundness.
12 For example, in both large private sector firms and in the bureaucracy, those individuals who failed to be promoted as they neared the top of the promotion ladder typically assumed lucrative posts in affiliated firms (for the private sector) or in private sector firms or quasi-governmental organisations (for the bureaucracy). An employee depended on the personnel office of his or her original employer to arrange this post outside the organisation, however. Thus, publicly exposing organisational problems meant risking the loss of this large financial pay-off (author interview with MOF official, 1998).
13 A deposit insurance system was introduced in 1971 but was insufficiently funded even to pay off depositors in the event of a regional bank failure.
14 Although civil servants are rotated into different positions on a regular basis in the Japanese bureaucracy, this rotation is often to different divisions within the same bureau. Furthermore, the MOF has long been distinctive for the way in which officials become branded members of the 'budget clique', 'tax clique', etc. and spend a disproportionate amount of time in a particular bureau.
15 This was particularly true in the 1990s when rescue mergers became increasingly difficult to arrange and media leaks foiled the rescues of Cosmo Credit Co-operative and Sanyo Securities.
16 Financial regulation until June 1998 was fragmented only in the case of special purpose financial institutions such as agricultural co-operatives, labour co-operatives, and consumer finance corporations.
17 See Amyx (forthcoming 2001) for more on the way in which the FSA's independence was compromised initially and the effect of the October 1998 legislation on the incentives of actors within this agency.
18 The latter change has spurred demand for bond and other asset-pricing data and at least one Japanese brokerage, Nomura Securities, has announced its intention to generate such data for the market, as a new business venture.
19 Prominent examples of successful lawsuits include those brought against the former management of Daiwa Bank and Chiyoda Mutual Life Insurance Company.
20 The FRC, for example, must issue regular written reports while the BOJ's Policy Board must disclose the minutes of its meetings. The FSA also documents extensively the content of discussions leading to new policies or interpretations on its web site. In April 2001, the implementation of a new Freedom of Information Act will open up government documents to further public scrutiny.
21 Notably, the bureaucracy is making a concerted effort to regain its legitimacy as a neutral provider of information by adjusting definitions and calculations of national statistical indices to bring them more in line with global standards.
22 Of course, foreign actors also bring with them their own interests, but these tend not to be status quo supporting.
23 FSA officials do report, however, that statements hurt organisational morale by undermining public perceptions of the FSA as an independent regulator.
24 Among the proposed measures is one that would establish a 'private' fund to purchase stocks from banks and hold these stocks for five years. Notably, although Finance Minister Kiichi Miyazawa has expressed his support for this measure, MOF civil servants have expressed scepticism of the plan. And, their scepticism is warranted. The coalition proposes a government-guarantee of

purchases made by this fund, thus effectively approving of any compensation for losses – a behaviour which brokerages were sanctioned for in the 1990s. Furthermore, the coalition suggests that banks buy into the fund at the same time that the fund is intended to buy shares from the banks. In short, the proposed fund would clearly distort the price function of the stock market, just as the MOF's injection of funds did in 1993.

25 The financial health of Japanese banks has long been inextricably tied to the stock market. Banks have long been large shareholders, holding approximately 20 per cent of total market shares on the Tokyo Stock Exchange and have been permitted to count 45 per cent of unrealised capital gains on these shares toward their capital bases.

References

Amyx, J. (2001). 'The Ministry of Finance (MOF) and the Bank of Japan (BOJ) at the crossroads', in Jennifer Amyx and Peter Drysdale (eds), *Beyond Japan, Inc.: Transparency and Reform in Japanese Governance*, Routledge, London.

Karube, K. and Nishino Tomohiko (1999), *Kensho: Keizai no Shissei (Examination: Economic Policy Failure)*, Iwanami Shoten, Tokyo.

Mabuchi, M. (1997), 'Financing the Japanese Industries', in Muramatsu Michio and Frieder Naschold (eds), *State and Administration in Japan and Germany: A Comparative Perspective on Continuity and Change*, Walter De Gruyter, New York.

Nikkei Net Interactive, various issues.

Ramseyer, J. Mark and Frances McCall Rosenbluth (1997), *Japan's Political Marketplace*, Harvard University Press, Cambridge, MA.

Rosenbluth, Frances McCall (1989), *Financial Politics in Contemporary Japan*, Cornell University Press, Ithaca, New York.

Tabb, W. (1995), *The Postwar Japanese System: Cultural Economy and Economic Transformation*, Oxford University Press, New York.

Vogel, Steven K. (1994), 'The bureaucratic approach to the financial revolution: Japan's ministry of finance and financial system reform', *Governance: An International Journal of Policy and Administration*, 7(3), July.

5 Changes in the J-type firm

From bank-centred governance to internal governance[1]

Hideaki Miyajima and Hidetaka Aoki

Introduction

The institutional characteristics of the Japanese firm, in particular the main bank relationship began to change in the 1990s. The long-standing practice of maintaining stable relations with a main bank changed following the liberalisation of capital markets; the strategy of inter-corporate shareholding was modified due to the sluggish performance of the stock markets in the 1990s; seniority-based wages structures were changed to accommodate merit-based pay incentives; and long-term employment practices changed as a result of vigorous restructuring of large firms, such as Nissan. According to conventional understanding, the main features of Japanese firm systems encouraged long-term investments by mitigating asymmetric information problem emanating from main banks, and solved the problem of managerial myopia through inter-corporate shareholdings (Abeglen and Stalk, 1985; Porter, 1992; Sheard, 1995). However, a contrary understanding of the J-type firm has gained popularity among researchers. They argue that the institutional features of J-type firms were of marginal economic significance,[2] and even negative in that these features led to excess investment in the late 1980s. From this perspective, the disciplinary role of capital markets and portfolio investors is desirable and a welcome source for improved corporate governance.

These issues have raised questions of J-firms converging on the Anglo-American system? Among journalists and critics of Japan's conventional industrial structure, the convergence scenario is not only plausible but also preferable. The purpose of this chapter is to investigate recent changes in corporate finance and assess the impact on governance of Japanese firms, by focusing especially on the presidential turnover. We review the convergence theory and suggest the possibility of internal governance mechanisms appropriate to the J-type firm that is also complimentary to the discipline of capital markets. After briefly summarising recent changes in corporate finance, we will, in the following section, consider developments in the bank-centred corporate governance structure of Japanese firms. We show that the role of main banks is declining and that the frequency of main bank intervention is less sensitive to corporate performance, in comparison to the 1980s. We show also that intervention has contributed less to improved firm performance. Further, we examine the rapid restructuring of the banking sector after the financial crisis in 1997. The next three sections highlight the effect of changes in corporate finance on corporate governance mechanism, focusing on the presidential turnover. We briefly summarise the changes of presidential turnover pattern in the 1990s compared to previous period, report the result of statistical test of presidential turnover regressed on firm performance, emphasising the effective function of internal governance mechanism based on the long-term employment, and investigate the effect of external environment on internal governance mechanism by dividing sample large firms into several categories, respectively. The penultimate section treats the effect of external stakeholder on internal governance mechanism, and is followed by a discussion on some of the results.

The changing structure of corporate finance in Japan

Following financial market deregulation that began in the 1970s, the finance strategies of Japanese corporations have undergone significant changes. Until the 1970s, firms had limited financial options due to strict regulation of bond markets. Collateral requirements made it prohibitively difficult for firms to issue bonds and the Bond Issuance Committee (the *kisaikai*) decided which firms could issue bonds and how many bonds were issued. In 1979 firms were allowed to issue unsecured straight bonds for the first time by the introduction of the accounting index and profitability index as the bond issue criteria. Initially, only two companies were eligible for issuing unsecured bond but as deregulation progressed, more firms gained eligibility to issue unsecured as well as secured bonds. This relaxation of the bond issue criteria was one of the conditions, besides other favourable macroeconomic factors, that made it possible for Japanese firms to raise money through equity-related bonds in either domestic or foreign markets. By the end of 1989, the number of firms that had any financial options increased to approximately five-hundred.[3] With new opportunities, large firms in particular, reduced their reliance on bank financing and diversified their financial resources. The average of total number of bonds issued between 1985 and 1989 increased by more than 140 per cent from ones issued between 1980 and 1984. Bank borrowing, in this same period, declined dramatically. In the 1990s, although the amount of debt capital

Table 5.1 Issued financial instruments by large Japanese manufacturing firms (1,000 million yen)

	Total debt	Bank borrowing	Bond	Equity
1980–4	3,241,682	2,071,125	1,170,557	210,397
1985–9	3,769,320	951,935	2,817,386	708,772
1990–4	3,424,088	1,604,373	1,819,715	151,769
1995–8	736,472	−532,982	1,269,454	133,832

Source: Compiled from the *Kigyo Keiei no Bunseki* by Mitusbishi Research Institute.

Note: Data is averaged for each period. The number of firms is X.

raised declined, bond issuance did not decline as drastically as bank borrowing. This is shown in Table 5.1.

The bond market was further deregulated in November 1990, when all except the rating criterion were lifted from the bond issue criteria. In April 1993, the lowest bound of the rating criteria for issuing unsecured straight bond was lowered to BBB. This was important because the main form of bond issuance drastically changed, from equity-related bonds in the late 1980s to straight bonds in the early 1990s. As a result of this relaxation, 184 listed firms became eligible to issue unsecured straight bonds. Finally, in January 1996 bond issue criteria and some other covenants were removed, freeing Japanese firms from regulations on debt choice.

In order to understand the choices between bond and bank finance, Miyajima and Arikawa (2000) present empirical evidence of the determinants of Japanese firm's choice between unsecured bond and bank borrowing in the 1980s and 1990s. They tested the hypotheses that firms did not use bank borrowing, with an implicit rescue-insurance, when default risk was low or when future profitability was high. They assumed that firms treat debt choice as one between debt without implicit rescue-insurances (NRI debt) and debt with implicit rescue-insurances (RI) debt, rather than the choice between public and private debt. Here, NRI debts includes unsecured convertible bonds, unsecured straight bonds, and non-bank-guaranteed warrant bonds, whereas RI debt is composed of bank borrowings, secured convertible and straight bonds, and bank-guaranteed warrant bonds. The main reason for classifying secured and bank-guaranteed bonds as RI bonds, similar to bank borrowing, was that defaulted corporate bonds with collateral were bought back by the trustee banks without any exception from 1955 to 1997, while bank-guaranteed warrant bonds were, by definition, guaranteed by banks.[4]

Their findings confirmed that, in the late 1980s, a firm's choice between unsecured bonds and bank borrowing was determined largely by default

Changes in the J-type firm 75

risk and future profitability. For firms that had a choice between unsecured bonds and other debt (secured bonds or borrowing), debt choice correlated with default risk and future profitability. Even among firms that could fully choose their financial methods, firms with high default risk and low future profitability still continued to borrow to keep implicit rescue-insurance, in spite of the fact that bank borrowings might incur hold-up problems and high interest rates.[5] For firms eligible to issue secured or bank-guaranteed bonds, the choice was again sensitive to default risk. Further, this choice was sensitive to future profitability only among firms having strong main-bank ties. The results show that when managers valued their managerial discretion, they tended to avoid bank borrowings to reduce, in turn, bank monitoring.

It is worth emphasising that these facts imply a deterioration of client firms in the banking sector in the latter half of the 1980s. As firms with low default risks depended on bond issuance, firms with high risks continued to raise external fund through bank borrowing. This rational self-selection led to a deterioration of bank clients. It was inevitable, therefore, that financially distressed firms would become a larger proportion of bank clients when the Japanese economy was affected by negative macro shocks in the 1990s.[6]

On April 1, 1993, the Financial System Reform Act became effective. This new law allowed banks and securities companies to set up their securities firms and trust banks, respectively. Furthermore, in 1996, the Japanese government announced the financial system reform programme known as the Japanese 'Big Bang'. With the completion of this programme in 2001, bank, security firm and insurance company will compete directly each other. Then, even firms having a strong relationship with the main bank might put more value not only on the bank lending but also on other financial services like security underwriting.

Changing patterns of corporate governance in Japan

As is well known, main banks played a disciplinary role in the Japanese financial system. However, with the decline in bank financing, as discussed above, it is important to understand whether bank-centred governance structures are being transformed into the market-based structures. It is clear from Table 5.2 that large Japanese firms have progressively become less dependent on their main banks since the late 1970s. As a measure of this decline, the ratio of borrowings from main banks to total assets decreased from 4.92 per cent in 1979 to 3.62 per cent in 1989. The share held by the main bank also decreased from 5.25 per cent in 1979 to 4.16 per cent in 1989.[7] In conjunction with this decline, the role of main banks in corporate

Table 5.2 Main-bank relationship and ownership structure

Fiscal year	1979		1984		1989		1995	
	Average	Std. dev.	Average	Std. dev.	Average	Std. dev.	Average	Std. dev.
MB borrowing ratio	17.96	13.24	18.36	12.08	19.24	13.60	19.26	13.08
MB dependence ratio	4.92	3.93	4.72	3.98	3.62	3.84	4.39	5.61
MB dependence ratio 2	16.82	13.00	15.26	11.21	12.24	12.09	13.92	12.31
MB shareholding	5.25	2.50	4.93	1.95	4.16	1.28	4.26	1.10
Borrowing and shareholding are top	47.00		41.00		17.00		25.00	
Borrowing and shareholding among banks are top	174.00		213.00		138.00		180.00	
Ownership structure								
Individuals (A)	30.70	11.44	25.00	10.25	19.97	7.34	22.00	9.11
Foreigners (B)	2.66	7.42	7.22	9.59	4.70	7.37	8.97	8.79
Security companies (C)	3.08	3.78	3.12	3.52	2.94	2.54	2.19	2.44
Financial institutions (D)	37.26	14.51	37.93	14.02	45.55	14.64	42.56	13.35
Non-financial companies (E)	26.29	16.53	26.71	16.83	26.84	15.87	24.26	15.07
ε (A+B+C)	36.43	12.49	35.34	11.59	27.61	9.52	33.16	10.08
γ (D+E)	63.56	12.50	64.64	11.60	72.38	9.52	66.82	10.08

Notes
1 MB borrowing ratio = MB borrowing/Total borrowing.
2 MB dependence ratio = MB borrowing ratio × (Total borrowing/Total assets).
3 MB dependence ratio 2 = MB borrowing ratio × (Total borrowing/Total borrowing + bond).

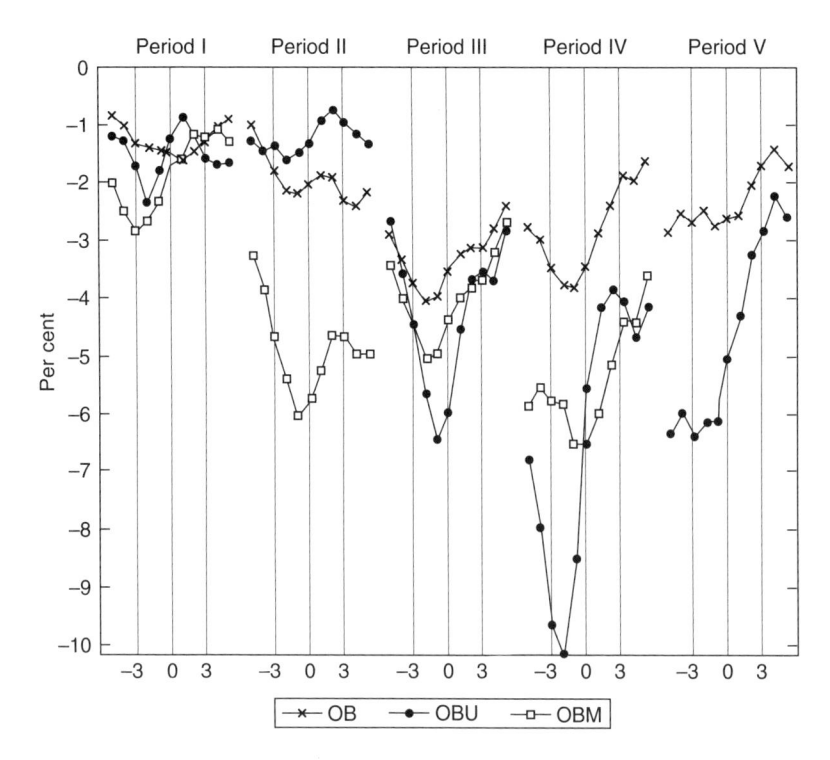

Figure 5.1 Dispatching directors and improvement of firm performance.

Note: Three periods moving average of NORR (standardised operating profit/sales). OB: all dispatched directors from banks; OBU: dispatched directors as higher than junior operating director; OBM: dispatched directors supposed to be based on monitoring incentive.

governance has faded, including bank intervention to rescue a client firm from financial distress. Miyajima *et al*. (2001) provided evidence that the frequency of banks dispatching their personnel to client firms performing poorly had declined in the 1990s. These same results were confirmed by Hirota and Miyajima (2001) for firms facing financial distress.[8] In the 1990s, as shown in Figure 5.1, the effect of dispatching bank managers to a client firm had little effect in terms of improved corporate performance. This is in contrast to evidence available for the period till the 1980s.

One reason is that Japanese banks, suffering from bad loans problem after the bubble economy, have adopted conservative lending policies to strengthen their capital base. These conservative policies led to fewer interventions to rescue borrowers in financial distress.[9] As a result, in the 1990s, fewer benefits accrued to borrowers from having long-term bilateral relationships with a main bank. Another recent development that influenced 'relational banking' was merger-mania, following the financial turmoil of 1997. Thus, in August 1999, Fuji Bank, Dai-Ichi Kangyo Bank and Industrial Bank of Japan announced a comprehensive consolidation to form the Mizuho Holdings. In October, Sumitomo Bank and Sakura Bank announced a merger, even though these two banks were at the centre of two separate Japanese *keiretsu* groups, Sumitomo and Mitsui.[10] As a result of mergers, by 2001 Japan had only four big bank groups and two city banks compared to nine city banks in April 1999.

These developments have affected relationship banking without, however, transforming a bank-based financial system into a market-based and arm's length system. There are several reasons to believe that the bank-centred governance will continue to exist, even if in a scaled down form. First, it is often pointed out that the information rent created by the long-term bilateral relationship between a bank and its borrower will disappear with bank mergers and that this will weaken relationship banking. However, as long as borrower-specific information created by the pre-merger bank is saved, the post-merger bank might also take a long-term strategy toward its borrowers (Aoki and Dinc, 2000). In other words, whether the specific firm–bank relationship becomes more arm's length will depend on how the mergers proceed and whether these will necessarily break the established relationship between lender and borrower.

Second, given informational advantage, main banks still play a positive role in Japanese large firms. According to Miyajima, Arikawa and Kato (2001), R&D expenditures still face liquidity constraints due to asymmetric information problem and main-bank relationships seems to mitigate this problem. This constraint is especially true for relatively young, and small firms. Consequently, for those with enough growth opportunity but likely to face asymmetric information problems, the main-bank system might still play a significant role in their long-term investment strategy. Third, the role of main banks in corporate governance appears stable for certain large Japanese firms. In 1995, the main-bank dependence ratio increased after the drop of 1989, with an increased standard deviation (Table 5.2). This means that some firms remain highly dependent on banks for their financial resources and the high commitment of main bank to client firms raises the probability of intervention when they face financial distress. Consequently, main banks still play a certain role in corporate governance in Japanese firms sectors.

At the same time, portfolio investors have enhanced their influence in Japanese corporate governance. The lower row of Table 5.2 shows the ownership structure of large firms since 1979. The share of 'stabilised shareholders' is defined as the aggregate share held by financial and non-financial institutions. The share of 'portfolio investors' is defined as the aggregate share held by individuals, foreigners and security companies. In the late 1980s, the share of 'stabilised shareholders' increased approximately 9 per cent and then decreased 6 per cent in the early 1990s. In 1998, the percentage share of portfolio investor and foreigners was 35.9 and 8.6 per cent respectively. These changes of ownership structure have influenced corporate behaviour and governance mechanism. As is well known, the characteristics of the board of directors in Japanese firm are: (1) the board is mainly composed of corporate insiders, (2) there are a very limited number of outside directors, (3) the firm's insiders have the power to determine the candidate for director. Therefore, shareholders could not effectively control management through the board of directors.

In the 1990s, however, relatively weak boards of directors began to emerge as major devices for corporate governance. The results of a survey by the Ministry of Finance in 2000 (see Arikawa and Miyajima, 2001) show that in more than 50 per cent of the sampled firms, directors were considering the introduction of outside directors as direct representative of investors. The significance of this is that Japanese firms are considering making the board of directors into a more independent structure for efficiently monitoring the firm's behaviour. According to the same research, 48 per cent of the sample Japanese firms had already introduced or were considering introducing stock options as part of executive compensation. Provided share prices contain enough information about future profitability, stock options are effective ways to ensure that managers pursue the interests of shareholders. These survey results suggest, therefore, that many Japanese firms are becoming more sensitive to shareholder's interest especially in the post-crisis period.

The pattern of presidential turnover in the 1990s

As outlined in preceding sections, economic institutions unique to Japan were substantially modified in the 1990s. In terms of governance structures, main banks have stepped back and portfolio investor become more influential. In order to assess whether this constitutes a complete transformation of J-type corporate system or just a modification to suit external circumstances, we will investigate presidential turnover, which is crucial for maintaining effective governance mechanisms. We focus on insider presidential turnover instead of outside or abnormal turnover, which was the main concern of previous researchers (Kaplan and Minton, 1994; Kang and Shivdasani, 1995).

First, let us review presidential turnovers of large Japanese firms since the 1970s. According to Figure 5.2, it is clear that turnovers increased

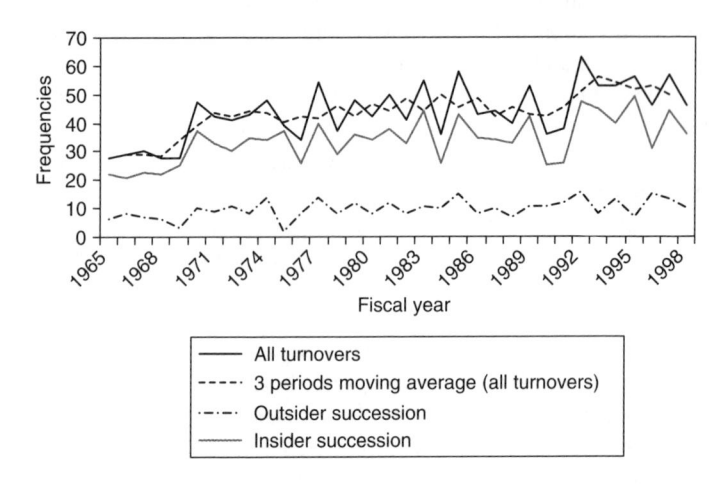

Figure 5.2 Presidential turnovers.

sharply around 1970 and the frequency of turnovers has shown cyclical rise and fall since 1977 when adjustment of oil shock almost ended. This cycle is also seen in outsider turnovers. It was after the oil crisis that turnovers based on seniority rule, such as two terms and four years, or three terms and six years, was established and became popular among large firms.

The seniority rule based turnover pattern is beneficial in two ways. First, regular presidential turnover is a signal of stable management and policy continuity to both outsiders and insiders. Second, seniority-based insider turnover is highly complementary to the incentive system of Japanese firms. Of course, long-term employment accompanies a moral hazards problems but, according to Aoki (1988), this incentive problem was solved by promotional competition through ranking hierarchy, which in turn made it possible for corporate insiders to invest in firm specific skill. However, the sustainability of this system required an ample supply of positions in the board of directors for corporate insiders. As a result, establishment and enlargement of promotional competition through ranking hierarchy resulted in increasing posts of directors and regular turnovers of these directors.

Seniority-based presidential turnover, however, has two potential drawbacks; (a) an incentive problem among junior directors who cannot aspire to presidential appointment, and (b) a leadership problem for the new president, because it is difficult to override the policy of a former president. Nonetheless, until the late 1980s, these costs were not serious because main-bank monitoring mitigated moral hazard problems of insiders. Under high debt–equity ratio, it was always possible for the main bank to intervene when firms faced financial distress due to mismanagement. Another condition that mitigated the leadership problem was relative environmental stability. As shown in Figure 5.3(a), ROA had recovered and its standard deviation decreased from the late 1970s onwards when the process of adjustment to oil crisis had been completed. Although ROA has been declining in the 1980s, its standard deviation remained stable. This understanding is supported by the trend toward greater diversification of firms. According to Figure 5.3(b), the entropy index, an index of the diversification, was relatively stable in the late 1980s. This implies that Japanese firms did not face a serious need to invest their resources in new fields.

However, in the 1990s, as economic environment changed so did the pattern of presidential turnover. Figure 5.2 shows that while frequency of turnovers increased in the 1990s, the cyclical rise and fall in presidential turnovers that was evident in earlier decades had disappeared. In the 1990s, a new succession pattern became evident. For example, prior to 1996 the

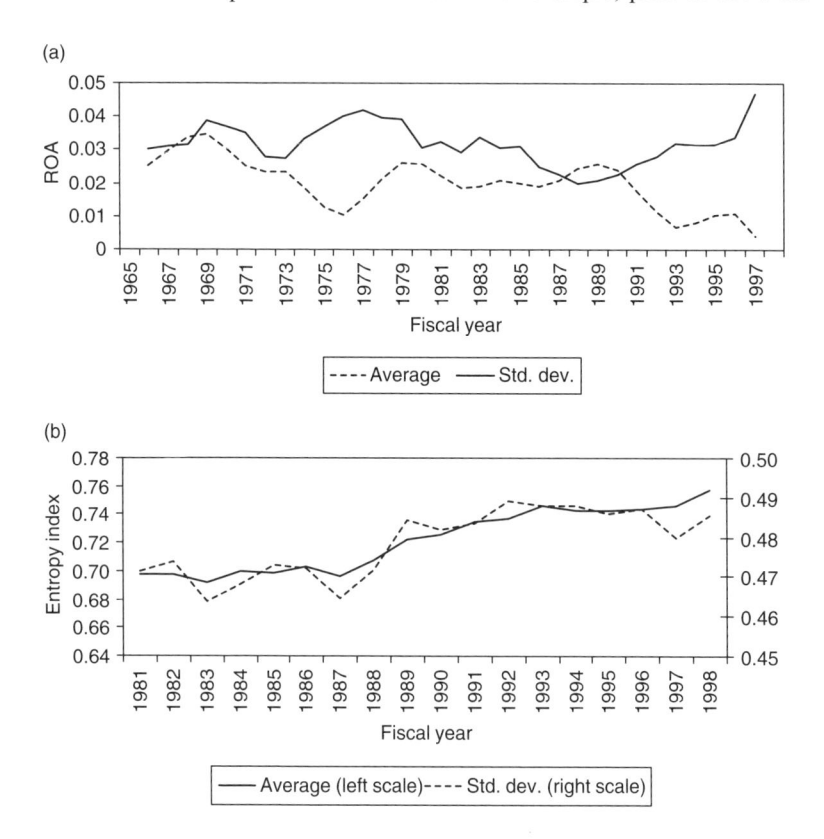

Figure 5.3 (a) ROA (3 periods moving average) and (b) Diversification.

President of Toshiba was selected from the Heavy Electric Division, but in 1996, Mr Nishimura from the International Division was appointed President. Also at Ricoh, known for its sales power, Mr Sakurai assumed the presidency from the Technical Division in 1996. However, from Table 5.3,

Table 5.3 Insider succession type
Panel 1 The previous division of new presidents[a]

Division	1970s Frequency	1970s Ratio (%)	1980s Frequency	1980s Ratio (%)	1990s Frequency	1990s Ratio (%)
Sales	48	19.4	49	15.2	63	19.9
Finance	14	5.7	15	4.6	8	2.5
Personnel	36	14.6	36	11.1	28	8.8
Production/factory	76	30.8	118	36.5	118	37.2
R&D	23	9.3	37	11.5	34	10.7
Management/secretary	20	8.1	35	10.8	40	12.6
Advertisement	2	0.8	0	0.0	1	0.3
International/trade	3	1.2	6	1.9	10	3.2
Relational company	25	10.1	26	8.0	14	4.4
Others (culture/social)	0	0.0	1	0.3	1	0.3
Sum	247	100.0	323	100.0	317	100.0

Panel 2 Number of turnovers and 'succession from enlarged candidates pool'

	1970s	1980s	1990s	Total sample
No Turns	2,867	2,838	2,522	8,227
All Turns	433 (13.1%)	463 (14.0%)	448 (15.1%)	1,344
Outside succession	96 (22.2%)	100 (21.6%)	105 (23.4%)	301
Inside succession	337 (77.8%)	362 (78.2%)	343 (76.6%)	1,042
Selection from 1 rank below the president	290 (86.1%)	294 (81.2%)	240 (70.0%)	824
Succession from enlarged candidates pool	47 (13.9%)	68 (18.8%)	103 (30.0%)	218

Note

a We investigated the division with *Yuka-Shoken-Hokokusho* (Japanese 10Ks). We could not cover all divisions. Unknown cases are 90 in the 70s (26.7 per cent), 39 in the 80s (10.8 per cent) and 26 in the 90s (7.6 per cent).

Changes in the J-type firm 83

Panel 1, which summarises the home division of new presidents, it is clear that 'unusual divisions' are not so common. Rather the division from which new president was selected was not very different from previous periods in the 1990s. As a succession rule, it was rare for successive presidents to be selected from the same division, as was the case at Toshiba. Usually, presidents were selected from different divisions on a rotational basis.

There is evidence also of 'exceptional promotion' where a lower-ranked director jumped over a higher-ranked director. For example, at Sony, Mr Idei a junior operating director assumed the presidency in 1995 after jumping over fourteen higher-ranked directors. Similarly, at Hino Motors, Mr Yuasa a junior operating director became president in 1997 after jumping over fourteen higher-ranked directors. These exceptional promotions were remarkable, but the important feature of insider successions in the 1990s was that the pool of successor candidates was enlarged to all members of the operating committee. We can now define those cases where a new president jumps over higher ranking directors as 'succession from enlarged candidates pool'. This succession pattern has increased from 47 in the 1970s to 68 in the 1980s, and reached 103 in the 1990s (Table 5.3, Panel 2). Figure 5.4 shows that 'succession from enlarged candidates pool' increased sharply in 1992 and has remained high since 1994. Yet, large-scale exceptional promotion

―― Succession from enlarged candidates pool (left side scale)
---- Ranks (right side scale)
·—·- Scale (right side scale)

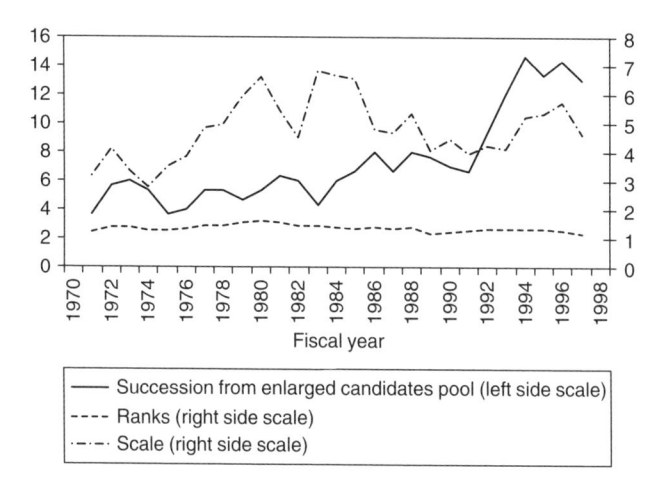

Figure 5.4 Succession from enlarged candidates pool (3 periods moving average).

Notes
(Ranks) the average number of ranks such as vice president or senior operating director, successor jumps over in each turnover.
(Scale) the average number of directors, successor jumps over in each turnover.

described above is not necessarily common. The average number of ranks (like vice-president and senior operating director) that a successor president jumped did not increase from that of the 1970s. Also its scale measured by average number of higher-rank directors who were jumped over by new president had become smaller compared to the 1980s. Therefore, large-scale exceptional promotion that captured social attention is one of the special cases of 'succession from enlarged candidates pool'.

This 'succession from enlarged candidates pool' is supposed to be an innovation, because it may mitigate the potential costs of managerial succession in the following sense. First, it puts pressure and discipline on higher-rank directors, because of the possibility of being jumped over and losing the opportunity of assuming the presidency if performance is not appropriate. On the other hand, it provides lower-ranked directors the incentive of rising quickly to the presidency. Thus, it is expected to mitigate the incentive problem of boards of directors based on seniority rule turnover. Second, an enlarged pool of candidates enables a firm to select a more suitable person as president than one who is selected solely on the basis of seniority. The flexible succession from an enlarged candidates pool is necessary and appropriate in the context of greater environmental uncertainty and demonstrates that Japanese firms were adapting to external shocks.

Determinants of managerial turnovers in the 1990s

To approach the above mechanism of internal self-discipline, we analysed the determinants of presidential turnovers in the 1990s relative to earlier periods. We chose a sample of 330 large firms in manufacturing sector covered in Mitsubishi Sogo Kenkyujo's *Kigyo Keiei no Bunseki*. These firms were selected on the criterion of availability of financial data for the period 1965–98. Accordingly, we excluded IPO (initial public offer) firms after 1965 and included typical J-type firms with an established history. For instance, our sample firms included 95 firms of from the Big Six Corporate Groups (Kigyo Shudan),[11] which account for 70 per cent of the Presidential Council (Shacho kai) firms of Big Six Corporate Groups in manufacturing sectors.[12]

We used multivariate logit model analysis, where presidential turnovers (outsider successions, insider successions and no turnovers), the dependent variable, was regressed on firm performance and the tenure of retiring president, which reflected the strength of seniority rule.[13] We defined an insider as a person who had worked for the company for more than four years, and an outsider as a person coming from another company, financial institution, or governmental institution and assuming presidency within four years. For independent variables, we used the ordinary profit ratio (OPR) as a performance measure, removing the effect of any special gain or loss without operational activities. Then, we standardised the OPR by each industry's average (two digit), because the focus here was whether or not the probability of turnovers was really affected by performance, a reflection of managerial capability. We did this to exclude idiosyncratic shocks from the performance index of each industry.

Figure 5.5 illustrates the concept of estimation. In Figure 5.5(a) presidential turnover is negatively correlated to firm performance. Where this relationship is statistically supported, we interpret it to mean the presence of effective governance in the sense that lower-performance increases the probability of presidential turnover. Figure 5.5(b) shows the case that turnover is positively correlated to the tenure of the former president. Where this relationship is statistically supported, we interpret it to mean

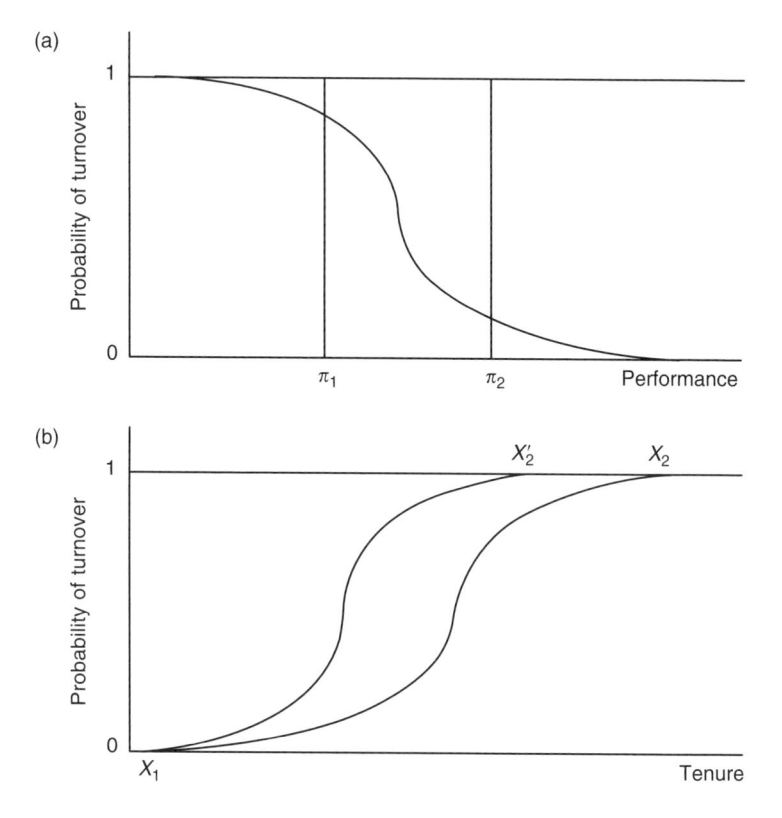

Figure 5.5 The concept of logit model I: (a) Presidential turnover and performance and (b) Presidential turnover and tenure.

that presidential succession is mainly based on the seniority rule, such as adhering to rule of two terms and four years, or three terms and six years interval. In this case, we assume that effective governance is weak and that selection from an enlarged candidates pool is relatively limited. The time frame of this study was of twenty-nine years (1970–98), which we divided into three periods; period I (oil crisis and its adjustment periods) is the 1970–9, period II (recession after yen appreciation and bubble) is the 1980–9, period III (after bubble) is the 1990–8.

Table 5.4 summarises the estimation results for each period. There are three points to be noted. First, for outsider succession, turnover was negatively correlated to firm performance in the 1970s, but this relationship became less clear in the 1980s, and it reappeared in the 1990s. The results for the 1980s were caused not only by changes in the disciplinary mechanism but also by shift of performance average. As shown in Figure 5.5(a), average performance of sample firms shifted from π_1 of the 1970s to π_2 of the 1980s. As average performance declined to π_1 again in the 1990s when Japanese economy faced serious recession, outsider succession became sensitive again to firm performance. The results indicate that external disciplinary mechanism, based mainly on financial institutions, was still functioning in the 1990s. This is consistent with our explanation in the section on the changing patterns of corporate governance in Japan.

Second, our most important and noticeable finding was that insider succession was negatively correlated to the firm performance (OPR) in the 1990s. The significance of the estimation result becomes clear when we compare the result of the 1990s with those of the 1970s when Japanese economy experienced external shock, much like in the 1990s. On one hand, in firms that performed poorly in the 1970s, similar or even worse than in the 1990s, insider succession was never sensitive to firm performance. On the other hand, in the 1990s, insider succession was negatively correlated to performance. This result is robust when OPR is replaced by operating profit ratio. From Table 5.4, a two standard deviations (6.9 per cent) decline of the OPR raised the probability of insider succession by 4.1 per cent, which is fairly high compared to 11.6 per cent the turnover ratio of the 1990s.

The results imply that J-type firms have a form of effective internal governance, in that low performance raises the probability of insider presidential turnover in the 1990s. According to Allen and Gale (2000) and Kawamura and Hirota (2000), the longer the employees worked for a firm and the more they invested their resources in firms specific skill, the higher the extent of voluntarily reform instead of exiting from them when firms performed badly.

Third, another important result of this estimation is that the effect of the tenure of former president increased in the 1990s. The results in Figure 5.5(b)

Table 5.4 Base regression (each period)

Column	1970–9						1980–9						1990–8					
	Average	Std. dev.					Average	Std. dev.					Average	Std. dev.				
Tenure	8.16	8.07					6.03	6.28					5.24	4.82				
OPR (standardised) (%)	0.00	4.93					0.00	3.99					0.00	3.02				
OPR (raw data) (%)	3.94	5.61					4.40	4.48					2.94	3.46				
	Frequency	Ratio (%)					Frequency	Ratio (%)					Frequency	Ratio (%)				
No turnovers	2,867	86.9					2,838	86.0					2,522	84.9				
Outsider succession	96	2.9					100	3.0					105	3.5				
Insider succession	337	10.2					362	11.0					343	11.6				
	Parameter	p-value		Marginal Effect			Parameter	p-value		Marginal Effect			Parameter	p-value		Marginal Effect		
Outsider succession																		
Tenure	0.02	(0.086)	*	0.001			0.03	(0.073)	*	0.001			0.07	(0.000)	***	0.002		
OPR	−8.37	(0.000)	***	−0.224			−4.77	(0.039)	**	−0.130			−14.22	(0.000)	***	−0.433		
Insider succession																		
Tenure	0.03	(0.000)	***	0.003			0.05	(0.000)	***	0.005			0.09	(0.000)	***	0.009		
OPR	−1.10	(0.363)		−1.79	−0.076		−0.210	(0.000)	***	(0.000)	−6.68	−0.156	−0.597					

Notes
Estimation formula: Turn = F(Sub, Tenure, OPR).
Turn: Presidential turnover; Sub: Subsidiary dummy (top shareholder is non-financial company and its share is over 10 per cent); Tenure: Tenure of former president; OPR: Ordinary Profit Rate.
(t −1) period of the OPR and subsidiary dummy are used for estimation.

show that the slope expressing the effect of the tenure of former president on insider succession rose from X_1X_2 to X_1X_2'. If the tenure of former president was five years longer than average, the probability of insider turnover increased 4.5 per cent comparing to the average turnover probability of 11.6 per cent in the 1990s. Furthermore, interestingly even outsider succession is also significantly correlated to the tenure of former president in the 1990s, showing the increased effect of the seniority rule.

Therefore, J-type firms, characterised by long-term employment and promotional competition through ranking hierarchy, include effective governance at the point that lower performance creates pressure for presidential turnover. On the contrary, however J-type firms accompanied the potential cost that managerial succession tends to excessively depend on the seniority rules. Our next concern then was to consider under what kinds of external conditions the cost became serious, and whether outsiders (main bank, shareholders) mitigated this cost or not.

Changes in external environment, increased uncertainty and restructuring of business

In the 1990s, the external environment has drastically changed. It is often said that globalisation has yielded hyper-competition in product market and that exchange-rate volatility, caused by international capital transfers, has increased the uncertainty of firms profitability. These changes in environment substantially raised business risk. As shown in Figure 5.3(a), economic performance (ROA) of Japanese firms declined and its difference among firms was enlarged in the 1990s. Which Japanese firms faced serious uncertainty is also confirmed in Table 5.5. This table shows the average and standard deviation of growth ratio (1990–8) of real sales in each industry. In assembly industry (such as machinery and transport equipment) and material industry (such as paper/pulp and metal/steel), the standard deviation is higher. Furthermore, growth ratio of real sales is negative in almost all industries. Therefore, firms in material industry faced enormous business risk in the 1990s.

At the same time, technological innovation and IT-revolution has changed the structure of business and enhanced the necessity of restructuring business activity. Firms are simultaneously required to concentrate their resources on high growth activities and to withdraw resources from less profitable activities. As shown in Figure 5.3(b), entropy index of sample firms increased in the 1990s, as a result of environmental change. Table 5.5 also shows the average annual changes of entropy index (1990–8) by industries. The diversification trend seems to be obvious in glass/cement, foods, machinery sector, while a specialisation trends is observed in paper/pulp,

Table 5.5 Business risk and diversification (1990–8)

Industry	Number of firms	Business risk Average (%)	Std. dev. (%)	Diversification Average (%)	Std. dev. (%)
Foods	24	−0.78	4.86	3.57	9.60
Textiles	31	−4.50	7.95	0.81	3.10
Printings/others	12	−1.02	7.08	0.07	2.20
Paper/pulp	14	−0.61	9.68	−1.61	4.75
Chemistry	45	−1.19	6.01	0.62	3.88
Pharmaceuticals	10	1.40	4.48	−0.32	2.67
Oil/rubber	11	−2.72	8.54	0.97	4.00
Glass/cement	19	−2.22	8.42	6.66	14.87
Steel	25	−4.44	8.27	1.73	4.33
Metal	21	−3.35	8.84	1.12	6.26
Machinery	42	−1.20	13.31	2.20	7.83
Electric appliance	32	−0.93	7.72	0.71	2.43
Transport equipment	30	−2.28	8.79	−0.19	2.60
Precision instrument	9	1.66	8.47	1.15	7.38
Construction	5	−1.62	10.68	5.05	7.00
Sum/average	330	−1.59	8.21	1.50	5.53

Notes
1 Business Risk: Sales (real value).
2 Diversification: Entropy index.
3 Entropy index: $\sum_{i=1}^{n}[P_i \times \ln(1/P_i)]$ from i to n means business of the firm, P_i is the ratio of sales of the i-th business.
  The classification of each business is based on the three digit classification of *Nihon-Hyojun-Sango-Bunrui* (Standard Industry Classification: Somucho: Ministry of Public Management).

pharmaceuticals, and transport equipment. In regard to external changes in the 1990s, we divided sample firms into two groups based on the following criteria: the extent of business risk and the corporate restructuring.

1   In order to capture the degree of uncertainty for a firm, we divided the sample into two groups by the average of coefficient of variation of real sales (1990–8): high business risk firms (119 firms) and low business risk firms (211 firms).
2   Calculating the average annual changes of the entropy index (1990–8), we categorised firms with an above average entropy index as diversification-oriented firms (DV firms) and firms with a below average entropy index as the specialisation-oriented firms (SP firms). In addition, we considered that environmental change in the 1990s required firms to concentrate their business in areas of high profitability. Using

Table 5.6 Base regression for sub-samples

Panel 1

	High business risk (no. of firms 120)			Low business risk (no. of firms 210)		
	Frequency	Ratio		Frequency	Ratio	
No turnovers	903	0.84		1,619	0.86	
Outsider succession	62	0.06		43	0.02	
Insider succession	115	0.11		228	0.12	

	Parameter	p-value	Marginal Effect	Parameter	p-value	Marginal Effect
Outsider succession						
Tenure	0.04	(0.025) **	0.002	0.10	(0.004) ***	0.002
OPR	−8.12	(0.055) *	−0.360	−21.46	(0.000) ***	−0.444
Insider succession						
Tenure	0.06	(0.000) ***	0.005	0.14	(0.000) ***	0.014
OPR	−9.57	(0.000) ***	−0.836	−5.09	(0.062) *	−0.445

Panel 2

	Diversified firm (no. of firms 179)		Specialised firms (no. of firms 151)	
	Frequency	Ratio	Frequency	Ratio
No turnovers	1,358	0.84	1,164	0.86
Outsider succession	54	0.03	51	0.04
Insider succession	199	0.12	144	0.11

	Parameter	p-value	Marginal	Effect	Parameter	p-value	Marginal	Effect
Outsider succession								
Tenure	0.07	(0.002)	***	0.002	0.07	(0.016)	**	0.002
OPR	−8.29	(0.067)	*	−0.216	−20.59	(0.000)	***	−0.678
Insider succession								
Tenure	0.08	(0.000)	***	0.009	0.10	(0.000)	***	0.009
OPR	−9.07	(0.000)	***	−0.909	−4.05	(0.150)		−0.294

Panel 3

	High restructuring (no. of firms 166)		Low restructuring (no. of firms 164)	
	Frequency	Ratio	Frequency	Ratio
No turnovers	1,275	0.85	1,247	0.84
Outsider succession	46	0.03	59	0.04
Insider succession	173	0.12	170	0.12

	Parameter	p-value	Marginal	Effect	Parameter	p-value	Marginal	Effect
Outsider succession								
Tenure	0.04	(0.120)		0.001	0.18	(0.000)	***	0.005
OPR	−14.49	(0.002)	***	−0.395	−14.82	(0.001)	***	−0.485
Insider succession								
Tenure	0.06	(0.000)	***	0.006	0.16	(0.000)	***	0.014
OPR	−6.18	(0.012)	**	−0.566	−7.09	(0.020)	**	−0.592

Note: Estimation formula is the same as that in Table 5.4.

the distribution of the entropy index, we categorised firms in first quartile (specialised firms) and fourth quartile (diversified firms) as the high-restructuring firms (hereafter HR firms) and firms in second and third quartile as the low-restructuring firms (hereafter LR firms).

According to Table 5.6, which summarises estimation results by grouping, the correlation between insider turnover and firm performance is less clear in firms with low business risk, although turnover was strongly affected by the tenure of former president. On the other hand, insider succession is negatively correlated to firm performance in high business risk firms, while the effect of the tenure of former president is relatively small. Among low risk firms, while two standard deviations decline in OPR increased the likelihood of turnover only by 2.7 per cent, prolonged tenure of former president (five years) increased the probability of turnover by about 7 per cent.

Concerning the high and low restructuring grouping, insider succession in DV firms correlated significantly to firm performance, but not in SP firms. Indeed, in SP firms, outsider succession correlated significantly to firm performance. When we compared HR firms with LR firms, although the sensitivity of turnovers to firm performance was not so different between the two groups, it was noticeable that the sensitivity of insider turnover to tenure of former president in HR firms was much lower than for LR firms. In LR firms, when the tenure of former president was extended five years, the likelihood of turnover increased 7 per cent, implying that insider succession of LR firms is mostly determined by seniority rule.

These results based on uncertainty and restructuring imply that characteristics of J-firm such as long-term employment and rank competition have a contrasting effect on governance through the pressure of external environment. For firms under high external pressure, long-term employment and rank competition result in insider succession being sensitive to performance, while its potential cost, that is, dependence on seniority rule is relatively weak. On the other hand, for the firms under low pressure from external environment, these characteristics intensified the succession based on seniority rule.

Effect of external governance on internal governance (main bank and portfolio investors)

As pointed out in an earlier section, the main bank has stepped back while portfolio investors, such as foreigners, have increasingly played an important role in corporate governance. In this section, we analyse the effect of changes in ownership structure and bank–firm relationship on insider managerial succession.

Changes in the J-type firm 93

In order to analyse the effect of these main-bank relationship and ownership structures, governance variables were added to the regression as constant terms as well as interaction terms with firm performance and the tenure of former president. Figure 5.6 illustrates the concept of this estimation. Here, the main point is whether or not the interaction term is statistically significant. Figure 5.6(a) shows the case where governance variable (for instance the share held by portfolio investors) exaggerates the sensitivity of turnover to firm performance (exaggeration effect on performance), and Figure 5.6(b) shows the case where it mitigates the sensitivity of the turnover to the tenure (mitigating effect on the tenure). If these relationships are statistically supported, we can conclude that portfolio investors play a positive role in governance.

We selected two ratios as governance variables: main-bank dependence ratio representing the strength of main-bank relationship and the percentage

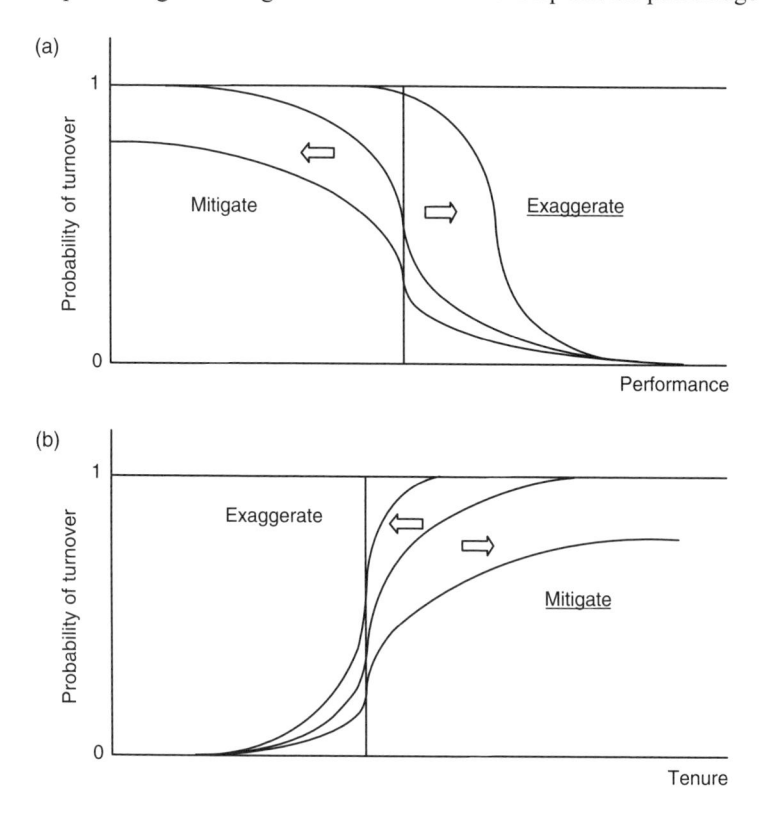

Figure 5.6 Concept of logit model II (interaction term): (a) Effect of governance on turnover performance and (b) Effect of governance on seniority rule.

Table 5.7 Effect of governance structure (MB, portfolio investor)

Panel 1 All samples (outside and insider succession)

	Outsider succession				Insider succession			
	Parameter	p-value	Marginal	Effect	Parameter	p-value	Marginal	Effect
Tenure	0.16	(0.004)	***	0.004	0.23	(0.000)	***	0.022
OPR	−25.01	(0.020)	**	−0.742	−14.74	(0.024)	**	−1.328
MB	3.05	(0.179)		0.106	−2.19	(0.348)		−0.224
MB × OPR	41.06	(0.396)		1.350	−9.64	(0.811)	−1.094	
MB × Tenure	0.05	(0.912)		−0.000	0.49	(0.106)		0.047
PI	−0.68	(0.658)		−0.030	2.05	(0.035)	**	0.201
PI × OPR	31.25	(0.405)		0.890	27.88	(0.146)		2.575
PI × Tenure	−0.23	(0.163)		−0.006	−0.45	(0.000)	***	−0.043

Panel 2 Sub-samples (insider succession)

	Parameter	p-value	Marginal	Effect	Parameter	p-value	Marginal	Effect
	High business risk				Low business risk			
MB × OPR	3.60	(0.942)		0.179	−17.35	(0.803)		−1.832
MB × Tenure	0.12	(0.780)		0.010	1.51	(0.005)	***	0.147
PI × OPR	2.82	(0.922)		0.128	45.65	(0.100)		4.314
PI × Tenure	−0.23	(0.141)		−0.020	−0.59	(0.002)	***	−0.057

	Diversified firms			Specialised firms		
MB × OPR	−110.96	(0.103)		70.66	(0.327)	
MB × Tenure	0.21	(0.577)		1.08	(0.084)	*
PI × OPR	42.44	(0.111)		42.79	(0.177)	
PI × Tenure	−0.46	(0.001)	***	−0.47	(0.020)	**
	High restructuring			Low restructuring		
MB × OPR	7.28	(0.903)		−25.06	(0.702)	
MB × Tenure	0.07	(0.853)		2.60	(0.000)	***
PI × OPR	20.71	(0.374)		16.11	(0.659)	
PI × Tenure	−0.30	(0.029)	**	−0.64	(0.014)	**

	Diversified firms		Specialised firms	
MB × OPR	−12.576		5.893	
MB × Tenure	0.028		0.089	
PI × OPR	4.240		3.822	
PI × Tenure	−0.047		−0.039	
MB × OPR	0.588		−2.698	
MB × Tenure	0.008		0.229	
PI × OPR	1.976		1.230	
PI × Tenure	−0.029		−0.054	

Notes
Estimation formula: Turn = F (Sub, Tenure, OPR, MB, MB*OPR, MB*Tenure, PI, PI*OPR, PI*Tenure).
Turn: Presidential turnover; Sub: Subsidiary dummy (top shareholder is non-financial company and its share is over 10 per cent); Tenure: Tenure of former president; OPR: Ordinary profit ratio; PI: Portfolio investor's share; MB: MB dependence ratio (ε: Table 5.6).

share held by portfolio investors (foreign investors, individual investors and security companies). According to Table 5.7, as expected, the likelihood of outsider succession increases when main-bank dependence ratio is high. However, neither exaggeration effect on performance nor mitigating effect on the tenure is confirmed in outsider succession. On the other hand, although main-bank relationship is not influential as constant term as well as interactive term with firm performance in insider succession, it shows some exaggeration effect on the tenure (but not statistically significant enough). Interestingly strong main-bank relationship does not mitigate but enhance the seniority rule of presidential turnover.

When sample firms were divided by external environment (Panel 2), the exaggeration effect of strong main-bank relationship on the tenure is the case for firms that are in a relatively stable environment. Interaction terms between main-bank dependence ratio and tenure is positive in firms with low business risk and low necessity of restructuring. It does not show any significant correlation in firms with high business risk and high necessity of restructuring.[14] Strong main-bank relationship intensified the seniority-based managerial insider succession for firms with low business risk and low necessity of restructuring.

Portfolio investors had a substitute effect for main bank. As shown in Panel 1, although the effect of portfolio investors is neutral to performance, it has a mitigating effect on the tenure (column 2). The magnitude is fairly large, because a two standard deviations (9.8 per cent) increase in share held by portfolio investors decreased the effect of tenure on turnover by 40 per cent. An important implication of this is that Japanese firms have an internal governance mechanism to facilitate management turnover in the event of poor performance. This mechanism, however, also has a potential cost, that is, to intensify the seniority rule of presidential turnover. Portfolio investors play an important role because they exert pressure to mitigate the seniority rule. Thus, capital markets are not a substitute, but rather complement internal governance initiated by insiders.

It is worth noting that the mitigating effect on tenure of portfolio investors is not caused by explicit intervention in managerial succession, but by their low evaluation of a firm that selects a president on the basis of seniority rule. In consideration of their investment behaviour, corporate insiders select the next president by ignoring the seniority rule. When we divide sample firms into sub-groups by business risk and restructuring, the mitigating effect of portfolio investor on tenure is significant only for low business risk firms, and LR firms. It was for these firms that portfolio investors play a substitute role to external pressure that mitigates the sensitivity of insider succession to tenure.

The effect of insiders' commitment on corporate governance

Lastly we discuss on the effect of employees' commitment on the insider presidential turnover in the 1990s. This is important because the autonomous mechanism for presidential turnover in Japanese firms is employees' commitment to their firm, which in turn intensifies the seniority rule. It is difficult to find the appropriate variable that directly represents the strength of employees' commitment. As a second best approach, we prepared two proxies, first the effects of the average tenure of employees as a proxy of insiders' sunk cost for their firm, and second, the employees stock ownership. Suppose an average tenure of employees and that employee stock ownership correctly reflect the extent of employees' commitment to their firm, we expect an exaggerated effect on firm performance or a mitigating effect on the tenure.

For the average tenure of employees, we introduced the average tenure at the previous year of turnover into regression as interaction term with firm performance and the tenure, and as dummy variable of each quartile of 1989. We investigated employee stock ownership, both in 1989 and 1995, from the list of 20 largest shareholder. In 1989, the number of firms where employee stock ownership was within largest 20 was just 100 out of the 330 sample firms and the average was 1.35 per cent. In 1995, the number was 155 and the average was 1.5 per cent. In order to capture firms with stable employees stock ownership, we give a dummy variable to firms, where employee stock ownership was within largest 20 in both 1989 and 1995 (dummy 1: 93 firms).[15]

According to Table 5.8 Panel 1, contrary to our expectation, employee stock ownership exaggerated the seniority rule for insider succession. For firms with stable employee stock ownership, insider turnovers were mainly based on seniority rule. Besides, column 3 shows that this result is also supported when it is defined by a stricter criterion (dummy 2). The employee stock ownership plan is different from stock option. One explanation is that although the employee stock ownership was originally introduced to enhance their participation to management, it encouraged stable shareholding in the end. Therefore, the estimation result rather reflects the manager's preference of entrenchment from external market.

Second, average tenure of employees does not have any significant exaggeration effect on performance and mitigating effect on tenure. However, the effect of the employees' commitment on presidential turnover may not be linear. In order to test this possibility, we set dummy variables to each quartile of the average tenure of employees in 1989. Second quartile is over 15.2 years, third quartile is over 17.7 years, and fourth quartile is over 19.5 years.[16] Although the employees' commitment does not have any

Table 5.8 Effect of employees (insider succession)

Panel 1 Effect of an average tenure of employees and holding institution of employees

Estimation formula: Turn = (Sub, Tenure, OPR, ATE, ATE*Tenure, ATE*OPR, ESO, ESO*OPR, ESO*Tenure), Turn: Presidential turnover; Sub: Subsidiary dummy (top shareholder is non-financial company and its share is over 10 per cent); Tenure: Tenure of the former president; OPR: Ordinary profit ratio; ATE: Average tenure of employees; ESO: Employees stock ownership dummy: Employees stock ownership is within the largest 20 in both 1989 and 1995.

	Parameter	p-value	Marginal	Effect
Tenure	0.07	(0.297)		0.006
OPR	−13.03	(0.194)		−1.186
ATE	−0.03	(0.354)		−0.003
ATE × OPR	0.35	(0.537)		0.032
ATE × Tenure	0.00	(0.848)		0.000
ESO	−0.60	(0.011)	**	−0.053
ESO × OPR	0.72	(0.882)		0.172
ESO × Tenure	0.09	(0.002)	***	0.008

Panel 2 *Effect of employees' commitment: Average tenure of employees quartile: 1989*

Estimation formula:Turn = F(Sub, OPR, Tenure, ATEQD, ATEQD*OPR, ATEQD*Tenure), Turn: Presidential turnover; Sub: Subsidiary dummy (top shareholder is non-financial company and its share is over 10 per cent); Tenure: Tenure of the former president; OPR: Ordinary profit ratio; ATEQD: Average tenure of employees quartile dummy (1989).

All samples

	Parameter	p-value	Marginal Effect
OPR	−6.09	(0.108)	−0.555
OPR × 1 quartile	1.04	(0.850)	0.117
OPR × 2 quartile	−4.21	(0.480)	−0.365
OPR × 3 quartile	0.49	(0.922)	0.061
Tenure	0.16	(0.000) ***	0.015
Tenure × 1 quartile	−0.05	(0.119)	−0.005
Tenure × 2 quartile	−0.08	(0.022) **	−0.007
Tenure × 3 quartile	−0.09	(0.007) ***	−0.008

High business risk

	Parameter	p-value	Marginal Effect
OPR	−5.15	(0.337)	−0.446
OPR × 1 quartile	−8.79	(0.283)	−0.807
OPR × 2 quartile	−5.75	(0.590)	−0.474
OPR × 3 quartile	−3.94	(0.565)	−0.360
Tenure	0.08	(0.032) **	0.006
Tenure × 1 quartile	−0.00	(0.982)	0.000
Tenure × 2 quartile	−0.02	(0.608)	−0.002
Tenure × 3 quartile	−0.03	(0.471)	−0.002

Low business risk

	Parameter	p-value	Marginal Effect
OPR	−9.38	(0.114)	−0.875
OPR × 1 quartile	11.83	(0.157)	1.165
OPR × 2 quartile	0.06	(0.994)	0.035
OPR × 3 quartile	6.23	(0.428)	0.642
Tenure	0.31	(0.000) ***	0.029
Tenure × 1 quartile	−0.18	(0.002) ***	−0.017
Tenure × 2 quartile	−0.18	(0.001) ***	−0.017
Tenure × 3 quartile	−0.18	(0.003) ***	−0.017

Diversified firms

	Parameter	p-value	Marginal Effect
OPR	−5.53	(0.314)	−0.596
OPR × 1 quartile	−3.98	(0.623)	−0.392
OPR × 2 quartile	−1.51	(0.851)	−0.033
OPR × 3 quartile	−5.74	(0.421)	−0.513
Tenure	0.16	(0.000) ***	0.016
Tenure × 1 quartile	−0.07	(0.149)	−0.006
Tenure × 2 quartile	−0.09	(0.044) **	−0.009
Tenure × 3 quartile	−0.10	(0.019) **	−0.010

Specialized firms

	Parameter	p-value	Marginal Effect
OPR	−4.99	(0.376)	−0.370
OPR × 1 quartile	2.97	(0.707)	0.278
OPR × 2 quartile	−12.62	(0.180)	−1.116
OPR × 3 quartile	5.65	(0.452)	0.471
Tenure	0.18	(0.000) ***	0.016
Tenure × 1 quartile	−0.07	(0.199)	−0.006
Tenure × 2 quartile	−0.07	(0.145)	−0.006
Tenure × 3 quartile	−0.10	(0.074) *	−0.008

significant effect on firm performance (Panel 2), it has significant mitigating effect on seniority rule. The effect of the tenure on insider presidential turnover is significantly decreased at second and third quartile of employees' average tenure. Therefore, higher commitment of employees is important for effective governance in the sense that it mitigates the probability of insider succession based on seniority rule. However, too much long tenure of employees intensifies the insider succession based on seniority rule. According to the estimation by groups, this mitigating effect of employees' commitment on the tenure of former president is statistically significant for firms with low business risk and firms with high necessity of restructuring. This result implies that, employees' commitment played a substitute role for the pressure from environmental change in corporate governance, and complementary role with the high necessity of restructuring.

Conclusion

As pointed out in the introduction, some researchers insist that there has been a convergence of the Japanese firm system toward the Anglo-American-style market-based system. However, as outlined in the preceding sections, it might not be appropriate to conclude that the Japanese firm system is totally converging toward the Anglo-American system, because there is clear evidence that aspects of the Japanese financial system still remain in place.[17] For large firms, which can raise financial resources from the capital market, the board of directors, or portfolio investors work well as corporate governance devices for implementing innovative management strategy, replacing the main-bank system. Among these firms, the issue will be the long-term employment system. As is often pointed out, market pressure for high stock prices might encourage managers in financial distress to reduce employment. As long as stock prices contain enough information about expected profitability of the firm, lay-offs induced by shareholders will improve the efficiency of firms. However, if capital market suffer from an asymmetric information problem, the increase of liquidity in labour market induced by shareholders' pressures might lead to a destruction of long-term formation of firm specific skill, which was one of the primary factors sustaining the high productivity of Japanese manufacturing. Thus far, there has been no evidence that firms have changed their long-term employment system in the manufacturing sector except for a few firms have that faced financial distress. This fact may be complimentary to the fact that the cross-shareholdings among firms still kept at a certain level.

Furthermore, in the 1990s reform initiated by insiders was implemented, which implies that a kind of internal governance mechanism is working in

Japanese firms. Boards reforms referred to in section three were not directly initiated by foreign investors, but mainly implemented by corporate insiders who realised the pressure of capital market. There is also some evidence that J-type firms have adapted to changing external circumstances through insiders' initiatives. The new president of J-firms has increasingly been selected within the enlarged candidates pool. In our estimation, the presidential turnover initiated by insiders became much sensitive to corporate performance in the 1990s, which is worth noticing as a new phenomenon because insider presidential turnover was not sensitive to firm performance in the previous period.

The internal governance mechanism is clearly observed in firms facing serious environmental change (high business risk and high restructuring firms). Insider succession in these firms is much more sensitive to their performance and less based on the seniority rule than those in firms with less business risk and HR. These facts suggest that J-type corporate system includes an effective internal governance mechanism based on insiders whose investment has already sunk in their firms and it evolves corresponding to environmental change. This understanding is in contrast to a recent popular understanding that Japanese firms have been and should converge on the Anglo-American model. On the other hand, we also noted that Japanese firms are characterised by long-term employment and promotional competition incurs costs associated with high dependence on seniority rule. These costs were serious in the 1990s, and crucial for firms facing stable environment (low business risk and LR firms). Furthermore, the costs were exaggerated by characteristics of J-firm systems (main-bank relationship and stabilised shareholdings). It is clear that firms which depend on a main bank for their financial resources try to stabilise shareholder through the employees stock ownership and tend to base presidential secession on the seniority rule.

On the contrary, the pressure from capital market played an important role on insider managerial succession by mitigating its seniority rule. It is statistically supported that insider succession is only weakly based on seniority rule in firms with high proportion of shares held by portfolio investors. This is especially the case for firms with low business risk and low necessity of restructuring. What has occurred in the 1990s is that the capital market (portfolio investors) can mitigate the cost of internal governance by evaluation of firms, with low dependence on the seniority rule, as good firms. Although the disciplinary mechanism based on capital market is often understood as a substitute one for J-type corporate system, it is worth noticing that the capital market in corporate governance should be rather complimentary to the internal governance mechanism. Further, the disciplinary mechanism based on capital market is especially important for firms with low business risk and with low necessity of restructuring. However, the results of this paper also indicate that the potential function of capital market for these firms do not automatically work. Firms that are free from pressures of external environment may not have any incentive to deviate from the seniority rule in selecting presidents. Further, main bank could support their financing, while portfolio investors evaluated them as modest firms. Then, they have little possibility of moving from seniority rule until the outsider intervenes into them when they face financial distress. Here exists the trap of long-term employment in managerial succession.

Reform of corporate governance for the twenty-first century has been discussed in Japan. Our results imply that one of the focus of corporate reform in Japanese firms is on firms with low pressure from environmental change, with high dependence on main bank, and with high average of tenure of employees. The results depend on whether insiders can solve the trap of long-term employment mentioned above by themselves otherwise pressure from capital market will be institutionally introduced into these firms.

Acknowledgements

We wish to thank Yasuhiro Arikawa and other participants and for their helpful comments. Our research was supported by a Waseda University Grant for Special Research Projects (2000A-114).

Notes

1 An earlier version of a paper presented at a workshop organised by Ministry of Economy, Trade and Industry.
2 See Weinstein and Yafeh (1998), Hall and Weinstein (1996), Hayashi (2000).
3 See Hoshi et al. (1993) and Hoshi and Kashyap (2000) for further detail of the deregulation process of Japanese capital market.
4 In 1997, for the first time after Second World War, the publicly issued unsecured convertible bond of *Yaohan* was defaulted and not bought back by the trustee bank.
5 Firms that depend excessively on their financial resources on banks plausibly face serious difficulty when banks cut off financing to them. This is the hold-up problem of bank borrowings. In this case, firms decrease the amount of bank borrowing resulting in under-investment, or they have to accept high interest rate for borrowing.
6 This understanding is partly contrary to conventional understanding on the causes of bad debt problems in the 1990s. See Horiuchi (1995), Miyajima and Arikawa (2000).
7 Main bank is defied by the first bank listed on Kaisya Shiki-Hou. When the borrowing is zero, main-bank dependent ratio is also zero. Main-bank dependent

ratio was investigated only in 1989 and 1995. The ratios of 1989 and 1995 are used for 1990–4 and 1996–8 respectively.
8 Here, financial distress means that a firm's operating income is below the interest payment for two years.
9 In addition, the capital adequacy requirements by BIS urged Japanese banks to reduce the total amount of lending. Due to the fall of asset prices, the unrealised gains from the shares banks contracted. As banks counted this gain as capital base to comply with the BIS banking regulations, the fall of share prices automatically reduced the capital bases and banks could not help reducing the loans they make. The disappearance of a long-term strategy taken by main banks might provide large Japanese firms with many financial options and more opportunity to be independent from main banks.
10 Furthermore, Sanwa and Tokai bank announced their integration under UFJ (United Financial of Japan) Group in March 2000. In April 2000, Bank of Tokyo–Mitsubishi announced the establishment of their holding company, Mitsubishi Tokyo Financial Group with the Mitsubishi Trust Bank.
11 This is not the same as vertical type of 'Keiretsu' such as Toyota and Matsushita group. Here, corporate groups are mainly characterized by a horizontal relationship by cross-shareholding and presidential council.
12 Syacho-kai is the meeting for presidents of the Big Six Corporate Group members.
13 We follow the method of Kaplan and Minton (1994), Kang and Shivdasani (1995), Miyajima (1998), Miyajima et al. (2001).
14 This result is also supported when main-bank dependence ratio is replaced by main-bank borrowing ratio and main-bank dependence ratio.
15 Besides, dummy variable was given in firms where its ownership was over average in both of the years 1989 and 1995 (dummy 2: 40 firms).
16 We need to improve this estimation formula further, because it does not consider the changes among 1990–8.
17 According to Miyajima et al. (2001), R&D expenditure still face liquidity constraints due to the asymmetric information problem, and main-bank relationships seems to mitigate that problem. This constrain is especially the case for relatively young, and small firms. Consequently, for those with enough growth opportunity but likely to face asymmetric information problems, the main-bank system might still play a significant role for their long-term investment strategy. This point is close to what Aoki and Dinc (2000) explained.

References

Abegglen, J. C. and Stalk, G. (1985), *Kaisha, the Japanese Corporation*, Charles E. Tuttle.
Allen, F. and Gale, D. (2000), *Comparing Financial Systems*, MIT Press.
Aoki, M. (1988), *Information, Incentives, and Bargaining in the Japanese Economy*, Cambridge University Press.
Aoki, M. and Dinc, S. (2000), 'Relational financing as an institution and its viability under competition', in Aoki, M. and Saxonhouse, G. R. (eds), *Finance, Governance, and Competitiveness in Japan*, Oxford University Press.

Arikawa, Y. and Miyajima, H. (2001), 'Corporate finance and its impact on corporate strategy after the bubble: is the long-term strategy of Japanese firms really changing?', mimeo.

Hall, B. and Weinstein, D. E. (1996), 'The myth of the patient Japanese: investment horizons in Japan and the US', NBER Working Paper 5818.

Hayashi, F. (2000), 'The main bank system and corporate investment: an empirical reassessment', in Aoki, M. and Saxonhouse, G. R. (eds), *Finance, Governance, and Competitiveness in Japan*, Oxford University Press.

Hirota, S. and Miyajima, H. (2001), 'Ginko kainyu gata gabanansu wa henka shitaka (Is the bank based governance really changing?: empirical test for 1970s to 1990s)', mimeo. Waseda University.

Horiuchi, A. (1995), 'Financial structure and managerial discretion in the Japanese firm: an implication of the surge of equity-related band', in Okabe, M. (ed.), *The Structure of the Japanese Economy*, Macmillan.

Hoshi, T. and Kashyap, A. (2000), 'The Japanese banking crisis: where did it come from and how will it end?', *NBER Macroeconomic Annual* 1999.

Hoshi, T., Kashyap, A. and Sharfstein, D. (1993), 'The choice between public and private debt: an analysis of post deregulation corporate financing in Japan', NBER Working Paper 4421.

Kang, J. and Shivdasani, A. (1995), 'Firm performance, corporate governance, and top executive turnover in Japan', *Journal of Financial Economics*, 38, 29–58.

Kaplan, S.N. and B.A. Minton (1994), 'Appointments of outsiders to Japanese boards: determinants and implications for managers', *Journal of Financial Economics*, 36, 225–58.

Kawamura, K. and Hirota, S. (2000), 'Employees discipline management: an alternative mechanism of corporate governance', mimeo.

Miyajima, H. (1998), 'Will the deregulation change J-type capitalism?: the impact of deregulation on corporate governance and finance in J-type firm', in Carlile, L. and Tilton, M. (eds), *Regulation and Regulatory Reform in Japan: Are Things Changing?* Brookings Institute, Washington, DC.

Miyajima, H. and Arikawa, Y. (2000), 'Relationship banking and debt choice: evidence from the liberalization in Japan', IFMP Discussion Paper Series 00A-07, Institute of Fiscal and Monetary Policy, Ministry of Finance.

Miyajima, H., Arikawa, Y. and Kato, A. (2001), 'Corporate governance, relational banking and R&D investment: evidence from Japanese large firms in the 1980s and 1990s', in *International Journal of Technological Management*.

Miyajima, H., Kondo, Y. and Yamamoto, K. (2001), 'Nihon kigyo ni okeru kigyo Touchi?Gaibu Yakuin?Kigyo Paformance: Nihon Kigyo System no Keisei to Henyo', (Corporate Governance in Japanese Firms, Outsider Directors, Firm Performance: The Formation and Metamorphoses of Japanese Firm System), *JCER Economic Journal, Nihon Keizai Kenkyu*.

Porter, M. E. (1992). Capital Disadvantage: America's Failing Capital Investment System, *Harvard Business Review* 70, 65–82.

Sheard, P. (1995) 'Long-termism and the Japanese firm', in Okabe, M. (ed.), *The Structure of the Japanese Economy*, Macmillan.

Weinstein, D. and Yafeh, Y. (1998). 'On the costs of a bank-centered financial system: evidence from the changing main bank relations in Japan', *Journal of Finance* 53, 635–72.

6 Continuity and change in Japanese human capital formation

Christopher Pokarier

Introduction

Until recently Japan's apparent success in developing and deploying human capital was celebrated at home and abroad. Indeed Japan's education and training systems have been frequently identified as one of the principal reasons for the nation's economic achievements over more than a century. Effective human capital formation appeared to occur through a judicious mix of education and training in state and private institutions, formal on-the-job training (OJT) and informal learning through well-managed employment. Yet many critics, both Japanese and foreign, now claim certain Japanese education and human resource management (HRM) practices hamper the nation's future economic prospects. Others suggest that the relationship between Japanese firms and employees are already changing to resemble supposed Western practices, with profound implications for individuals' investments in skill formation.

In 2001, Japanese mass media gave considerable attention to the notion that the society was becoming more meritocratic (*jitsuryoku shakai*), with recruitment and reward increasingly dependant on skill, rather than academic credentials, age or personal contacts. In an environment of concern about corporate restructuring (*resutora*) there was discussion also about the need for individuals to take greater personal responsibility for education and training. This in turn drew attention to the state of Japanese higher education. The prolonged economic problems of the 1990s, in contrast to the so-called 'new economy' dynamism of the United States, also rekindled old debates about whether Japanese education and employment systems foster sufficient creativity and critical capacities perceived as vital to success in knowledge-intensive industries.

This chapter first notes the centrality of accounts and theories of human capital formation to past interpretations of Japanese economic success. These accounts centred on blue-collar workers in manufacturing enterprises.

Yet, such employees represented only a small proportion of the Japanese workforce. Substantial changes in both the composition of the labour force and participation in formal education are noted, along with the questions this raises about influential skill formation and theoretical explanations of Japanese economic performance. In this context, evidence of change in Japanese HRM practices of long-term employment and seniority-based wages are surveyed. This reveals little change in the commitment of firms to maintain long-term employment and only modest shifts towards a system of performance-based pay. These findings have profound implications for human capital formation in Japan.

Since the mid-1990s young Japanese have found insufficient fulltime employment and skill formation opportunities while firms continued to hoard and reward older labour. Interestingly, in conjunction with commitment to long-term employment for a core of generalist management employees, firms have increased their dependance on outsourced specialist skills. This has included a reliance on foreign specialists in areas such as information technology (IT). This raises questions about the capacity of Japanese higher education system to produce graduates who possess the requisite skills. Although competition among Japanese educational institutions provides an impulse to innovation, many are hampered in their capacity to do so by the same commitment to established HR practices that constrain firms. Japan's stock of dynamic human capital is high but questions remain about whether it can be a source of competitive advantage in the future.

Human capital formation and Japan's development

Japan's success in fostering ongoing human capital formation over the last century figures prominently in most accounts of its economic development. Observers have emphasised the achievements of the education system in developing human capital that could be deployed and further developed by enlightened HRM practices (Galenson and Odaka, 1976). This fostered an interest in learning from Japan, which peaked in the late 1980s, just the time when more critical voices were being raised there about the continuing efficacy of established education and HR practice. Poor economic performance in the 1990s added fuel to these criticisms in Japan and led the foreign media to give them more attention. The extremes of commentary on what might loosely be called 'the Japanese human capital formation model' have obscured both the extent of continuity and change and several of the biggest issues.

Japan's establishment of a widely accessible national education system in its early modern period was doubtless a key feature of its development. Yet, the weaknesses of technical training during a period of rapid industrialisation early in the twentieth century was a major factor in the decisions of large enterprises to create substantial OJT programmes for blue-collar workers (Gordon, 1985). This became a key feature of Japanese enterprise in the postwar period. The practice of long-term employment (the 'lifetime employment' term is a misnomer) was also established in this period because high turnover of skilled workers led firms to fear that they would not capture an adequate return on investments in the OJT skill formation (Dore, 1973). Although the concept of long-term employment was readily couched in long-established Japanese loyalty and paternalism its immediate adoption was driven by the reality of skilled workers being prepared to quit in response to better offers elsewhere. Through a mix of financial inducements, evolving social expectations and an element of entrapment – through implicit no-poaching agreements, non-portable employment benefits and the like – long-term employment became a major feature of large manufacturing and some service sector firms.

It is now widely understood that long-term employment created a positive structure of incentives for both employers and employees to invest in competency building. Koike provided an influential account of a virtuous cycle of investments in skill formation, increasing firm productivity, and employee rewards, as explaining Japanese HR practices and the successes of Japanese manufacturers in the postwar period (Koike, 1987, 1988). Seniority-based wages had become another major feature of Japanese HR practice in the postwar era. Koike (1988) explained the steep age–wage profile as incentive/reward for skill formation. Over time, workers gained skill through formal and informal OJT, made greater contribution to the firm, and were paid more as a consequence. He also maintained that the tendency to mid-career changes of employers was attenuated by a significant firm-specific component to the skills employees developed. This, he argued, was in no small part because Japanese firms liked to train generalist employees through a job rotation system. At the same time, he rejected the view that length of service was the overriding determinant of pay, emphasising mechanisms that manufacturers had developed to recognise and reward skills and effort amongst blue-collar workers. With the rising productivity and competencies of Japanese firms, blue-collar workers did fewer manual tasks and developed 'knowledge intensive or intellectual skills' (Koike, 1988: xiii). This gradual 'white-collarisation' of the work experience of particular employees (Koike, 1987: 290) suggests the fallacy of recent popular distinctions drawn between 'new economy' and 'old economy' enterprises.

While the experience of firm-centred human capital formation in the manufacturing sector was positive, it cannot be taken as indicative of the Japanese economy as a whole. Even in 1990, only 13 per cent of the total

Japanese workforce was employed in manufacturing, with another 10.5 per cent in 'machinery', with a prediction that it would decline to 8.5 per cent in 2010 (Watanabe, 2001: 3). Moreover, a decreasing proportion of employees in manufacturing are in the factory floor roles that Koike and others characterised in the 'skill formation thesis'. It does not automatically follow that effective OJT has been delivered to white-collar workers in successful manufacturing firms just because their blue-collar training has been effective. Employment growth is currently in industries outside manufacturing, and in the services sector in particular (MHLW, 2001; Management and Coordination Agency, 1999). Emphasis on firm-based staff training certainly helped the service industry firms realise more consistent quality in interactions with customers but there have been criticisms about the overall productivity and strategic capabilities of the services sector (Porter *et al.*, 2000: 149). This implies that OJT has significant limitations and that the higher education system has failed to meet the gap.

Recession and employment scarcity

Although the Japanese media has given much attention to victims of corporate restructuring ('resutora'), large Japanese firms have generally avoided firing core employees. The long-term employment commitment is seen as too fundamental to employee morale and the established model of training and general management to be readily dispensed with (Gordon, 1985, 1999). Yet, even without recession, the long-term employment practice must have put considerable pressure on firms' balance sheets during this period. Ageing of the large baby boomer cohort coupled with seniority-based wages, would have increased labour costs at a time when many industries are in a maturing and rationalising phase. Normally, firms would have brokered the placement of core workers in their early fifties not destined for senior management ranks into 'post-retirement' employment with related firms but the low growth environment of the 1990s diminished the scope for doing so. Partly for that reason, the average retirement age in the private sector rose throughout the 1990s, despite poor business environment curtailing the growth of firms (Genda, 2000: 7).

In earlier recessionary periods, firms resorted to hiring freezes to lower the high fixed costs entailed in long-term employment. With the onset of recession in the early 1990s firms did the same and were reticent to hire new graduates in large numbers. When economic conditions worsened in 1997–8 that tendency became even more pronounced (Japan Institute of Labour, 2000a: 1, 3). Large Japanese firms have offered proportionately few young people the skill formation and career path associated with being a regular employee (*seishain*) than previously. Genda (2000) explored how companies with a high ratio of employees over the age of 45 tended to curb new hiring, effectively displacing young people. Total active job openings to applicants fell from 1.5 per job to each job searcher in 1990 to 0.5 in 1998 (Japan Institute of Labour, 2000c: 39).

Despite claims that more Japanese workers were prepared to change employers, there was little rise in the rate of persons changing employers between 1992 and 1997 (Japan Institute of Labour, 2000c: 45). Despite the Japanese mass media's fixation on the plight of older workers, the consequences of a weak labour market have been most significant for young job-seekers. The Management and Coordination Agency's annual labour force survey report revealed a 10.3 per cent unemployment rate for males aged 15–24 in 1999, in contrast to 3.2 per cent for males in the 45–54 age group and 6.7 per cent in the 55–64 age bracket (Japan Institute of Labour, 2000c: 48).

In 1998, only 65.6 per cent of an increasing number of new university graduates found fulltime work, compared with 81 per cent in 1990 (Japan Institute of Labour, 2000c: 31). This might partly be attributed to more graduates proceeding to graduate schools but about 10 per cent of total university graduates did not make the ready transition to fulltime employment in the late 1990s as they might have expected a decade earlier. There is also evidence that a larger proportion of newly employed graduates were dissatisfied with their employment. This was a reflection of the paucity of available positions and has significant implications for post-secondary human capital formation, given the centrality of OJT in even white-collar roles. Corporate Japan is taking a long-term gamble retaining expensive but ostensibly high value-adding senior employees at the expense of new recruits.

White-collar skill formation and performance

Until recently, most analysts believed that the positive experience of skill formation with blue-collar manufacturing workers also applied to white-collar employees. Koike (1988: 206), for instance, rather blithely declared as evidence of effective development and management of white-collar labour that '… the business performance of large Japanese companies is hardly inefficient'. The skill formation issue is particularly significant for white-collar workers because firms' commitment to long-term employment means that the vast majority of managers in larger Japanese enterprises have no experience with another firm or external management training.

In recent years many firms have moved from seniority-based wages for white collar employees towards a more skills and performance-based remuneration system (Sato, 1995). The immediate imperatives were the need to ration management positions among an ageing workforce and to slow down the associated rising labour costs (Watanabe, 1999: 11; Yamakawa, 1999: 7). Yet, the greater focus on performance also reflected a recognition by senior managements that firms had not avoided the moral hazard problems associated with guaranteeing employment and pay rises. While moral suasion and sanctions for poor performance – through such mechanisms as the transfer system – may have diminished outright shirking, there have not been sufficient rewards for individual application and competency development (Morishima, 1999).

The shift away from seniority-based pay, although still tentative in many enterprises, was a significant concession by firms that there was no simple and direct relationship between length of service, skill formation and value-adding to the enterprise. An ageing employee profile did not correlate directly with the realisation of greater productivity or product innovation and, consequently, raised questions about the reliance on in-house trained white-collar management. The value of OJT and general experience for white-collar workers is often difficult to measure in any environment. These issues have vexed Labour Ministry officials for a number of years and, since 1994, it has promoted the Business–Career system for appraising white-collar skills, through the Japan Vocational Ability Development Association. In areas such as personnel management it attempts to enunciate the professional knowledge expected, certifies educational and training institutions to offer relevant courses and certifies the skills this ostensibly attained (Sato, 1995: 3).

Employers have increasingly encouraged technical workers to take external skills tests although they are reticent to place much weight on them for general white-collar workers, especially in relation to promotion, owing to a concern for more general personality attributes (Ministry of Labour, 1992; Naganawa, 2000: 2). Skill testing and grading systems are hardly alien to the Japanese. In fact, they are central to training in certain traditional crafts and martial arts, and so are a familiar process. While in some circumstances they can reward and exacerbate credentialism there is an established set of norms about sustained effort for skill formation and tests to provide a foundation for a merit-based management system. By 1994, about 800,000 people a year were being tested for nine major white-collar qualifications (Sato, 1995: 6) To some extent, however, performance-based pay and promotion system masked the reality of a continuing emphasis on length-of-service, because development of competencies depends critically on opportunities for training and experience of higher level tasks. Thus, even as many Japanese enterprises were adopting the formal trappings of a merit-based promotion system it is still too early to judge whether they had moved away from a seniority-based approach to allocating staff development opportunities.

Firm-specific management

The parlous state of some large firms in the 1990s, in services sectors like banking and finance in particular, has raised doubts about the quality of firm-centred management training in Japan. Replication of the job rotation system deployed so effectively amongst blue-collar workers in Japanese manufacturing firms for many white-collar workers has created a class of generalist managers having broad familiarity with a range of aspects of the business. Yet, by sourcing management and most core staff internally, and by making only limited use of external training and consulting, firms deny themselves learning from the experiences of other enterprises and this made benchmarking profoundly difficult.

The appropriate balance between 'generalist' and 'specialist' training is currently being debated in Japan but the former is still generally understood in firm-specific terms. This is in stark contrast to the North American conception of general management skills being transferable across particular enterprises and industries, and encapsulated in the model of MBA training. A large survey conducted by the Institute of Labour in 1995–6 of middle managers in Japan, America and Germany was illuminative. Only 18 per cent of Japanese middle managers had worked for another firm while about 82 per cent of Americans and 70 per cent Germans had (Japan Institute of Labour, 1998a; Sato, 1999). In all three countries most managers who had worked elsewhere had done so for several other firms. Japanese employees are much more likely to have had substantial experience in functional areas outside the one in which they become a section chief than either American or German workers (Sato, 1999: 4–7). Interestingly, German and American managers considered their specialised experience to have been an important preparation for their current role while Japanese managers considered their generalist background valuable.

Continuing faith within Japanese organisations in the promotion of firm-specific generalists has found expression in the formal vision of future HR practices expressed by Nikkeiren, the national employers' federation (Nikkeiren, 1995; Yamakawa, 1999: 7–8). It envisaged the retention of long-term employment for, and management by, a core workforce to be recruited largely from new graduates. Contracted specialist staff would meet the growing need for specialist skills and a degree of overall labour cost flexibility would be maintained through contract clerical and other general staff. Although there was some dissent within Nikkeiren, support for an essentially *status quo* model was reaffirmed under the presidency of former Toyota Motor president Okuda (Yamakawa, 1999: 7–8). In 1999, he criticised firms for resorting to lay-offs of core staff; although firms that had done so were generally not in the healthy position of Toyota Motors

(Ushio and Dore, 1999). Widespread support remains for an essentially firm-specific management model. In this context, the shift of many firms to a more performance-oriented pay and promotion system looks merely to be an attempt to attenuate the financial, moral hazard and adverse selection problems associated with long-term employment rather than the beginning of a wholesale shift away from 'Japanese-style management'.

The continuing commitment of many large firms to long-term employment should not be taken as strong evidence in itself of its efficacy in promoting human capital formation and its effective deployment. It may be consistent with academic accounts of how weaker corporate governance pressures from shareholders in Japanese firms allow core workers to become a larger stakeholder in decision-making (Yamakawa, 1999: 8; Aoki, 1987). Until the economic malaise of the 1990s many observers saw this as a positive attribute that allowed firms to be more long-term oriented and which delivered both better human capital development and economic growth over time. More recently, inadequate corporate governance is seen to have caused unhealthy high debt levels and a low return on capital in many firms (Porter *et al.*, 2000: 150–2). It may also be the case that suboptimal employment practices persist under the guise of skill retention that in reality reflect capture of enterprises by baby boomers.

There was always a simple irony in the argument that seniority-based remuneration reflected high levels of skill formation in the context of long-term employment. In essence it was being argued that firms pay a substantial premium to retain human capital whose real value is not readily gauged in the labour market because it is rarely traded. The skill formation thesis would be credible if firms imparted portable skills in employees that they then needed to reward in order to retain in the firm, and that external market conditions were close to the salaries employees were getting by staying with the firm. In fact, a large literature attests as to how Japanese firms did not poach staff from their rivals and how employees leaving a large enterprise mid-career often had to settle for lesser wages and conditions. This may be because, as Koike (1987) suggested, firm-specific skills were a significant part of the competency mix that employees acquired while working in large firms. Yet, in such circumstances, a profit-maximising firm need not pay a substantial seniority premium to employees in order to retain non-portable skills. Moreover, many Japanese employees have also faced a degree of entrapment because, until recently at least, retirement and other non-salary benefits were not readily portable to another employer. Concern for a high quit rate but not profitability is consistent with an account of firm capture by core employees who do not want the viability of their vested entitlements diminished by the loss of talented employees.

114   Christopher Pokarier

Changes in HR practices, to better reward performance, can help existing middle-aged employees, controlling a firm, to secure its economic prospects in order to protect their entitlements. As noted above, the cost of avoiding large-scale rationalisation of expensive senior employees is a sharply reduced capacity to recruit and invest in the training of young workers (Genda, 2000). If the skill level and consequent value-adding of older white-collar workers has been exaggerated then they have been accruing significant benefits, in the form of secure income and benefits, at the expense of both shareholders and actual and potential young employees. Even if those senior employees were very productive, and one would expect better firm performance if that was the case, then a larger proportion of young Japanese have nonetheless missed out on the skill formation opportunities than in the past. That would not matter so much if education institutions and a strong economy presented alternative skill development and associated employment opportunities in emerging enterprises and sectors. A serious question persists as to whether that is the case, with significant implications not only for young people but also for established enterprises in the longer term.

Japan's future skills base

Concerns naturally arise about Japan's future skills base given the predominance of OJT in regular employment and the growing numbers of young people who do not hold such employment. The Japanese mass media have recently given considerable attention to the so-called *freeter* phenomenon of young people who hold non-regular casual employment and have high quit rates. The 2000 White Paper on Labour estimated the number of freeters at 1.51 million, double the figure for 1987 (Japan Institute of Labor, 2000b: 1). They include high school graduates but also junior college and university graduates, especially women. Although the broader social dimensions of the phenomenon are of greatest interest to the popular press, some academics and the Ministry of Labour have warned about the implied national failure to develop fully the stock of human capital (Ministry of Labour, 2000). However such commentary blames the freeter for lacking self-discipline to apply themselves to a career and to develop appropriate skills. The Japan Institute of Labour (2000a: 4), summarised the 2000 White Paper on Labour's judgement of the freeter phenomenon that 'behind the recent employment pattern of young people is their lack of commitment to working and a kind of unfounded optimism created by the economic affluence in which they grew up'. Similarly, Yamada (1999) situated freeters in the context of a broader phenomenon of so-called 'parasite singles'. Some 10 million single Japanese between the ages of 20 and 34, many more than in other developed economies, live with their parents and, consequently, have a higher material standard of living (Genda, 2000: 2). This is certainly not a new phenomenon and discourses about a new generation (*shinjinrui*) with a weak work ethic and attracted to service industries have been heard for at least two decades.

Still, too little consideration is given to how Japanese firms have employed fewer young people as regular employees while retaining much more expensive older workers despite a poor business environment. Collectively, the freeter have provided labour cost flexibility to facilitate new business development and cost reductions in established ones. The young workers bear a significant cost in terms of skill development, income and other benefits although a surprising proportion seemed to accept their status. A 1998 Monbusho survey revealed that 21.5 per cent of freeters who participated were pursuing personal goals simultaneously and were content with their modest employment status while another 27.1 per cent were freeters because they had no particular goals at all (Japan Institute of Labour, 2000b: 2). The other half aspired to regular employment. Far from its negative portrayal, the freeter phenomenon may have minimised the negative social consequences of Japanese HR and education practices that have diminished rewarding employment and training opportunities for young people. Genda (2000: 2) offered rare support for the freeters, and criticised baby boomers' complicity in their plight, arguing that 'the truth is not that parasite singles enjoy vested rights as handouts from their parents, but that young people 'scrounge' the vested rights that society affords the older generations'.

Over time the displacement of the young from regular employment with substantial skill training opportunities may end with simple demographics, especially if there is sustainable economic recovery. Substantially fewer young people will enter the labour market over the next decade and Japanese firms may then be forced to pay a price for having allowed baby boomers to influence HRM, such that fewer numbers of young talented and skilled individuals can be called upon within the boundaries of the firm. Yet, by then the baby boomers will have retired and a subsequent generation of core employees will have to struggle with the challenge of fostering a firm's competitive advantages while being increasingly reliant on outsourced specialist skills. This new generation of managers may revisit the appropriateness of established recruitment, training and promotion policies. Yet, in the absence of rigorous corporate governance pressures management capture of enterprises may persist at the expense of their future competitiveness.

Over the last decade, large firms have made much greater use of contract and temporary labour, leading to rapid growth in businesses specialising in supplying staff (Yamakawa, 1999: 7–9). The capacity will, therefore, exist to supply general staff to lean firms on a contract basis but recruiting those staff will become more difficult in time. A tighter labour market will have social positives as it will become feasible for women to return to substantial employment after having children, as is already being seen in nursing in response to staff shortages. Japan currently fails to earn a good return on that very large store of accumulated human capital represented by women who have little or no participation in the labour market (Japan Institute of Labour, 2000c: 61). Future shortages of skilled labour may also improve the career prospects for new female entrants to the labour market whose collective standing, despite better legal protection against discrimination from the late 1990s, has been weakened somewhat by the prolonged economic malaise (Japan Institute of Labour, 2000c: 60). Firms are also likely to utilise workers to a later age, although not at very senior wages, and may also become more receptive to mid-career hires (Watanabe, 2001: 2). The Chairman of Keizai Doyukai, Ushio Jiro, predicted that by 2010, 30 per cent of labour movement will be 'lateral', that is, across firm boundaries, rather than 'vertical', up from the current 10 per cent (Ushio and Dore, 1999: 32). Foreign skilled employees are also likely to become more important to the Japanese economy as they are in the United States and a number of East Asian economies (Iredale, 2000). This is already evident in IT. The IT Strategy Council, in support of the government's grandiose commitment to make Japan the leading IT nation within five years, estimated that 30,000 foreign professionals would be required (Watanabe, 2001: 9–10). There is greater official recognition of the contribution that foreign specialists can make to the Japanese economy. If Japan faces substantial skills shortages in the future that constitute a brake on the rate of economic growth then it will be principally the consequence of private and public economic governance during the 1990s that favoured ageing baby boomers at the expense of young graduates. This is just as true of education institutions, crucially important in meeting Japan's future human capital needs.

Education reform and human capital formation

Calls for education reform figure prominently in contemporary Japanese and foreign discussions of the Japanese economy and why it has not shared the apparent dynamism of the American 'new economy'. Opinion-leaders are increasingly expressing the view that the current education system is a factor in Japan's perceived failure to match the economic dynamism of the American 'new economy' during the last decade. At the same time there is a popular perception that Japan is becoming a *meritocracy* (*jitsuryoku shakai*), which implies that individuals must take greater personal responsibility for the development of valuable skill sets. Prominent instances of older workers losing their employment through corporate restructuring have been the main reason for this growing belief. The pressing need for educational institutions to assist in addressing the current shortfall in employment-based skill formation opportunities confronting younger Japanese attracts less attention. Intense debates, nonetheless, rage over whether both the school and post-secondary education systems are adequately preparing young Japanese to face contemporary economic and social challenges. Deep cleavages of opinion amongst policy-makers, opinion-leaders and the Japanese community make the ultimate direction of current education 'reform' initiatives unclear. The Obuchi and Mori cabinets, nonetheless, placed education reform at the forefront of the national policy agenda and Koizumi's ascendancy to the prime ministership does not appear to have changed that.

Many of the criticisms levelled at Japanese educational institutions, for example, the failure to impart particular competencies and skills in student, are long-standing ones but given added currency and political salience by a decade of economic stagnation. New economy and knowledge economy discourses have rekindled debates about creativity and the role of the education system in hindering or fostering its development in individuals. The creativity theme became the focal point for deliberations by most business and university participants in the Mori Government's so-called Citizen's Forum on Education Reform (Kyoiku kaikaku kokumin kaigi, 2000b). Quite radical ideas about how to reinvigorate the culture of higher education institutions through promoting student diversity are now being floated. It has even been suggested that Tokyo University should admit a proportion of new students by lottery (Tachibana, 2001: 180–1). Yet, both the real extent of creativity in Japan and the ease by which it might be further cultivated through education institutions, understandably, are challenged.

Certain business proponents of fostering greater creativity may have a rather constrained notion of what its realisation entails. Prolonged training in firm-specific organisational procedures and norms for new white-collar employees can be antipathetic to the professed qualities and outcomes sought in young people showing initiative and 'creativity'. Conservative critics see passivity, laziness and poor manners as an intertwined consequence of affluence, current child-raising practices and naïve liberals in education institutions spoiling youths. Debate over school education reform, examined, in detail, in another paper in this volume, has been coloured by popular perceptions of rising problems of juvenile delinquency, and violent crime by youths (Kyoiku kaikaku kokumin kaigi, 2000). One conservative Tokyo University academic advocated education reform to teach the 'proper meaning of freedom and democracy' in order to address Japan's perceived 'descent into depravity' (Nakanishi, 2000: 5). Such 'reform' does not promise to be a well-spring of creativity for a knowledge-intensive economy.

A newer element in criticisms of the education system is to fault it for not instilling a greater sense of entrepreneurialism in students. This is a direct reaction to the apparent 'new economy' dynamism of the United States. Statistics still show a much lower level of new business establishment in Japan, perhaps not surprising given the parlous state of the macroeconomy, but both the Japanese and foreign media have focused much more attention on evidence of entrepreneurialism. There has been particular interest in e-business entrepreneurs and those who have left large companies to start their own businesses. Although, many business identities publicly lament a perceived lack of entrepreneurial zeal among younger Japanese, it is doubtful that they would all welcome more of their best and brightest employees leaving to start new enterprises. More Japanese firms do appear to be considering the internal structures of incentives that have militated against 'intrapreneurialism'. Yet, until they have been addressed it is premature to lay the principal blame for personal aversion to risk-taking and innovation upon education institutions. Attitudes to entrepreneurialism are related to broader opinions about differentiating oneself from others and equality. Central to debates over education reform, especially at the school level, is the extent to which excellence should be encouraged at the expense of promoting equality of educational attainment (Kyoiku kaikaku kokumin kaigi, 2000). Inoguchi (1999) argued that improved outcomes in areas such as a supply of professionals proficient in English was not likely until 'collective advancement obsession' had been discredited. While the shift towards more performance-based rewards in firms might, at first glance, suggest that attitudes in Japan towards equality of outcomes are diminishing, such developments might strengthen popular support for ensuring a high common level of skill attainment in the school system.

The expansion of many Japanese firms abroad over an extended period and the liberalisation of Japanese markets have made 'internationalisation' an issue for some time. Recently discourses on globalisation have become acutely influential in Japan though, reflecting both their currency in other countries and prominent instances of foreign acquisitions of failed Japanese enterprises. Viewers of the Japanese mass media could be forgiven for concluding that foreign firms currently were provoking a shake-up of management practices in Japan. Discourses about a 'third opening', after Perry in 1854 and the occupation forces in 1945, are common. This is despite the fact that, in 1996, there were only 230,000 people, or 6 per cent of company employees working for foreign-affiliated enterprises in Japan (Watanabe, 1999: 6). Nonetheless, while a notion of 'internationalisation' is difficult to define and to measure, there are many indicators that the Japanese had become more receptive to foreign influences. In 1997, 17 million Japanese travelled overseas and large numbers of Japanese are studying abroad, although many in short courses (JTB, 1998: 1). Contemporary Japanese lifestyles reveal readiness to borrow eclectically from the world. Critics argue that, despite the internationalisation of Japanese consumers, firms and employees were not adequately equipped by the education system to work well with foreigners. One ongoing concern is the level of English language attainment despite its significant weight in the high school curricula and considerable public resources devoted to deploying native speakers in schools (Hadley, 1999). Yet corporate English language training needs are served by a substantial private education industry that is evolving to also offer a 'one stop global skills shop'. The leading example of this is Glova, a subsidiary of the huge Nova English conversation school group that now offers in-house language courses, interpreting and translation services, bilingual temporary and permanent staff placement and internationalisation consulting services.

More specific demands for better educational outcomes are also heard from business constituencies. There are calls for more off-the-job training capacity, public and private, to address looming skills shortages in certain sectors. Predictions of future employment growth in the Japanese economy, such as conducted by the Institute of Labour, reveal that the largest relative growth is in areas where existing training capacities remain under-developed or at least under-accessed. In addition to the expected strong employment growth in the IT and healthcare areas, the other services categories of information, research and advertising services are projected to increase total employment by almost a million to 1.8 million in 2010 (Watanabe, 2001: 3). There are now strong calls from industry for better measures of the level of skill attainment of graduates. Firms want new employees with a demonstrated capacity to learn relevant new skills quickly. Ironically many firms are more concerned about the capacities of new employees partly because they are recruiting fewer of them owing to the heavy cost burden of retaining older workers benefiting from the long-term employment promise. The university sector currently faces profound challenges that make adoption of standard measures of graduate skill outcomes a vexing issue.

Porter *et al.* (2000: 144) declared that 'the roots of Japan's uncompetitive industries can often be traced back to its universities ... .' They blamed the conduct of research in universities for hampering the emergence of new industries and for not providing graduates with appropriate marketable skills. This view accords with a growing perception among opinion leaders that tertiary institutions had to adapt to meet the changing economic and social needs of the country. This in turn has influenced central government policies for tertiary institutions. An advisory group under the aegis of The

University Council produced an influential report in 1997 on 'the future vision for higher education' that explicitly acknowledged the need to re-examine universities' roles in HR development in the context of a changing economy and society (University Council, 1997). In the closing years of the 1990s, the nature and future of the higher education system emerged as a major issue of debate for another reason as well. A simple demographic trend threatens the very existence of some universities. The college/university student age cohort is shrinking precipitously in the wake of the second baby boomers' graduation. These two pressures on universities entail a number of contradictions that, combined with rather resilient features of university management and practice, are profoundly difficult for institutions to resolve.

It is a popular perception abroad that, in relation to Japanese human capital formation, schools provided a good academic education, universities provided a good break, and Japanese companies did the rest. While, not without substance, there is considerable variety across education institutions and in what they provide to students and employers. A shrinking student base compounds the differences between universities and colleges. The most prestigious institutions continue to attract the top students but others face a bleak future. Many institutions with little reputation and limited resources have closed their junior colleges as students adjust their expectations upwards in light of easier university entry. Total enrolled junior college (*Tanki daigaku*) student numbers peaked in absolute terms in 1995 at 499,000 and by 1998 had fallen to 417,000 (Japan Institute of Labour, 2000c: 80).

The 1997 University Council report envisaged more competition among tertiary institutions, leading to improved course quality and responsiveness to changing economic and social needs (MEXT, 2001; University Council, 1997). Yet, while the better-run institutions will certainly do more to sell themselves to prospective students it may actually be more difficult to realise higher graduate skill outcomes. Whether students take the easy path of enrolling in a relatively unchallenging programme or are prepared to invest considerable effort in a demanding one promising better competency development will depend largely on signals from employers through their recruiting practices. More companies are formally placing more emphasis on the skill sets of graduates yet there is still insufficient evidence to draw firm conclusions about how seriously this is pursued by firms in practice. Likewise, recent determinants of university choice have not been systematically studied although anecdotal evidence suggests, not surprisingly, that established institutional reputations are still seen as the best guarantee of good employment upon graduation.

The Ministry of Education has gradually loosened its regulatory grip on public and private institutions to give institutions more discretion to innovate offerings. Japan's ninety-eight national universities soon will be formally made autonomous, although still subject to considerable bureaucratic constraints (Umezu, 2001). If national universities transcend caps on enrolments and formidable internal hurdles to innovation then lesser private institutions will face even more intense competition. Policy provision for the creation of new 'professional schools' at the postgraduate level reflect an understanding in education policy-making circles that Japan will face series of skills shortages in the medium term owing to the current limitations of the OJT system. Greater emphasis is also being placed on partnerships between tertiary institutions and the private sector in skill development and fitting individuals to roles, such as through internship programmes (Japan Institute of Labour, 1998b: 2).

Individual Japanese universities must make effective responses in the near future to the need for better courses and teaching in order to avoid serious financial troubles. Yet they are hampered by seniority-based remuneration and ageing staff profile, much the same way that firms have been hampered in their important role in human capital formation. Institutions have avoided staff redundancy, leaving insufficient resources for innovate programmes (Kawanari, 2000). There are limited employment opportunities for young academics, hampering both short-term programmatic innovation while threatening longer term staff shortages across the sector. With the exception of languages departments and a few IT schools in more enlightened institutions, non-Japanese academic staff are strikingly scarce. The potential consequences for the Japanese economy of these substantial barriers to innovation in the higher education sector are significant given that it should be the principal means of ameliorating the increasingly evident problems with national reliance upon firm-centred human capital formation.

Conclusions

Japan's twentieth century model of human capital formation – sound universal schooling and OJT – and effective deployment of those HRs were perhaps its principal sources of national competitive advantage. Yet a decade of relative economic under-performance has revealed a range of weaknesses in that model. There are now serious questions being raised about whether Japanese education and training is adequately equipping the nation's youth with skills needed to be competitive in globally competitive knowledge-intensive industries. Heavy reliance upon OJT served Japan well at a time when the economy and businesses were growing rapidly. However, the last decade has revealed that a danger of diminished national human capital formation during a period of low economic growth. This risk has been greatly compounded by larger firms' continuing commitment to long-term employment and seniority-based remuneration for a core workforce. This commitment has been frequently rationalised by both managers and academics as necessary to promote the development and retention of valuable employee skills. Yet the firm-specific nature and limited external labour market for the skills developed is not fully consistent with the large wage premium paid to older employees. Instead it suggests that in the absence of strong corporate governance the management of firms have been captured by certain employee interests, currently the baby boomer generation. In guarding the employment and benefits of existing older employees at the expense of new hires, firms are taking risks with their future skills base. Although, firms are hesitant to hire new employees in great numbers they have become more focused on recruiting and rewarding competent individuals who might contribute to revitalising firms, in turn securing the vested rights of more senior core employees.

Young people unable to secure regular employment, offering considerable skill formation opportunities, are the neglected victims of continuity in Japanese HRM practices during a period of low economic growth. Japanese higher education institutions have inadequately compensated for the insufficient on-the-job learning opportunities although negative social consequences have been diminished by the preparedness of many families to subsidise their adult children in various ways. Higher education institutions are constrained in their capacity to innovate their offerings and practice by the very same tendency to 'baby boomer capture' that plagues Japanese corporations. Simple demographics – fewer young people – may attenuate over time their displacement from skill formation opportunities by ageing workers while also force higher education institutions to make some tough decisions about what they offer and how in a highly competitive market for education. Whether or not Japan's human capital continues to be a significant source of national competitive advantage will largely depend on the calibre of strategic responses over the next decade by both Japanese HR managers and education institutions to changed circumstances.

References

Aoki, M. (1987), 'The Japanese firm in transition', in Yamamura K. and Yasuba Yasukichi (eds), *The Political Economy of Japan: Volume 1 – The Domestic Transformation*, Stanford University Press, Stanford, California.

Dore, Ronald P. (1973), *British Factory–Japanese Factory: The Origins of National Diversity in Industrial Relations*, George Allen and Unwin, London.
Genda, Y. (2000), 'Youth employment and parasite singles', *Japan Labor Bulletin*, 39(3), e-version at www.jil.go.jp.
Galenson, W. and Odaka Konosuke (1976), 'The Japanese labor market', in Patrick, H. and Henry Rosovsky (eds), *Asia's New Giant: How the Japanese Economy Works*, Brookings Institution, Washington.
Gordon, A. (1985), *The Evolution of Labor Relations in Japan: Heavy Industry, 1853–1955*, Harvard East Asian Monographs 117, Harvard University Press, Cambridge, MA.
Gordon, A. (1999), 'Scaring the salaryman isn't the Japanese way', *New York Times*, 30 October.
Hadley, Gregory S. (1999), 'Innovative curricula in tertiary ELT: a Japanese case study', *ELT Journal*, 53(2).
Inoguchi, T. (1999), 'Japan's failing grade in English', *Japan Echo*, October.
Iredale, R. (2000), 'Migration policies for the highly skilled in the Asia-Pacific region', *The International Migration Review*, 34(3) 882–906.
Japan Institute of Labour (1998a), *A Comparative Study of Human Resources Development of College Graduates in Industry*, Japan Institute of Labour, Tokyo.
Japan Institute of Labour (1998b), 'The Kobe jobs conference', *Japan Labor Bulletin*, 37(1) (*http://www.jil.go.jp/bulletin/year/1998/vol37-01/08.htm*).
Japan Institute of Labour (2000a), 'The 2000 White Paper on labour: a summary of the analysis', *Japan Labor Bulletin*, 39(9), e-version at www.jil.go.jp.
Japan Institute of Labour (2000b), 'The "freeters" issue', *Japan Labor Bulletin*, 39(11), e-version at www.jil.go.jp.
Japan Institute of Labour (2000c), *Japanese Working Life Profile 2000: Labor Statistics*, The Japan Institute of Labour, Tokyo.
JTB (1998), *JTB Report 1998: Nihonjin kaigai ryokou no subete* (All about Japanese travellers), Japan Travel Bureau, Tokyo.
Kawanari, You (2000), *Daigaku houkai* (University Collapse), Takarajimasha Shinsho, Tokyo.
Koike, K. (1987), 'Human resource development and labour–management relations', in Yamamura K. and Yasuba Yasukichi (eds), *The Political Economy of Japan: Volume 1 – The Domestic Transformation*, Stanford University Press, Stanford.
Koike, K. (1988) *Understanding Industrial Relations in Modern Japan*, Macmillan Press, Hampshire.
Kyoiku kaikaku kokumin kaigi (2000), 'kyouiku kaikaku kokuminkaigi hokoku: kyouiku o kaeru 17 no teian' (Report of the National Panel on Education Reform: 17 proposals to change education), accessed at www.kantei.go.jp.
Management and Coordination Agency (1999), *Rodoryoku chosa* (Labor Force Survey), Statistics Bureau, Tokyo.
MEXT (2001), 'The final report on the future vision for higher education after the fiscal 2000', Summary, Planning Division, Higher Education Bureau, Tokyo, accessed at www.mext.go.jp.

MHLW (2001), 'Final report of monthly labour survey – January 2001', March 16, Statistics and Information Department, Minister's Secretariat, accessed at www.mhlw.go.jp.
Ministry of Labour (1992), *1992 Rodohakusho* (White Paper on Labour), Tokyo.
Ministry of Labour (2000), *2000 Rodohakusho* (White Paper on Labour), Tokyo.
Morishima, M. (1999), 'Procedural fairness in evaluation systems for Japanese white-collar employees', *Japan Labor Bulletin*, 38(1), e-version at www.jil.go.jp.
Naganawa, H. (2000), 'Employability as expertise of white-collar workers', *Japan Labor Bulletin*, 39(1).
Nakanishi, T. (2000), 'Goals for Japan in its "Second postwar period"', *Japan Echo*, April, 2000.
Nikkeiren (Nihon keieisha dantai renmei) (1995), *Shin jidai no nihon teki keiei* (Japanese Style Management in a New Era), Nikkeiren, Tokyo.
Porter, M., Takeuchi Hirotaka and Sakakibara Mariko (2000), *Can Japan Compete?* Macmillan, Hampshire.
Sato, H. (1995), 'New education and training system for white-collar workers', *Japan Labor Bulletin*, 34(2), e-version at www.jil.go.jp.
Sato, H. (1999), 'A comparison of career and skill development among white-collar employees in three countries', *Japan Labor Bulletin*, 38(2), e-version at www.jil.go.jp.
Tachibana, T. (2001), 'Todaisei wa baka ni natta ka?', *Bungeishunju*, March, pp. 180–190.
Umezu, K. (2001), *Tsubureru daigaku, nobiru daigaku, keieishindan* (Bankrupt Universities, Growing Universities: Management diagnosis), Yell Books, Tokyo.
University Council (1997), *Final Report on the Future Vision for Higher Education after the Fiscal 2000*, Report submitted to Minister of Education on 29 January.
Ushio, J. and Ronald Dore (1999), 'Constancy and change in Japanese management', *Japan Echo*, 26(2).
Watanabe, H. (1999), 'Recent trends of foreign-affiliated companies in Japan', *Japan Labor Bulletin*, 38(8), e-version at www.jil.go.jp.
Watanabe, H. (2001), 'Employment projections for the 2000–2010 period', *Japan Labor Bulletin*, 40(1), e-version at www.jil.go.jp.
Yamada, M. (1999), *Parasaito singuru no jidai* (*Days of the Parasite Single*), Chikumashobo, Tokyo.
Yamakawa, R. (1999), 'The silence of stockholders: Japanese labor law from the viewpoint of corporate governance', *Japan Labor Bulletin*, 38(11), e-version at www.jil.go.jp.

7 Changing environmental policy agendas

Japan's approach to international environmental problems

Jeffrey Graham

Introduction

Over, approximately, the last thirty years the significance of international environmental problems (which includes those of a transboundary, regional and global nature) have risen from virtual obscurity within the sphere of international relations and politics to that of the highest concern. Similarly, over the same period of time, the expectations placed on Japan to play a significant international role commensurate with its economic growth and status have risen dramatically, and this has placed increasing pressure on the Japanese government to expand the scope and depth of its contributions to the welfare, development and prosperity of the international community. Putting this simply, there has been dynamic change in terms of the expectations of the international community in relation to solving environmental problems, and in relation to Japan's international contributions, particularly in regard to the environment.

Understandably, the priority placed on environmental protection by the Japanese government, and by Japanese industry and the general community, has risen significantly since the early 1970s. In fact, by the 1990s, environmental concerns had become central to the government's domestic political and foreign policy agenda; an increasingly noticeable aspect of the community contributions, operational guidelines and promotional campaigns of Japanese companies; and a common theme of community cooperation activities. The question is, however, has government policy; the administration of that policy, and the tools of policy implementation, changed at the same pace, and in a way appropriate, to the dynamic change in the deterioration of the environment and the expectations of the international community in regard to Japan's contribution towards solving environmental problems.

The key objectives of this paper are to examine how Japan's international environmental policies have evolved since the early 1970s, and in doing so provide an insight into the drivers and mechanisms of this policy reform process. A second objective is to reveal the primary strengths and weaknesses of the changing policy position and attitude of the Japanese government in relation to international environmental protection. In achieving these first two objectives, this chapter sets out to provide a clear picture of where significant policy changes have occurred, and also where inadequate policies or unbalanced policy priorities continue to prevail.

There are four main sections to the chapter, each of which explores a particular issue concerning Japan's international environmental policy development. The first and most extensive of these sections involves an examination of Japan's diplomatic performance, with a particular focus on Japan's approach to the United Nations (UN) and the policies which have formed the backbone of this approach. The second and third sections deal with the more recent issues of the Kyoto Conference on Climate Change, and areas where changes have occurred in relation to key legislation and administrative bodies. While the fourth section highlights Japan's approach to environmental protection in the context of its Official Development Assistance (ODA) programme.

The underlying argument of this chapter is that while the complexities and challenges of policy reform for Japan over the last thirty years in relation to international environmental protection have been immense, it has only been in very recent years that Japan has provided any clear indication of self-motivated and progressive policy reform efforts. Furthermore, it is argued that while Japan has achieved almost leadership status in terms of its financial and technological contributions to international environmental protection, the focus of its environmental policies are yet to reflect what many consider to be the necessary balance across the whole spectrum of international environmental problems.

The policy foundations of Japan's environmental diplomacy

The early 1970s were certainly an interesting and important period for Japan in relation to environmental policy. The government's overall policy agenda, as had been the case throughout the postwar period, was understandably still very much dominated by domestic and international economic concerns. However, along with a number of previously ignored social welfare issues, the environment, or more specifically, domestic industrial pollution, was now emerging as a central element of the government's policy agenda.

The transformation of Japan's environmental policies during the early 1970s included the introduction and amendment of key legislation, such as changes to the 1967 Basic Law for Environmental Pollution Control (ridding that law of a clause which placed environmental protection second to economic priorities), the enactment of world's first legislation in relation to compensation for pollution-related disease victims, and new legislation for nature conservation, not to mention a range of other regulatory reforms which by the mid-1970s placed Japan at the forefront of pollution control standards, especially in regard to air pollution. Similarly, there were important administrative changes, the most significant being the establishment in 1971 of the Environment Agency (EA).

These early domestic environmental policy and administrative developments, and the pollution incidents which preceded them, are well documented in both Japanese and Western literature. What is relatively less well documented are the challenges which began to emerge during the early 1970s for Japan in relation to environmental policy at an international level, and the ways in which Japan responded to these challenges. As Japan had only just begun to take the necessary steps against severe domestic industrial pollution problems, its initial approach to the diplomatically complex and more financially challenging issues of transboundary environmental problems was one which largely reflected a resistance to change, not to mention a significant lack of policy initiative, especially for a country which was already gaining so much economically from the world's natural resources.

It is fair to say that at the beginning of the 1970s, Japan's environmental concerns were not only very much domestically oriented, but also that the concept of global-scale, or even regional environmental problems, was yet to be embraced by Japanese bureaucrats, politicians or even non-government organisations (NGOs). As one former high-ranking Environment Agency bureaucrat has stated, the government feared that the development of policies other than those needed for dealing with domestic industrial pollution problems would 'dilute' those measures that had already been established (Kato, 1990: 21).

Internationally, the largest and arguably most important environmental forum during the 1970s was the 1972 United Nations Conference on the Human Environment (UNCHE). The task of presenting the nation's record of dealing with environmental problems up to that point was not an easy one for the Japanese delegation, in the sense that its notoriety as possibly the most polluted country in the world by the end of the 1960s, and the severity of a number of pollution-related disease incidents which had occurred in Japan during the 1950s and 1960s, were still far more significant in the minds of most than the policy reforms which were enacted once the situation had reached crisis proportions.

On the positive side, Japan was supportive either verbally or financially towards the main aims of the UNCHE. This included support for the establishment of a UN environment committee, which became the United Nations Environment Programme, and a pledged contribution of 10 per cent towards a proposed $100 million UN environment fund, a percentage which was second only to that pledged by the United States. While this was a higher percentage than Japan had previously contributed to any other international organisation, it was only half the percentage for which the conference organisers had been hoping (Kumao, 1972). Japan also displayed much enthusiasm towards the establishment of an extensive bilateral network on the protection of migratory birds, a network which it had already started to build through an agreement with the United States earlier that year.

On the negative side, however, there was one issue raised at the UNCHE which placed Japan in a particularly difficult situation diplomatically, and which created conflict between Japan and many other nations, as well as environmental activist groups, not only during the conference, but also for many years to come. This issue involved a resolution to introduce a ten-year moratorium on commercial whaling. Although the resolution was adopted by a majority vote, the Japanese government not only refused to accept it, but also stated that it did not recognise the UN's authority to ban whaling, and that any such decision could only be made on the basis of scientific findings within the International Whaling Commission (IWC), a body which had managed the whaling industry since 1946. While the UNCHE resolution did lead to the introduction of stricter regulations within the IWC, which in turn brought about a reduction in Japan's whaling operations during the 1970s, Japan continued to defend its pro-whaling stance. Furthermore, it was not until the mid-1980s that Japan, under direct economic pressure from the United States, agreed to accept a total moratorium on international whaling (*Japan Quarterly*, 1972: 393). This, of course, did not end the controversy for Japan, which since that time has continued to take advantage of the so-called 'scientific research whaling' loophole within the moratorium, and has persistently argued its case for the sustainability of renewed commercial whaling.

The UNCHE was a starting point for more frequent and progressive multilateral discussion for most nations on a broad range of environmental issues. Apart from the whaling issue, this conference was also very much the starting point of Japan's international environmental diplomacy, and its efforts to transform its policies and international contributions more towards protection of the environment both within and beyond its own borders.

Japan's approach to the UNCHE and other environmental issues during the 1970s was the beginning of a trend, which continued into the 1980s and 1990s, where the Japanese government has focused its efforts, not so much on the actual debate over international environmental issues, but more so on making financial contributions and offering its services as a host of major international meetings. That is, Japan has used its strong economic position as a way of supporting progress in the debate over international environmental issues, but not as a motive to actively participate in that debate, or necessarily provide negotiating solutions.

In the 1980s, Japan's EA began investing time and money into understanding what should and needed to be done in relation to global environmental issues from a broad perspective. In this regard, its main achievement during the early part of this decade was the establishment in September 1980 of an advisory committee of academics and government officials, namely the Ad Hoc Group on Global Environmental Problems. This advisory group produced two reports, in December 1980 and in April 1982. Of the recommendations, the most significant was that Japan should assume a leading role within international environment protection efforts (Environment Agency, 1982: 405). It could be said, however, that the overall significance of this exercise was rather limited, in terms of its immediate policy impact, or in the sense that these reports contained more rhetoric than they did concrete objectives, as with many other Japanese government reports and policy guidelines before and since this time.

Progressively through the 1980s, Japanese politicians also became more directly involved in discussions on international environmental issues. For example, in September 1988, the Liberal Democratic Party's (LDP) Environment Committee formed a special sub-committee on global environmental problems, consisting of eighteen Diet members. The most prominent political voice in Japan, though, during the 1988–9 period, on international environmental issues was without a doubt Takeshita Noboru. Although his promises that the Japanese government would take the initiative in becoming a leader in the protection of the global environment were often regarded as having little substance, his persistence in raising the issue, ability to gather media interest, and his position of influence within industry circles where environment cooperation was needed most, were important factors in the development of broader support for a more positive Japanese position (Kitamatsu, 1989: 1, 6). One of Takeshita's initial efforts was to propose that Japan host a major international conference on the global environment. As a result such a conference did occur in September 1989 in the form of The Tokyo Conference on the Global Environment and Human Response Toward Sustainable Development (Kato, 1990: 55). While the conference was a major organisational effort for the EA and Ministry of Foreign Affairs (MFA), and involved sixty environmental experts from twenty-three countries, it was criticised for not producing any fresh or concrete proposals on how to deal with issues such as tropical deforestation and the funding of environmental protection in developing countries. Also, despite the fact that there was now a great deal expected of Japan as a financial power, and despite the fact that the Japanese government was the organiser and host of the conference, there were no bold funding proposals forthcoming from Japanese government representatives. The strongest positive point to make about this conference, is that Japan was making an effort to actively include Asian countries in international debate over global environmental issues and to assist in finding solutions to their problems, as the leading economic power in Asia would be expected to do. However, the main achievement of the conference, if any, was the enhancement of Japan's international environmental diplomacy and image (Lincoln, 1993: 151).

In a more coordinated fashion, however, the Japanese government also raised the profile of discussion on international environmental protection at the multi-agency and political levels through the establishment in May 1989 of the 'Council of Ministers for Global Environmental Conservation'. This council included the participation of nineteen ministry and agency heads, and high-ranking officials of the LDP (Environment Agency, 1991: 12). In just over a month this council produced a set of six basic guidelines for the government as a whole, such as those which recommended that Japan pursue the development and transfer of technology for global environmental protection, make efforts for the expansion of ODA in the field of environmental protection, and strengthen the consideration of environmental protection within the implementation of ODA. As stated above in relation to guidelines developed by the Ad Hoc Group on Global Environment Problems during the early 1980s, these guidelines could also be described as little more than vague rhetoric that allowed for a great deal of scope in the actual degree of policy reform and the effectiveness of policy development, and to a large extent could be summed up as broad aims that provided no real certainty of any concrete policy changes within any particular time frame.

However, it needs to be emphasised that these guidelines were actually drafted by the then EA in consultation with all relevant agencies and ministries before being presented to the Council of Ministers for Global Environmental Conservation for approval. Moreover, in regard to each guideline, even though the wording is seemingly open to a wide range of interpretation, it was necessary for the EA to receive consent (whether it be somewhat reluctantly) from all relevant ministries and agencies, because such wording could determine the course or focus of many of these agencies' future activities (Environment Agency Official, 1994). Hence, although the official adoption of these guidelines by the Council of Ministers was little more than a formality, the fact that it involved representatives from all relevant ministries and agencies, as well as the governing party, was at least an indication that the government as a whole was now reaching a clearer consensus on the nation's appropriate policy priorities in relation to international environmental issues.

Throughout the 1980s Japan was on the receiving end of much international criticism, especially for its relatively poor performance in relation to controlling trade in endangered species, the scale of its industrial waste dumping operations at sea and plans to dump low-level radioactive wastes; its involvement in the rapid pace of tropical deforestation, particularly in Southeast Asia; its controversial harvesting of minke whales for the purpose of so-called 'scientific research whaling'; the impact of its driftnet fishing operations, and its failure to satisfactorily consider environmental concerns within the context of its huge development assistance programme (Lauber, 1993: 42–3). By the end of the 1980s, this criticism began to weigh heavily on the policy makers within the EA.

Largely as a result of this international criticism, during the late 1980s the EA, in particular, began a process of rapidly re-developing both its administrative structure and policy guidelines in relation to international environmental protection. For example, in August 1988, the EA established a 'Global Environment Protection Board', headed by the agency's Deputy Director-General, for the purpose of following up on the recommendations outlined in the June 1988 report of the Ad Hoc Group on Global Environmental Problems. Hence, the new board was faced with the challenge of planning and drafting ways of dealing with a wide range of international environmental issues, somewhat wider and now considerably more serious than the range of issues considered only six to seven years earlier (Environment Agency, 1988: 4). Another centre of activity was the EA's Planning and Coordination Bureau. At this time, its efforts were almost entirely directed towards tackling global environmental problems. Between late January and early March of 1989, a wide range of specialists, such as ecologists, biologists, journalists, international lawyers, economists, etc., were asked to pass on their advice to the Planning and Coordination Bureau in relation to the appropriate policies and diplomatic approach that should be taken by the Japanese government.

There were a number of viewpoints in common among these various advisers. They included the suggestion that Japan should actively tackle global environmental problems; that it would be appropriate for Japan to focus its international contributions in the environmental field; that different ministries and agencies cannot be seen to be tackling global environmental problems in different directions; and that the EA should be given the central coordinating role. It was also recommended that environmental problems in developing countries should not be dealt with in the same way as they had been in Japan; that development assistance should be directed towards training more environmental experts in developing countries; that NGOs should be included in such a training process; and that Japan should further develop its global scientific research base by establishing interconnections with international research organisations, universities and the private sector (Environment Agency Official, 1994).

In the lead up to the June 1992 United Nations Conference on Environment and Development (UNCED), the issue of 'Japanese leadership' was frequently discussed in official and media circles, with questions raised as to whether such leadership should simply involve a commitment to provide large sums of money, or whether it should involve a more diverse set of contributions. The debate often centred on the 'cheque-book diplomacy' which had characterised Japanese efforts in other areas such as its contributions to the UN endorsed military activities during the 1991 Persian Gulf crisis. The MFA, for example, considered UNCED to be a starting point for a more diverse and acceptable Japanese contribution to the international community which would not be complicated by some of the more negative political issues associated with military and economic aggression, and which offered opportunities for Japan to go beyond its 'cheque-book diplomacy' reputation (Newhouse, 1992: 68, 76).

However, as UNCED drew near, it was the expectation that Japan would contribute a large sum of money to global environmental protection which attracted the maximum media attention. In preparatory meetings the real expectations of officials from various countries actually centred on Japan being able to make the sort of financial commitments that would help to dispel North–South tensions over global environmental protection. Even the chairman of these meetings, Tommy Koh (a Singaporean diplomat), was quoted as saying to Japan's EA Director-General, 'if Japan does not make a commitment to cooperate financially at UNCED, then we will not be able to make the developing countries agree to anything' (*Asahi Shinbun*, 1992b). In addition, based on his comments leading up to UNCED, the Secretary-General of UNCED, Maurice Strong, expected Europe to act as the leader in negotiations by applying pressure on other countries to agree to the most progressive and environmentally sound treaties possible, but in the case of Japan, his main concern was its capacity to provide the necessary funding (*Daily Yomiuri*, 1992).

The UNCED, held in June 1992, in Rio de Janeiro, Brazil, was not only a testing ground for Japan's international environmental diplomacy, but also the first real testing ground for Japan's expected and often talked about global environmental role and leadership. There were mixed reports, though, about Japan's performance at UNCED. Some articles described Japan as one of the heroes; indicated that Japanese government officials had made positive contributions to behind-the-scenes negotiating sessions; and stated that the government was very much satisfied with its overall efforts (Linden, 1992). Other reports, however, described Japan's performance as low profile; as having reflected a failed leadership opportunity; and as being restricted by the negative position of the United States. NGOs also criticised the Japanese delegation for being typically silent during meetings with other delegations (Schwarz, 1992: 61). On the whole, though, while it can be said that Japan gained a great deal of attention at UNCED, it did not turn out to be the diplomatic success that Japanese EA and MFA officials, as well as Takeshita and his group of environmentally oriented LDP politicians (the so-called 'environment-tribe'), would have preferred.

The basic commitments that were made by the Japanese government at UNCED involved the signing of the Framework Convention on Climate Change and the Convention on Biological Diversity; support for the Rio Declaration, Agenda 21 and the Statement of Forest Principles; and a pledge to allocate between ¥900 billion and ¥1 trillion (approx. US$6.9 billion and $7.7 billion) in ODA in the environmental field over a five-year period beginning FY1992 (*Japan Economic Survey*, 1992). Japan's ODA pledge, the largest nominal financial commitment made by any country at UNCED, was particularly significant in that it meant there would be an increase of 30 per cent over the annual average amount of environment-related ODA that Japan had dispersed between FY1989 and 1991 (*Yomiuri Shinbun*, 1992). In comparison, for example, the United States announced plans to double its bilateral assistance for forest protection in 1993; increase its environment-related aid by 66 per cent above its 1990 level; and, in addition, provide US$2.5 billion through development banks for the realisation of Agenda 21 (Brock, 1992). While not necessarily as impressive in nominal financial terms, the United States at least provided a somewhat more focused and detailed outline of their approach; and to some extent this is where much of the criticism has stemmed from in relation to Japan's environmental ODA.

While the Japanese government was willing to substantially increase the amount of ODA it allocated to environmental protection, it was not ready to announce any new policies or approaches to environment-related funding within its ODA programme. Any element of real policy reform, if one can call it that, in terms of Japan's approach to international environmental protection within the context of development assistance, did not occur as part of this financial pledge at UNCED.

The Kyoto conference on climate change

In December 1997 Kyoto, Japan played host to the Third Session of the Conference of the Parties to the UN Framework Convention on Climate Change (COP3). This was not only an administrative duty for Japan, but also an important test of its ability to provide meaningful and positive input into the process of brokering a multilateral agreement aimed at solving a major international environmental issue. At a domestic level, Japanese policy on climate change had commenced some years earlier with the announcement in 1990 of the Action Plan to Arrest Global Warming, which set a target of stabilising the nation's per capita carbon dioxide emissions at 1990 levels by the year 2000, a target which was consistent with the aims of the 1992 Framework Convention on Climate Change. At the Kyoto conference in 1997, Japan entered negotiations with a proposal for developed nations to reduce their emissions of three key greenhouse gases (GHGs) by 5 per cent below that of 1990 levels by 2008–12.

Many in Japan, including scientific advisors, opposition party politicians, and the more environmentally inclined government bodies such as the EA, believed that Japan could and should have set a much higher target for itself, not to mention other industrialised nations. For example, Dr Shuzo Nishioka, Director of Global Environment Research at Japan's National Institute for Environmental Studies, indicated that anything less than a 10 per cent per decade reduction in GHGs was unacceptable (Naito, 1998). While there were clearly arguments for setting a more aggressive target, by 1996 there were already indications that Japan would not even meet its initial year 2000 Action Plan target. Between 1990 and 1996 Japan's carbon dioxide emissions had increased 9 per cent, and this was in the midst of an economic downturn, which one would assume would lead to a reduction in energy consumption, and hence a reduction in GHG emissions (Environment Agency, 1998b: 2).

In the end, Japan's so-called 'Kyoto Initiative' represented a middle ground approach, not only in terms of domestic interests, but also in terms of where Japan placed itself relative to the proposals put forward by other major GHG-contributing nations. It was an effort on Japan's part to keep all parties at the negotiating table. At one extreme was the United States which put forward a 'zero per cent' target, leaving the way open for developed nations to make their own 'best efforts' to curb emissions by 2012, while at the other extreme the European Union nations pushed for a 15 per cent emission cut. Essentially, it was Japan's target formula (with the inclusion of three additional GHGs) that became the central element of the proposed Kyoto Protocol, a protocol agreed to by over 160 nations (although the ratification of the treaty is yet to be achieved). For itself, Japan set a target of 6 per cent.

Beyond the differing positions of industrialised nations was the mammoth task of effectively incorporating developing nations, who were not about to make any significant short-term sacrifices to their economic growth prospects for the sake of overcoming an environmental problem that they believed had been largely created by the developed nations. In this regard,

Japan's 'Kyoto Initiative', while not calling on reductions by the undeveloped world, did outline plans to assist developing countries in building their capacity to deal with climate change issues, such as additional technical training and technology transfer, and loans with very concessional conditions (Environment Agency, 1998a: 4).

Fundamental legislative and administrative change

Fundamental legislative change, as well as major adjustments to the bureaucracy for the purpose of addressing international environmental problems more effectively and with a clear set of priorities, have been relatively slow in coming. As discussed above, the development of guiding principles and priorities in the form of advisory committee recommendations has occurred since the early 1980s. However, it was not until the late 1980s that elements of the Japanese government, primarily senior officials in the EA, began realising that the country's fundamental legislation for dealing with environmental problems, namely the Basic Law for Environmental Pollution Control, introduced in 1967, and the Nature Conservation Law, introduced in 1972, were no longer satisfactory (Interview, 1994). As mentioned above, these pieces of legislation were more-or-less directed towards the problems of domestic industrial pollution or domestic conservation issues. However, by the late 1980s, and especially in the early 1990s, it was realised that Japan's basic environmental legislation needed to cater also to a wider range of environmental problems such as international or global-scale environmental issues. For instance, The Basic Law for Environmental Pollution Control made no mention of international environmental issues, or the contribution expected of Japan towards overcoming environmental problems beyond its borders. Although international environmental problems had been dealt with since the early 1970s on the basis of bilateral or multilateral cooperation, the ratification of multilateral conventions, ODA activities, or the introduction of other independent pieces of domestic legislation, there needed to be a basic legal responsibility, on the part of the Japanese government at all levels, to address such issues (The Central Council, 1992: 3–5; Environment Agency, 1994).

Deliberation on the issue of new basic environmental legislation was initiated within the EA's two main advisory committees, the Central Council for Environmental Pollution Control and the Nature Conservation Council, in December 1991. Also, within political circles, Takeshita Noboru, along with members of his 'environment tribe', such as Hashimoto Ryûtaro, Kaifu Toshiki, and Takemura Masahisa, held a number of so-called 'round-table' meetings (*Jimintô no kankyô kihon mondai kondan kai*) from early February 1992 which focused, in particular, on the possible introduction of a globally oriented basic environmental law. In March 1992, support for such legislation was received from the highest political level when then Prime Minister, Miyazawa Kiichi, announced to the Lower House Budget Committee that the drafting and introduction of new basic environment legislation was necessary (The Central Council, 1992: 24; *Asahi Shinbun*, 1992a). These developments reflected a shift in the priorities of Japan's political elite from the domestic focus, which existed until at least the late 1980s, to that of a more worldly outlook on environmental issues. The role of politicians such as Takeshita, however, extended no further than prompting the legislation's development.

The greatest challenge for the EA, despite its jurisdiction over the drafting process, was the need to gather the necessary support from other government bodies such as Ministry of International Trade and Industry (MITI), the Ministry of Construction, and the MFA. In this regard it is interesting to note that during the early stages of the drafting process the MFA was actually opposed to the inclusion of any statements concerning 'international cooperation' because it was concerned that such statements could lead to a loss of jurisdictional power, and possibly government funding for the MFA, whereas for the EA, it could mean potential gains. Similarly, any inclusion of basic principles relating to ODA were flatly refused by the MFA. It was only through continual persuasion by EA officials, as well as growing LDP and public support for a globally oriented Basic Environmental Law, that the MFA agreed to a number of carefully worded, that is, jurisdictionally non-intrusive, paragraphs on the importance of promoting international cooperation, at various levels, and through certain means.

One important aspect of international cooperation which was included in the legislation was that concerning the role of local governments. Until the drafting of this law, it had been generally assumed from a legislative perspective that international environmental cooperation was the role of the central government, and that at a local level it was not expected that the people's taxes would be used to assist other countries in combating their environmental problems. On the other hand, there had already been some local governments especially those with previous experiences of tragic environmental pollution, and success in overcoming the worst of such pollution, such as Yokkaichi, Kita Kyushu and Tokyo, which had taken the initiative in cooperating with other countries and providing various forms of assistance in the area of pollution control. The Basic Environmental Law, however, made it clear that the role of local governments in this particular area of international cooperation was now considered 'important' and that they were expected to become actively involved in providing the relevant resources and services to developing countries. With forty-seven prefectural governments and some 3,300 municipalities in Japan, the legislative promotion of their potential efforts in the area of international environmental cooperation is not something to consider as insignificant.

Japan's new Basic Environmental Law, after being submitted to the Diet in March 1993, was unanimously approved by the Upper House, and came into effect, in November of the same year. Although Japanese supporters of the Basic Environmental Law saw it as 'a base that formalises an overall sustainable development ethic in Japanese legislation', there were those who had only limited praise for this legislative milestone (Murdo, 1993: 10). For example, in addition to the EA only being partially satisfied with the legislation's final format, many observers, especially those from the West and within environmental groups, criticised its 'vague and round-about' language, which generally involved suggestions, as opposed to strict and clear-cut requirements (Sakurai, 1994). This was especially the case in areas relating to environmental impact assessment; public access to information and decision-making; control of natural resource consumption; and the introduction of an environment tax (Murakami, 1993). Some of these inadequacies have been addressed in the subsequent Basic Environmental Plan.

Another significant environmental legislative milestone during the 1990s, although not relating to international aspects of environmental protection, was the enactment in June 1997 of the Environmental Impact Assessment (EIA) law. What makes this legislation significant is that initial efforts by the EA to introduce an EIA law began as far back as the mid-1970s and were eventually abandoned in 1983 due to resistance from other parts of the bureaucracy, as well as the LDP. In its place there existed throughout the 1980s and early 1990s EIA guidelines which had been drafted by individual ministries and local governments. It was not until 1993 that official deliberations on the introduction of an EIA law were recommenced. Pressure to introduce such legislation, however, had been mounting for some time, especially when one considers that by the early 1990s Japan was virtually the only OECD country to not have an EIA law (Ohkura, 2000: 352–5, 373).

As part of the Japanese government's administrative reform process, effective from January 2001, the former EA is now one of a dozen ministries. The significance of this transition for Japanese environmental policy-making is not absolutely clear. There are, however, a number of important points to take into consideration. From the time of its establishment in July 1971, as a part of the Prime Minister's Office, and as the Japanese government's central coordinating body in relation to environmental issues, the EA was troubled by numerous problems in its attempts to introduce more effective environmental protection or pollution control policies. Moreover, despite the fact that the Director-General of the EA was a member of the cabinet and had the same rank as a minister, the EA, in comparison with other government bodies, especially the so-called 'line' ministries, suffered from a number of basic bureaucratic or jurisdictional weaknesses. In brief, these weaknesses included relatively low funding and staff levels, an inability to submit a bill directly to the Diet without consultation with, and agreement from, other relevant ministries and agencies; and a majority of higher ranking staff who were temporarily transferred from other more powerful and less environmentally inclined government bodies as part of the government's staff rotation system (Barrett and Therivel, 1991: 12–15).

Some of these weaknesses were compensated from the early 1990s by the growing urgency surrounding global environmental issues, and the importance of Japan's role in dealing with such issues (Barrett and Therivel, 1991: 9, 15). However, the problem still remained that the EA was a weak government body in terms of fundamental policy-making, and in terms of its ability to effectively operate as the central 'spokesperson' and coordinator of Japan's efforts to protect the environment, whether domestically or abroad. Furthermore, for the established and committed officials within the EA who have come to appreciate the urgency surrounding international environmental problems and the importance of Japan's role in promptly dealing with such issues, other government bodies such as MITI and the MFA have often been viewed, not as cooperative members of the same national government, but more so as 'bureaucratic enemies'. This is not surprising when one considers the resistance to change that was faced by EA officials in their efforts to develop policies in relation to issues such as global warming, environmental ODA and the transboundary movement of hazardous wastes. In the case of these issues, for example, there have been long and tedious inter-ministerial negotiations where more often than not the environmentally progressive proposals of the EA have been either watered down or completely rejected by the somewhat inward-looking, jurisdictionally conscious, and sector-based demands of more powerful ministries. With growing domestic and international pressure on Japan to act more promptly and efficiently in relation to international environmental issues, and with increasing frustration among EA officials over their incapacity to introduce the necessary legislation, discussion and proposals within a number of governmental and political forums began to arise in the early 1990s in relation to the possible elevation of the EA's status to that of a ministry (*Nikkei Shinbun*, 1991; *Japan Times*, 1991).

This transition in the status of Japan's key environmental administrative body brings with it a number of important changes. The EM is able to independently submit policy proposals to the Diet; its budget is four times that of the former EA, and its administrative responsibilities now include waste management and recycling. On the negative side, it needs to be emphasised that the EM has the smallest number of staff among the twelve ministries, and in fact only one-fifth the number of personnel of the next smallest ministry (Corliss, 2000). Some also argue that the effectiveness of the EM will depend on its ability to integrate environmental policy with the government's economic priorities, and its capacity to operate within the still jurisdictionally conscious and vertically orientated bureaucracy (Corliss, 2000).

ODA reform and Japan's regional role

At an international level, the financial and technological challenges that have arisen with problems such as sustainable development in developing countries, climate change (or global warming), and the development and support of collaborative efforts at a regional level have been the more promising areas of policy reform, and in turn the keys to Japan's leadership potential (Kohno, 1991). This has been particularly evident in relation to Japan's approach to environmental protection within the context of its foreign aid programme. The central issue of concern in relation to Japan's foreign aid programme, most of which involves what is known as ODA, is how the Japanese government has used this programme for the purpose of extending its environmental policies to an international level through assisting developing countries in their efforts to protect the environment. In addition, there is also the question of whether the environment-related initiatives in Japan's aid programme actually represent effective and satisfactory environmental protection measures, and also reflect the stated objectives of Japan's international role in the environmental field. Based on criticism Japan received during the late 1980s it is clear that many considered, at least at that time, that Japan's environmental policy reform efforts in regard to ODA were either too slow, insufficient or superficial. Specific points of criticism included a lack of specially trained staff within the aid administration; the delay but never disapproval of projects for environmental reasons, an emphasis on projects involving advanced technology or 'hardware' solutions; insufficient allocation of time for development surveys due to the one-year budgeting system for ODA; and inadequate implementation of environmental impact assessment procedures (Forrest, 1989: 43–6).

Since the late 1980s there have been a series of environmental policy reforms, or what could be called, guideline reform developments in relation to Japan's ODA, the majority of which are summarised in Table 7.1. One aspect of this policy reform process relates to the task of making the whole system more 'environmentally friendly'. Putting it simply, this means

Table 7.1 Environmental policy and administrative reform in the context of Japan's ODA

Date	Policy and administrative reform
September 1986	The Environment Agency (EA) commenced the government's first inquiry into appropriate environmental reforms to the aid programme, through the establishment of 'The Committee on Development Assistance and Environmental Protection'
August 1987	The above EA committee produced a report called 'Basic Directions for Environmental Consideration in Development Assistance'
June 1988	The Japan International Cooperation Agency (JICA), one of two Japanese government aid implementation bodies, commenced its own enquiry into specific procedures for incorporating greater environmental consideration and an increased number of environment-related projects into the aid programme by establishing an 'Aid Study Group on the Environment'
October 1988	A report was submitted by the above JICA study group which provided a number or recommendations on environmental consideration and environmental ODA projects
April 1989	The Overseas Economic Cooperation Fund (OECF), Japan's other aid implementation agency (until October 1999 when it was merged with the Export Import Bank of Japan to form the Japan Bank for International Cooperation) established an Environment Committee for reviewing possible reforms to the process of environmental consideration within the loan aid programme
September 1989	The Japanese government announced at the G-7 Summit a three-year environmental aid budget of ¥300 billion (US$2.2 billion)
November 1989	The OECF published its first guidelines on environmental consideration
1989–93	JICA made a number of administrative changes including the establishment of an Environment Office in August 1989; appointing an environment officer to each project division and overseas office in 1990; and replacement of the Environment Office with the Environment, Women in Development, and Other Issues Division in May 1991
1990–3	The introduction by JICA of environmental guidelines for specific types of development projects, such as agricultural, mining or infrastructure projects
July 1991	The Japanese government outlined at the G-7 Summit its priorities in terms of environmental aid (priorities consistent with the JICA and OECF guidelines)

(Continued)

Changing environmental policy agendas 141

Table 7.1 (Continued)

Date	Policy and administrative reform
June 1992	The Japanese government announced at UNCED it would allocate between ¥900 billion and ¥1 trillion (approximately US $6.9 billion and $7.7 billion) of ODA funds to projects in the environmental field between FY1992 and FY1996
June 1992	The Japanese government announced its ODA Charter, within which Japan's commitment to environmental protection is outlined as part of the nation's 'aid philosophy', and as one of the 'basic principles' and 'priority issues' of the aid programme
October 1993	The Environment and Social Issues Division was established in the OECF
June 1997	As part of Japan's 'Green Initiative' proposal for dealing with global warming in developing countries, the Japanese government proposed the promotion and expansion of specially designed project funding under the tag of 'Green Aid'. The government also announced its so-called 'Initiatives for Sustainable Development Toward the Twenty-First Century'
December 1997	As part of its so-called 'Kyoto Initiative' the Japanese government announced that it would grant ODA loans with the most concessional terms available internationally (0.75 per cent annual interest rate, forty-year repayment period) to fund projects designed to combat global warming
August 1999	Environment conservation was included as a priority task in the Japanese government's medium-term policy on ODA
October 1999	An Environment and Social Development Department was included as part of the newly established Japan Bank for International Cooperation

Sources: Forrest (1989); Aid Study Group on Environment, JICA (1988), *Sectoral Study for Development Assistance: Environment*, December; OECF (1994), *Annual Report 1993 OECF*; OECF (1989), *OECF Environmental Guidelines (1st Version)*, October; JICA (1994); Ministry of Foreign Affairs, Japan (1993), *Japan's ODA Official Development Assistance, Annual Report 1992*; Ministry of Foreign Affairs, Japan (1995); Government of Japan (1992); Ministry of Foreign Affairs, Government of Japan (2000); Environment Agency (1998a,b).

reducing as much as possible, or to an agreed and reasonable extent, the negative environmental impact of any project which is funded under the government's aid programme.

Due to the sheer size of Japan's overall aid programme, and in particular Japan's increasingly integrated trading and investment relationships with developing and high-growth Asian nations, many would consider this to be the most important area of policy reform. The other area of policy reform, as demonstrated at UNCED, relates to the task of directing as much of the aid programme as possible towards projects which are specifically designed to protect and enrich the environment, or at least enhance efforts to do so.

Although during the late 1980s and early 1990s definite progress was made by Japan's aid administration in developing recommendations and drafting its initial environmental guidelines, these efforts were, in fact, several years behind relatively more concrete measures which had been taken by a number of other advanced countries. For example, by the late 1970s the US government had already introduced its own system of environmental impact assessment legislation which applied to development assistance. This was followed in the same year by the United Kingdom, and then in 1983 by West Germany, with both countries developing guidelines which obligated them to carry out environmental assessments when providing foreign aid. Then in 1984, Canada also introduced legislation, which set out the same obligations. In addition to Japan's relatively laggard and reactive approach to environment consideration within ODA, the environmental guidelines developed by Japan's aid implementation agencies have been criticised for their vagueness and inconsistencies. In addition, there has also been criticism of the disparity between the grandiose promises of policy rhetoric and the number of truly beneficial environmental projects, as well as the lack of improvements to the bureaucracy's procedural practices in relation to assessing projects and dispersing aid funding (Dauvergne, 1997: 30–1).

In recent years Japan's environmental ODA has become an increasingly important and prominent aspect of the nation's overall strategy to combat environmental problems at an international level. Despite the tightening pressure on Japan's overall aid budget, the policy momentum of the early 1990s has been maintained through the announcement of new initiatives such as 'Green Aid' and the 'Initiatives for Sustainable Development Toward the Twenty-First Century' (see Table 7.1). However, these new initiatives do not appear to be much more than the 're-badging' of existing efforts, or the sorts of projects that Japan's environmental aid has targeted for some time. Furthermore, rather than being a testing ground for innovative and progressive environmental protection measures and decision-making processes, the aid programme continues to reflect or incorporate the less-than-impressive aspects of Japan's environmental policies and administrative practices, such as a bias towards technology or infrastructure-based solutions, non-transparent decision-making procedures, and inter-ministerial rivalry as opposed to open cooperation (Potter, 1994: 207–9). Until such problems are actively addressed by the Japanese government, and are shown to be addressed within policy announcements, criticism will continue to be directed towards the aid programme, especially by the international NGO community, media and other observers, and a question mark will remain over whether Japan's foreign aid as a whole can be considered environmentally friendly, or whether that portion of the ODA programme targeted specifically at 'environment-related' projects simply compensates, if only marginally, for the environmental harm caused by the rest of the programme.

One aspect of Japan's international environmental policy which has evolved significantly since the early 1990s, and could be described as relatively proactive and positive, has been its involvement in regional environmental protection initiatives. These initiatives, which are largely unattached to Japan's ODA and which during the 1990s were coordinated predominantly by the EA, and hence now the EM, essentially involve efforts by the Japanese government to establish and support regional cooperative management programmes. The four key initiatives are:

- the Environmental Congress for Asia and the Pacific
- the Northeast Asian Conference on Environmental Protection
- the Asia-Pacific Seminar on Climate Change; and
- the Acid Deposition Monitoring Network in East Asia.

All four of these regional forums were established in the 1990s, through the initiative of the Japanese government, and have been strongly supported by Japan's scientific community, and by the Japanese government financially and administratively, on an ongoing basis. In making some general observations about these initiatives, it can be said that their short-term goals involve primarily exchanging information, and achieving a greater awareness among all parties concerned of the problems that exist, and the strategies that are needed to overcome these problems. One of the major criticisms, however, which has been directed at these forums, especially by NGOs and other more environmentally aggressive observers, is that these forums provide little in the way of concrete measures to overcome regional environmental problems. For example, the Japanese government, in relation to all four forums, including that of acid deposition, has made no indication that a legally binding agreement is the ultimate objective. NGOs, for example, would like to see a more direct connection between the discussions at these forums and the policy-making of the countries involved.

On the other hand, Japanese bureaucrats emphasise that their main priority is that of 'continuity', in other words, establishing a close and long-lasting dialogue among the relevant parties, as opposed to achieving immediate progress towards some form of legally binding or policy-connected agreements. The concern of the Japanese government of course is that overly aggressive moves towards concrete measures would most likely result in the break down of these forums, or at least limited participation. While these regional initiatives are the creations of a more focused Japanese agenda on international environmental protection, especially since the early 1990s, they still reflect elements of Japan's international environmental diplomacy that have remained largely constant since the early 1970s, such as a non-aggressive negotiating style, an emphasis on the provision of financial and technological support, and a lack of contributions in regard to instigating concrete policy solutions.

Conclusion

Throughout the 1970s, Japan displayed only limited efforts to cooperate on a multilateral level within the field of international environmental protection, especially in the area of international conventions. Its economic concerns overshadowed any potential commitment to international environmental protection, and no significant administrative changes to the central government were made in order to specifically foster a more balanced international agenda. While Japan's efforts were not completely negative, and a number of long-term international arrangements were established in the form of bilateral environment-related agreements with other advanced countries, overall Japan's efforts to cooperate at an international level in the environmental field were still only based on a fairly fragile network of agreements and institutional memberships which did not obligate it to take any substantial action against international environmental issues.

The 1980s, and in particular the latter part of that decade, were a transition period for Japan in terms of international environmental policies. It was the first period in which the Japanese government experimented with the responsibilities of its new-found global economic status in the context of international environmental politics. By the late 1980s, Japan began to shape a recognisable role for itself as a financial and technological supporter of environmental protection activities.

Unfortunately, though, the overall intentions and significance of Japan's international environmental policies during the 1980s still maintained an unfavourable image through Japan's lack of cooperation towards, and reluctance to make positive or innovative policy recommendations within, a number of international environmental regimes which dealt with more specific, controversial and commercially associated issues such as trade in endangered species, tropical deforestation and whaling. During this period Japan's contributions towards the formation and support of issue-specific international environmental regimes were limited compared to its administrative and financial contributions in other areas. Moreover, it was expected by not only foreign governments, environmental activist groups and international organisations, but also a growing of number of politicians and government officials in Japan itself, that there should be a more even balance between Japan's economic status and any positive political manoeuvres it could carry out within international environmental negotiations.

In the 1990s, Japan's international environmental policies involved an increasingly diverse array of regional and international contributions and initiatives. On the one hand, some of these activities, such as the hosting of meetings of signatory nations to nature conservation-related conventions, and Japan's involvement in the UNCED preparation process, further exposed the weaknesses of Japan's international environmental policies and its approach to multilateral negotiations. On the other hand, Japan's performance at UNCED, its coordination of the Kyoto Conference, and its cooperation initiatives within the Asian region, have highlighted the conscious efforts that Japan has made in recent times to strengthen its leadership role. Such efforts, although in some cases yet to produce quantifiable results, are a clear indication of the transition which has occurred in Japan's international environmental policies from that of reactive or limited compliance, to more innovative policy-making and significant contributions. The extent to which Japan maintains and further improves its current international environmental policies and diplomacy will depend a great deal on the extent to which it acts on the mandates of its Basic Environmental Law, its ability to meet the prescribed targets of policies within areas such as climate change and deforestation, and the capacity of the EM to capitalise on its new-found status. These policy and administrative developments will either prove to be significant turning points, or simply smokescreens for the ongoing deficiencies in Japan's environmental policies and the processes by which it develops those policies.

References

Asahi Shinbun (1992a), 'Kankyô Kihonho seitei ni Sekkyoku Shisei Shimesu Miyazawa Shusho' (Prime Minister Miyazawa indicates positive stance in relation to establishment of Basic Environmental Law), 17 March.
Asahi Shinbun (1992b), 'Naze takeshita san ga' (Why Mr Takeshita?), 7 April.
Barrett, Brendan F. D. and Therivel, R. (1991), *Environmental Policy and Impact Assessment in Japan*, Routledge, London, New York.
Brock, B. (1992), 'Bush defends U.S. environmental stance', *The Daily Yomiuri*, 14 June.
Corliss, M. (2000), 'Environment Agency rises a rank', *The Japan Times*, 9 December.
Daily Yomiuri (1992), 'Who will finance summit plans', 5 June.
Dauvergne, P. (1997), *Shadows in the Forest: Japan and the Politics of Timber in Southeast Asia*, The MIT Press, Cambridge, MA.

Environment Agency, *Japan Environment Summary*, Government of Japan (various issues).
Environment Agency, *Japan Environment Quarterly* (various issues).
Environment Agency (1982), *Quality of the Environment in Japan 1981*, Tokyo, Japan.
Environment Agency (1988), 'Global environment protection board established', *Japan Environment Summary*, 8(9), 10 September.
Environment Agency (1991), *Quality of the Environment in Japan 1990*, Tokyo, Japan.
Environment Agency (1994), 'Enactment of the Basic Environment Law', *Japan Environment Summary*, 21(5), 10 January.
Environment Agency (1998a), *Japan Environment Quarterly*, http://www.eic.or.jp/eanet/en/or/jeq/v003-01.html, 3(1), March.
Environment Agency (1998b), *Japan Environment Quarterly*, http://www.eic.or.jp/eanet/en/or/jeq/v003-02.html, 3(2), March.
Environment Agency Official (1994), Extract from personal papers of a senior EA official, (A draft of his recollections of international environmental policy formation during the late 1980s and early 1990s in preparation for later publication as a journal article or book).
Forrest, Richard A. (1989), *Japanese Economic Assistance and the Environment: The Need for Reform*, National Wildlife Federation, revised edition, Washington, DC, November.
Government of Japan (1992), *Japan's Official Development Assistance Charter (Copy)*, 30 June.
Interview (1994), Former high-ranking official of the Environment Agency, 10 August, *Japan Economic Survey* (1992), 'Japan fares well at UNCED', 16(7), 1–3 July.
JICA (1994), *Japan International Cooperation Agency, Annual Report 1993*, Tokyo.
Japan Quarterly (1972), 'A whale of a problem', 19(4), October–December.
Japan Times (1991), 'Agency is chronicled', 6 October.
Kato, S. (1990), Kôgai taisaku kihon hô to sono sekai (7) – ckikyû kankyô mondai no kakudai, shinka – (Issues surrounding the Basic Law for Environmental Pollution Control (7) – The expansion and deepening of global environmental problems), *Gesuidô kyôkaishi*, 27(308), January.
Kitamatsu, K. (1989), '"Save the Earth" initiative launched – Takeshita promoting "environmental diplomacy"', *The Japan Economic Journal*, 29 April.
Kohno, M. (1991), 'Japan at UNCED – taking a leadership role', *GISPRI Quarterly*, no. 3.
Kumao, K. (1972), *Ningen kankyô sengen (Declaration on the Human Environment) Only One Earth*, Nihon sôgô shuppan kikou, Tokyo, 16 October.
Lauber, S. (1993), 'Japan and International Environmental Law – economic over environment', *Japanese Studies Bulletin*, 13(3).
Lincoln, Edward J. (1993), *Japan's New Global Role*, The Brookings Institution, Washington, DC.
Linden, E. (1992), 'Rio's legacy', *Time* (Australia), 7(25), 22 June.

Ministry of Foreign Affairs (1995), *Japan's ODA Official Development Assistance, Annual Report 1994*, Association for Promotion of International Cooperation, Tokyo, March.

Ministry of Foreign Affairs (2000), Japan's environmental cooperation, http://www.mofa.go.jp/policy/oda/category/environment/2000/coop.html.

Murakami, A. (1993), 'Environmental law takes effect', *The Japan Times*, 20 November.

Murdo, P. (1993), 'Japan steps up activist approach to environment', *JEI Report*, no. 46B, 17 December.

Naito, Y. (1998), 'Proposed emissions targets falling short, expert says', http://www.japantimes.co.jp/cop3/indepth/series1b.html, 29 May.

Newhouse, J. (1992), 'The diplomatic round earth summit', *The New Yorker*, 1 June.

Nikkei Shinbun (1991), 'Kankyô chô minaoshi teigen' (A proposal to reconsider the Environment Agency), 19 September.

Okhura, Y. (2000), 'Environment impact assessment in Japan: evolution of the system and critical appraisal of the environmental impact assessment law of 1997', *Asia Pacific Journal of Environmental Law*, 4(4).

Potter, D. (1994), 'Assessing Japan's environmental aid policy', *Pacific Affairs*, 67(2), Summer.

Sakurai, K. (1994), 'Basic Environmental Law and international cooperation', *INTEP Newsletter*, no. 4, February.

Schwarz, A. (1992), 'Back down to earth, Global summit fails to live up to ambitions', *Far Eastern Economic Review*, 155(25), 25 June.

The Central Council for Environmental Pollution Control and The Nature Conservation Council, Environment Agency (1992), *Establishing a Basic Law on the Environment*, (tentative translation), 20 October.

Yomiuri Shinbun (1992), 'Kankyô ODA, itchô en kibô' (Environmental ODA of the order of 1 Trillion Yen), 14 June.

8 Crusaders of the lost archipelago

The changing relationships between environmental NGOs and government in Japan

Mike Danaher

Introduction

Since the early 1970s, an increasing number of environmental groups have emerged as significant agents of change in the politics of global environmental management. This phenomenon reflects the increasing complexity of environmental issues but the reality is that governments and environmental groups have not always been able to work well together. The importance of a cooperative working relationship between governments and environmental non-governmental organisations (NGOs) was highlighted by Agenda 21 of the 1992 United Nations Conference on Environment and Development (UNCED) in Rio De Janeiro. Chapter 27 of Agenda 21 (*Strengthening The Role of Non-Governmental Organizations: Partners For Sustainable Development*) provided clear justification for the involvement of NGOs (not only environmental) in national decision and policy-making mechanisms. It emphasised that NGO involvement constituted a bottom-up source of strength, which should be harnessed by governments and other groups to bring about sustainable development.

In 1993 the Japanese government devised its own *Japan Agenda 21*, which states 'Japan intends to restructure its own socio-economic system into one which will enable sustainable development' and as part of this is committed to supporting NGOs (GEIC, 1997). Furthermore, Japan's passing of the Basic Environment Law (BEL) in November 1993 and Basic Environment Plan (BEP) in December 1994 also include the objective of establishing and nurturing productive government–NGO relationships, and came about as a response to Agenda 21. It will be argued that most state sponsored strengthening of the government–NGO relationships in Japan is owing to international pressure (*gaiatsu*) and the Japanese leadership's decision that the environment is an important foreign policy area, such as the case with *Japan Agenda 21* and the BEL. In this chapter, I will examine the changing relationships between the government and environmental NGOs in Japan in order to explain outcomes and achievements. Examining Japan's NGO–government relationships is significant also because it provides a further dimension in understanding the changing power dynamics between Japan's bureaucrats, politicians and general public.

The recent history of environmental politics in Japan shows evidence of both top-down and bottom-up developments in environmental policy-making. The importance of the bottom-up approach should not be underestimated as it was critical to the adoption of strict anti-pollution laws and regulations from the early 1970s. In the context of the government's public commitment since the mid-1990s to be supportive of environmental NGOs and to incorporate their advice in policy formulation, I will attempt to explain whether achievements have been significant or superficial. The analysis is based on corporatism (Schmitter, 1981) which argues that some countries can contain political discontent through a system of institutionalised bargaining between interest groups (such as business associations and labour unions) and the state. We know Japan has medium to high corporatist structures with Keidanren (Federation of Economic Organisations) and the General Federation of Labour Unions (Rengo) involved in political bargaining. Environmental interests however, were largely marginalised and environmental protection policies and enforcement remained inadequate.

A cross-national analysis of Japanese environmental NGOs

At the outset, it is important to define environmental NGOs. Morris-Suzuki (2000) and Princen and Finger (1994) provide some useful generic features of an NGO that can be applied to environmental NGOs in Japan. NGOs are flexible and decentralised, and are either formally or informally structured. They may participate in cross-border civil society and play key roles as independent bargainers and as agents of social learning. Even though they are non-government, some may still rely on government funding. NGOs vary greatly in terms of size and membership. According to Elliot (1998) NGOs can be organised as research institutes and think tanks, or as lobby and pressure groups. Environmental NGOs can be broadly classified as focused either on nature conservation or on issues of climate change and pollution. The nature conservation NGOs used as illustrative case studies in this paper are the Japan branch of the World Wide Fund for Nature (WWFJ); the Japan branch of Friends of the Earth (FOEJ); the Wild Bird Society of Japan (WBSJ); environmental groups belonging to the Japan Wetlands Action Network (JAWAN); Greenpeace Japan; and the Nature Conservation Society of Japan (NCSJ). Japanese environmental NGOs have a small membership base, in comparison to similar NGOs in other developed

Table 8.1 Cross-national membership of environmental NGOs

	Japan	UK	US	Australia	Germany
Greenpeace	4,000 (95)	380,000 (95)	1,600,000 (99)	94,000 (00)	75,000 (85)
WWF	7,000 (90)	247,000 (90)	1,200,000 (99)	16,000 (00)	
FOE	300 (98)	110,000 (95)	20,000 (99)	4,500 (00)	
NCS	14,000 (89)		830,000 (99)		
WBSJ	55,000 (00)				

Sources: Holliman, 1990; Barrett and Therivel, 1991; Department of Environment, 1992; Greenpeace Japan, 1996; Ormsby, 1998; Connelly and Smith, 1999; Shaiko, 1999; Walker, 2000; WBSJ, 2000; WWFJ, 2000.

Note: The number in brackets represents the year for that membership.

countries. The literature (Schreurs, 1996; Broadbent, 1998) indicates that environmentalism in Japan, that is public willingness to be active on environmental issues, is weak compared to the West.

In the West, environmental NGOs were established in the 1960s to 1970s. These include the Sierra Club (currently with a $43 million annual budget), the National Wildlife Federation, the Natural Resources Defense Council and the Nature Conservancy (to name a few) in the US, and the Australian Conservation Foundation (ACF – established in 1962) and Wilderness Society in Australia. The environmental movement in Australia began as protest groups but successfully transformed itself, during the 1980s, as important members of the policy community in matters relating to the exploitation of natural resources (Doyle and Kellow, 1995). It did this by building solidarity among its members and forming coalitions among specific environmental protest groups, so that national lobby groups such as the ACF became the accepted 'voice' of the movement. Since the 1960s, membership of environmental groups expanded rapidly in western countries and membership levels in Britain, for example, doubled each decade since 1960 to stand at approximately 4.5 million at present (Connelly and Smith, 1999). There are a number of transnational environmental NGOs established in Japan, but despite their memberships more than doubling in the 1990s, their foothold is not as strong as it is in other countries.

Despite their size limitations, it is interesting that Japanese NGOs have been reluctant to affiliate with one another to form a more powerful national lobby and be included in national delegations, as has occurred in many western countries. Japanese NGOs are financially and organisationally weak, mainly because public support is under-developed. The activities of Japanese environmental NGOs are supported not only by private membership dues but also small-scale government and non-government grants; funds from the Grassroots Grant Assistance (established by the Ministry of

Foreign Affairs (MFA) to provide modest assistance to NGO field projects in developing countries, Japan Fund for the Global Environment (JFGE) and the Keidanren Nature Conservation Fund (KNCF); their own entrepreneurial activities (e.g. the WBSJ manages bird sanctuaries); and donations from private corporations and individuals (e.g. FOEJ attracts some funding from the Toyota Foundation, but these are rare). Environmental NGOs which are registered as *Kôeki Hôjin* (public service corporations) under the EA, and which are non-profit organisations, are generally waived from income taxes. However, they do pay tax on all revenue making activities. The Japanese government established the Green Donation programme, which collects donations mainly on Green Day (29 April) and during Green Week (23–9 April). These funds are available for forestry management and reforestation domestically and internationally.

The way the NPO/NGO Tax and Corporation Laws in Japan affect NGO funding is somewhat complicated (certainly compared to Australia and the US), and environmental NGOs argue that it requires simplification and other modifications to make it work more in their favour. At present the system discourages individuals from making donations to environmental NGOs. Depending on the function and nature of specific NGOs, individual donations either do not qualify for tax deduction or the tax deduction is limited to only 25 per cent. Donations to schools, disaster relief and other special service groups are tax deductible but not to environmental NGOs. Businesses enjoy greater benefits because all their donations, up to a certain amount, are tax deductible. Not surprisingly, NGOs advocate tax reforms to treat individual contributions on par with corporate donations. In the 1990s, the Ministry of Posts and Telecommunications introduced a new system to allow depositors in Japan's Postal Savings system to donate interest earned on accounts to NGOs.

Japanese environmental NGOs are wary of accepting corporate donations and donations from other sources, like the JFGE and KNCF, because of concerns that corporate links could compromise their social credibility, integrity and political influence. This wariness extends even to donations by individual corporate employees, especially if the company in question is seen as working against the aims of the NGO. Still, in the interest of enhancing their international image, industry groups in 1991 made the surprising suggestion of working together with environmental groups and even offered to fund their activities. To this end they organised a meeting to which they invited several of the more 'socially accepted' environmental groups in Japan. Their proposal intrigued many of these groups, but in the end it was voted down by the NGO Forum Japan, a newly organised body representing approximately one hundred NGOs ranging from anti-pollution movements to international NGOs (Schreurs, 1996). A majority of NGOs continue to be reluctant about receiving funds from industry, which is sometimes referred to as 'greenwashing'. An example of greenwashing in Australia was the announcement, in October 2000, of an alliance between BHP and the ACF, which critics claimed was simply to pre-empt share holder backlash over its dubious environmental reputation (Beder, 2000). In the US, many large national environmental NGOs such as the Sierra Club, Nature Conservancy, WWF and Natural Resources Defense Council now receive significant corporate contributions. Japan may ultimately follow the example of the US and if this becomes the dominant international trend, it will confirm Sklair's (1994) argument that central parts of the 'green movement' are in the process of being incorporated, and those that refuse incorporation will be marginalised.

In Japan, an important domestic constituency is the media, which is generally supportive of environmental issues. The media, particularly the *Nikkei Shimbun* and the *Asahi Shimbun* have called for a more progressive NPO Law (Pekkanen, 2000). They view such a law as integral to administrative reform and they do have influence within the ruling Liberal Democratic Party (LDP). However, the media is less sympathetic about unconventional protest tactics. For example, FOEJ used to lobby by conducting marches and disrupting the operations they were targeting but they have since stopped those lobbying tactics because of media and public disapproval.

Changing dynamics of government–NGO relationships

While NGOs are wary of being compromised by corporate linkages, they have been willing partners of the Environment Ministry (EM), which has primary responsibility for environmental regulation and management. The EM takes into consideration opinions from the general public and the NGOs when formulating and implementing basic policies about the environment and sustainable development. However, the capacity of NGOs to engage the EM in dialogue and consultation is limited by their relative weakness. There are, as well, areas of environmental activity not effectively covered by existing NGOs.

Initially, the Japanese government paid little attention to the environmental NGO issue. Broadbent (1998) shows how the ruling triad of LDP, big business and the powerful economic ministries in the 1960s publicly denied the growing wave of pollution complaints emanating from local citizens' movements. However, privately they worried about the political implications. The ruling triad attempted to break the protesters with offers of compensation and bribes (and even community pressure tried to dissuade protesters from going to court), but this was not very successful and finally in 1970 they had to answer to their desperate demands, and began regulating industrial pollution. Since then, local government politics has gone under the banner of politics in accord with citizen participation (Abe *et al.*, 1994). This was a corporatist development to bring in environmental issues under the broad LDP 'catch-all' umbrella. This, in turn, can partly explain the absence of elected members of green political parties.

The formal process of extending corporatist structures to environmental NGOs is based on a Civil Code enacted in the late nineteenth century. The Civil Code maintains that before an NGO/NPO can have legal corporate status as an NPO, its founders must obtain authorisation from each concerned agency of the national government. In Japan there are a limited number of public service corporations (*Kôeki Hôjin*), and these include some of the older and larger environmental NGOs such as WWFJ, WBSJ and NCSJ. They are arbitrarily perceived by the bureaucracy as being in the public interest, and, therefore, have been able to obtain legal status. These environmental *Kôeki Hôjin* fall under the jurisdiction of various bureaus within the EM, including the Nature Conservation Bureau. This means they have been sponsored by the competent government agency in order to get legal corporate status. By having legal corporate status they can attract government grants because this status enables them to legally sign contracts. These grants together with membership dues help to fund their operations. They also provide the NGOs with valuable experience in scientific data gathering on environmental projects, and this serves to keep them closer to the actual state of the environment. Smaller NGOs, however, were unable to achieve corporate status because of the requirement that each NGO must have an asset base of Yen 300 million.

As well, legal corporate status means the NGO has tax-exempt status for their non-profit activities. However, there is also a high degree of bureaucratic control over these *Kôeki Hôjin* such as close supervision of, and intervention in, their daily operations (Okabe, 2000). Most small environmental NGOs, and they are the majority, have historically not been able to achieve legal corporate status in Japan because they are not perceived by the bureaucracy as being of public interest, and have remained as unincorporated organisations (*Jinkaku naki Shadan*) or voluntary informal groups.[1] Examples are FOEJ, Greenpeace Japan and JAWAN. Without legal status, they cannot operate legitimately in society.

Sponsorship of NGOs by the government can be interpreted as rendering NGOs less autonomous and influential because it brings them under tight control of the government. However, WWFJ does not concede that it is compromised by ministerial sponsorship or because some of their funding comes from government contracts. They reject criticisms that the process of incorporation has stifled their capacity to articulate their own position, and reject the notion that instead of influencing policies they are subject to governmental influence. Its main sponsor, the EM, holds similar views on the importance of nature conservation, and insists that there is no intention to undermine the activities of WWFJ and other NGOs. At the same time, it should be noted that the number of citizen movements, which displayed radical resistance to the government in the 1960s, has declined and this may suggest that incorporation has had a disempowering effect. Citizens movements of the 1960s and NGOs since the 1980s are fundamentally different because the latter are permanently mobilised and take on a wide range of issues.

In 1998, a significant amendment was made to the NPO legislation in Japan. On 19 March 1998, the Japanese Diet passed the Law to Promote Specified Nonprofit Activities (commonly referred to as the NPO Law). This was a Member's Bill to allow small civic groups, including many environmental NGOs to incorporate for the first time (with no requirements of minimum asset holdings), subject only to approval from the relevant prefectural government (the 'competent authority'). Thus, approval of a central government agency is no longer mandatory and the approval process is much faster and more liberal than under the former Civil Code. There is no longer any arbitrary discretion in approving legal status. Prefectures can draft their own implementing legislation which is expected to vary considerably between prefectures (Pekkanen, 2000). Environmental protection is one of twelve categories for incorporation under the new Law. Incorporation still does not give them tax-exempt status, and this remains a major limitation of the new Law. The Diet, however, made a special resolution when passing the Law to review tax benefits and other NPO support measures within two years of the implementation of the Law. In 2001, the Diet was still considering better tax incentives for NGOs and we can expect the issue to be resolved favourably, following negotiations with the Ministry of Finance (MOF). Those *Kôeki Hôjin* already with legal status granted under the Civil Code will remain under the control of their present government agencies.

Although there may be no financial benefit to small environmental NGOs under the NPO Law, the politicians, as well as some NGOs argue that benefits lie in prestige and greater social acceptance (Okabe, 2000). The Law gives NGOs greater ability to participate in society, and legitimises interest group activity in domestic politics. There is also greater freedom from bureaucratic supervision and discretion, meaning the bureaucrats will have less control over civil society. The relevant prefectural governments will now assume the supervisory role of the groups. The NGOs will have the ability to become a legal party of contacts rather than an individual group leader taking legal responsibility for the group and its assets, and there is enhancement of freedom of association. Social acceptance is also believed to lead to more donations. It is considered that this Law is just the first stage of developing non-profit NGO infrastructure in Japan. Not all environmental NGOs consider seeking corporate legal status under the new Law as worthwhile because the Law still does not allow tax-deductible status to individual contributions, whether monetary, motor vehicle or real estate (FOEJ, 2000). But, to the extent that donations can now be seen to go to legal NPOs rather than to non-incorporated entities, individuals and companies may be more inclined to give donations.

Pekkanen (2000) argues that the NPO Law is a result of pressure from citizen groups and media, as well as from politicians responding to new electoral incentives since 1994, which provided extra incentives for politicians and political parties (especially the smaller ones) to promote NPO formation and to receive their support, in return. There was also strong support for the Law from the Keidanren and the General Federation of Labor Unions (*Rengô*). Diet members and citizen groups engaged in a lot of cooperative consultation on drafting the final Bill. The bureaucrats generally opposed the Law and were excluded from participating directly in the drafting process.

Relationships between the government and environmental NGOs occur on a number of levels (international, national, prefectural and local), and involve politicians as well as bureaucrats in various ministries and agencies. This chapter does not intend to give an exhaustive coverage of all these relationships, rather will touch on the areas, which provide clearer examples of change and/or significance. For example, the EM is now very positive towards environmental NGOs in general, and is often the first point of call for NGOs' dealings with the government (Koyama, 1998).

Despite limited resources and other handicaps, some NGOs, have produced convincing scientific and other technical documentation to influence politicians and bureaucrats, and to modify existing government policy affecting a number of species and environments, although these cases are in the minority. Two recent cases provide good examples of this. The first is the case of Fujimae tidal flat. The Ministry of Land, Infrastructure and Transport (MLIT), which has jurisdiction over harbours; the Ministry of Health, Labour and Welfare (MHLW), which regulates waste management; Aichi prefectural government; and the Nagoya City government, for many years proposed to convert Fujimae tidal flat in Nagoya harbour into a landfill site for municipal waste. The project was cancelled in January 1999 and the tidal flat is set to become a Ramsar site (wetland of international importance) in 2002.

The decision by the Ministry and local governments to look elsewhere for a landfill site came after the public outcry concerning the destruction of

Isahaya Bay in 1997, Japan's largest tidal flat. As well, JAWAN and Save Fujimae Association consistently lobbied for its protection (JAWN, 1999). The Save Fujimae Association (a very small environmental NGO), organised independent data to be collected by ordinary volunteers with the assistance of specialist scientists into the impacts on fauna such as migratory birds, and water and air pollution from possible leaks in the landfill. This became known as *shimin no kagaku* ('citizen science'). This data gave actual proof of the damage that would be done if the project was to go ahead, and included survey work that was not included in the government environmental impact assessment (EIA) (Tsuji, 2000). This represented an independent EIA, which argued the environmental cost to Fujimae would be great. Moreover, the EM in December 1998 made it publicly clear that it did not approve the proposed mitigation plan and would issue a strong opinion critical of the government EIA if it was submitted as planned to the Ministry of Transport (MOT). These factors as well as the persistence of the EM and the independent scientific data that was gathered, were able in the end to influence the local governments (particularly the Mayor of Nagoya) and the MLIT to abandon the whole plan. The powerful MLIT, in the end made a public decision to respect the wishes of the EM, if the latter disapproved of the EIA.

The second case is where the WBSJ was successful in fighting an ecologically problematic government policy on a wetland issue. In 1982, the MLIT set up the Chitose River Diversion Channel Plan for flood control in a central part of Hokkaido. The plan was also approved by the Hokkaido prefectural government, despite alleged negative effects on the nearby Lake Utonai and Bibi River wetland which was declared Japan's fourth Ramsar site. The WBSJ linked up with local NGOs, academics and lawyers to organise public symposiums calling for a halt to the plan. One such symposium in December 1992 attracted international NGOs, as well as staff from the Ministry. The WBSJ also made representation at the 5th Conference of Parties (CoP) to the Ramsar Convention held in Hokkaido in 1993 and later organised a small group of technical experts on sustainable flood control to speak with Ministry staff. These technical experts communicated the weaknesses in the flood control project, and the points that they raised were carried on the news media with the aim of making the public more aware of the dangers of the plan. These 'experts' were effectively the third party intermediary in the dispute, and they commanded sufficient power and respect from both opponents. The ability of environmental NGOs to involve third party intermediaries of sufficient respect and power in the dispute was a key to their success. In 1997, the MLIT announced that public consensus had to be prioritised, and this bureaucratic back down forced the local politicians to follow suit. The WBSJ identifies two main innovations, which helped their campaign to halt the project; the discussions were

Environmental NGOs and government in Japan 157

open to the public and the discussions involved neutral third party experts. These two cases illustrate similarities; that local politicians are often the strongest critics of NGOs despite a common view that NGOs have considerable local government support.

Policy advisory roles for NGOs

The policy advisory role for Japanese environmental NGOs is limited despite the potential of NGOs to contribute meaningfully to policy formation. Environmental NGOs in Japan feel that they have a broad base of expertise, skill, experience and networks which urgently require reflection in climate and nature conservation governance. GEIC (1997) identified possible ways for NGO involvement, including:

- implementing international environmental regime obligations
- providing public access to information
- facilitating public participation and developing adequate responses
- monitoring and evaluating national and local policies
- providing important inputs into draft national official documents.

GEIC (1997) also identified specific policy options and proposals in order to increase the involvement of NGOs in general environmental governance, and these include:

- all environmental NGOs need appropriate legal status as a first basic step in ensuring equal parity between the major interest groups in climate change (and other environmental domains). Non-legal status effectively hinders NGO involvement at both national and international levels;
- appropriate and equitable representation needs to be afforded to Japanese NGO groups in the main committees related to climate change (and to other environmental domains);
- all environmental NGOs need to raise their own professional profiles and memberships;
- all environmental NGOs need to further develop mechanisms which can provide needed technical and scientific back-up for proposals and inputs.

Constraints faced by environmental NGOs

The two cases mentioned earlier illustrate the political influence of environmental NGOs in Japan. Although cases which show environmental NGOs having direct influence on major government policy are not numerous, they do exist. In assessing success and failure of NGOs, we can identify a number of important constraints on environmental NGOs in Japan. The difficulty for many Japanese NGOs in attaining corporate legal status and/or tax-free status is that it impinges on their ability to become better informed and more socially accepted, and therefore to lobby from a stronger position. Corporate legal status is difficult to achieve and often requires a high degree of affinity with government ministries and a substantial asset base. In recognition of this problem, and after sustained lobbying by NGOs, the Keidanren, media and politicians, efforts have been made, with the passing of the NPO Law in 1998, to provide for registration of environmental NGOs. Individual membership fees to environmental NGOs in Japan are still not tax deductible, and this limits membership. Difficulty in obtaining tax-free status has hindered accreditation of Japanese NGOs at international conventions, such as CITES and Ramsar, because accreditation requires proof of non-profit status. Moreover, despite the new NPO Law, Japanese environmental NGOs are often unable to provide such documentation since many do not yet have access to corporate legal status. In effect, deprivation of legal personality can lead to an inability to participate in international and national processes.

There are financial constraints associated with a relatively small membership, and this restricts their lobbying capability. Another constraint is not having access to official policy-making channels, to senior bureaucrats, and the responsible minister. Unlike the more influential lobbying powers of the farmers, fishermen and doctors, for example, who can gain access to a more senior level inside their respective ministries and agencies because they represent tangible voter groups and political donors, environmental NGOs simply do not have the same bargaining capability because they lack a powerful domestic constituency.

GEIC (1997) found that non-legal status effectively hinders NGO involvement at both national and international levels because without it, these NGOs are not on an equal footing with the major interest groups in regard to the relevant issue. Even though the government passed the NPO Law in 1998, the benefits are not yet very clear. The new Law provides legal status and social acceptance for NGOs with small assets and distant affinities with the government, but no better tax breaks. Also, most unincorporated NGOs are adopting a wait and watch approach, so it is difficult to evaluate the impact of the Law. Improved tax breaks within the Law would probably pave the way for more NGOs to apply for legal status. Japanese environmental NGOs also claim that the current practice of inviting individuals and 'experts' to sit on key environmental and policy-making committees should be more open, to ensure that environmental NGOs, with appropriate expertise are invited to occupy committee positions.

As well, until the enactment of new Freedom of Information (FOI) Law in 1999, there was no equivalent to the Australian and US Freedom of Information Acts in Japan. The NGOs and even the EM have argued that they have been at a strong disadvantage in influencing policy because of this. For example, they are left in the dark as to how MITI establishes its long-term energy supply and demand forecast (Schreurs, 1996). Since energy policy is closely tied to global climate change response options, this has put the EM and NGOs at a strong disadvantage in establishing their own proposals for action. Government agencies generally release information and data at their own discretion, and often suppress critical information. The LDP was, for many years, reluctant to legislate in this area but the national Information Disclosure Act (IDA) was passed on 7 May 1999 and should contribute to greater societal openness and to reduced powers of the central bureaucracy.

Conclusions

The Japanese government has enhanced its domestic environmental research capacities and strengthened the position of the EM in relation to international environmental issues. Recognising also that environment is an important foreign policy issue area, the government has reconsidered the role of NGOs. The Diet has initiated legislative changes to remove some of the barriers to NGO formation and maintenance in Japan. However, most of the new initiatives appear biased towards enhancing the quality of Japan's foreign aid, and to counter criticisms of it. Many of the schemes and funds which the government and Keidanren have set up clearly favour providing most support for Japanese NGOs which are working on issues in developing countries.

This chapter makes three main conclusions. First, government mechanisms still do not allow environmental NGOs to play a genuine partnership role in achieving sustainable development and environmental protection responsibly, effectively and fully. Specifically, NGOs have very limited input into decision-making and policy-making and feel that there is little meaningful dialogue between NGOs and government, at the national level. Second, it seems that any improved outcome for environmental protection owes more to tenacious lobbying on the part of NGOs than to government (top-down) initiatives and cooperation. Despite the government's public commitment to incorporate NGO proposals into policy-making as a means of achieving sustainable development, the reality is that rhetoric has not been matched with action. As a result, NGOs have to struggle to make their voices heard against unsound practices.

Third, while change is gradual and slow paced, there are signs to suggest that new legislative initiatives such as the NPO Law, EIA Law and IDA will act to strengthen the NGO community by challenging and curtailing bureaucratic power. Underlying these main changes are micro-level attitudinal changes among the political elite, who recognise that NGOs are here to stay, and can be useful to policy development, their own electoral prospects, and to Japan's image in the world. Even so, a well developed NGO community with access to policy-making, alone, is not enough to ensure adequate environmental protection. That requires more of a paradigm shift in social attitudes and behaviours, but determined and principled NGOs, independent of compromising influences, represent the ideal crusaders for such a paradigm shift. For economic reasons, Keidanren has also moved to embrace NGOs since the early 1990s. The changes are directing Japan's political economy towards one with fewer ties to a regulatory bureaucracy (which often inhibits expeditious and effective policy responses), extremely conservative politicians, and overly protected industries.

There are still no strong national environmental lobbies in Japan. Instead, there are loose partnerships among certain NGOs on certain issues at certain times. It seems they are reluctant to sacrifice their independence and autonomy for the greater good. The strength of the environmental NGOs is seen to lie in their autonomy. As units separate to the national government, environmental NGOs feel that they have the ability to express a human voice and perspective to an issue, and can, therefore, represent a community pulse. They are excellent disseminators of information at community and national levels, and consequently maintain a strong networking capability. Through their autonomy, environmental NGOs are able to act as watchdogs in monitoring and evaluating governmental actions and policies and changes in the natural environment. They have demonstrated an occasional ability to involve 'citizen science' and other providers of technical information, independent of the government. One of the main issues for environmental NGOs in Japan now appears to be attracting membership and finances commensurate with their international counterparts, and to get a new tax law sympathetic to their needs and in line with laws in other countries such as Australia and the US (with such a law also encouraging greater public membership). Their operating budgets are considered minuscule. Their budgets limit how many paid staff they can afford, as well as their access to technology for communications and scientific investigations. Finally, despite the political rhetoric and some late legislative changes, there appears to be resistance on the part of the state (mainly the bureaucracy) to fully embrace environmental NGOs and allow them to contribute to policy-making, which is perhaps symptomatic of resistance and procrastination by some to actual political reform on a wider scale. We have to remain cautious about the changes not going far enough, but we can also be hopeful that they will still improve opportunities for environmental protection, and that more progressive changes (e.g. a new Tax Law and an extended role in policy-making) will be implemented in the future.

Acknowledgement

The author wishes to thank the participants at the Workshop on Continuity and Change in Japan (18–19 January 2001, Brisbane), especially Dr Jeffrey Graham, Professor Tessa Morris-Suzuki and Professor Purnendra Jain, who kindly provided helpful comments on an earlier draft of this essay.

Note

1 According to an EA survey, Japan had 4,506 environmental NGOs in February 1995, and more than 70 per cent surveyed did not have full-time staff (*Japan Times Weekly International*, 1996: 15).

References

Abe, H., Shindo, M. and Kawato, S. (1994), *The Government and Politics of Japan*, University of Tokyo Press, Tokyo.
Barrett, B. and Therivel, R. (1991), *Environmental Policy and Impact Assessment in Japan*, Routledge, London.
Beder, S. (2000), ABC Radio interview, 18 October.
Broadbent, J. (1998), *Environmental Politics in Japan: Networks of Power and Protest*, Cambridge University Press, Cambridge.
Connelly J. and Smith, G. (1999), *Politics and the Environment: From Theory to Practice*, Routledge, London.
Department of Environment (1992), *The Common Inheritance: The Second Year Report*, HMSO, London.
Doyle, T. and Kellow, A. (1995), *Environmental Politics and Policy Making in Australia*, Macmillan, Melbourne.
Elliot, L. (1998), *The Global Politics of the Environment*, Macmillan Press Limited, London.
FOEJ (2000), *Yoku Aru Shitsumon to Kotae*, <http: //www.foejapan.org/faq.html> (accessed 14 November 2000).
Global Environment Information Centre (GEIC) (1997), *NGOs and Climate Change in Japan*, United Nations University, Tokyo, <http: //www.geic.or.jp/jp-ngo-cc.html> (accessed 15 November 2000).
Greenpeace Japan (1996), *Greenpeace Action Campaign Report*, 1(68), January 1996, Greenpeace Japan, Tokyo (in Japanese).
Holliman, J. (1990), 'Environmentalism with a global scope', in *Japan Quarterly*, July–September.
JAWAN (1999), *Save The Tidal Flats*, JAWAN, Tokyo.
Koyama, M. (1998), Wildlife Protection Division, Environment Agency, interview, June, Tokyo.

Morris-Suzuki, T. (2000), 'For and against NGOs: the politics of the lived world', *New Left Review*, 2 March–April.

Okabe, A. (2000), *Overview of Nonprofit Sector in Japan*, <http: //www.igc.org/ohdakefoundation/npo/npojp.htm> (accessed 15 November 2000).

Ormsby, P. (1998), Member of FOEJ, interview, June, Tokyo.

Pekkanen, R (2000), 'Japan's new politics: the case of the NPO Law', *The Journal of Japanese Studies*, 26(1), Winter.

Princen, T. and Finger, M. (1994), *Environmental NGOs in World Politics*, Routledge, London.

Schmitter, P. C. (1981), 'Interest intermediation and regime governability in contemporary Western Europe and North America', in Berger, S. (ed.), *Organising Interests in Western Europe*, Cambridge University Press, Cambridge.

Schreurs, M. (1996), *International Environmental Negotiations, The State and Environmental NGOs in Japan*, <http: //www.eic.or.jp/eanet/en/index.html> (accessed 31 October, 2000).

Shaiko, Ronald G. (1999), *Voices and Echoes for the Environment: Public Interest Representation in the 1990s and Beyond*, Columbia University Press, New York.

Sklair, L. (1994), 'Global sociology and global environmental change', in Redclift. M. and Ted Benton (eds), *Social Theory and the Global Environment*, Routledge, London.

Tsuji A. (2000), Leader of Save Fujimae Association NGO, correspondence.

Walker, C. (2000), FOE Australia national Liaison Office, email correspondence.

WBSJ (2000), <http: //www.wbsj.org/index2.html> (accessed 20 November 2000).

WWFJ (2000), <http: //wwfjapan.aaapc.co.jp/> (accessed 20 November 2000).

9 Immigration and citizenship in contemporary Japan

Tessa Morris-Suzuki

Towards the end of 1999, an advertisement appeared on subways and commuter trains throughout Japan, reminding passengers that this was something called 'tax awareness week'. The advertisement featured a photograph of the smiling face of Brazilian-born soccer star Ramos Rui, who had recently acquired Japanese citizenship. In the accompanying text, Rui informed the advertisement's readers that, as good Japanese nationals they, like him, should be conscious of their duty to pay taxes promptly and in full.

This advertisement seemed to me a striking illustration of some of the key paradoxes of the issues of migration and citizenship in contemporary Japan. At one level, it represented an unmistakable step forward in the recognition of Japan's social and cultural diversity. By using a 'foreign looking' face in the context of a statement about civic duties, the Japanese tax authorities were not just making a statement about tax-paying: they were also consciously making a statement about the increasingly 'multicultural' character of Japanese society. But at the same time, this bland association of citizenship and tax-paying carried some rather less comfortable overtones. For one thing, it obscured the fairly obvious fact that non-citizens who live and work in Japan are also, in most cases, required to pay Japanese taxes. The advertisement might also be read as conveying a subtext which ran approximately as follows: if you look 'foreign' and yet possess Japanese citizenship, you had better make *extra* sure that you are an exemplary, loyal, law-abiding, tax-paying citizen.

Challenges to the '1899 system'

Some of the most profound challenges to our contemporary notions of citizenship, sovereignty and the nation state come from the growing worldwide movement of people. In the early 1990s, about 80 million people (1.5 per cent of the world's population) were believed to be living outside the countries of their birth. Today, the figure is estimated to be around 120 million (Harding, 2000: 3). While governments and international agencies struggle to apply (often outmoded) laws, conventions and concepts to these accelerating currents of human movement, media panics over waves of 'illegal immigrants' or over rising levels of 'migrant crime' have acquired a powerful political force in many countries. How is the Japanese state, with its long history of restrictive immigration policies, reacting to a world order in which the cross-border movement of people has become an integral part of social existence? To answer this question, it is first necessary to say a little about the historical background to Japan's migration and citizenship policies.

The postwar political order centered on the dominance of the Liberal Democratic Party (LDP) was commonly referred to in Japan as the '1955 System' (a reference to the year in which the LDP was created from a merger of right-of-centre political parties). Some commentators now refer to the contemporary Japanese political order as the '1999 System'. (Kang and Yoshimi, 2001: 64) By analogy, one might refer to Japan's migration and nationality structures as the '1899 System'. This title highlights the extent to which these structures, even today, bear the imprint of Meiji period nation-building.

In 1899, with the dismantling of the Unequal Treaties imposed by the Western powers in the mid-nineteenth century, Japan was emerging as a fully fledged participant in the international order, and found it necessary to introduce a variety of domestic laws to adjust to this new status. Among these were the first Nationality Law, which came into force in April 1899, and Imperial Ordinance No. 352, the first general set of regulations governing immigration, issued just three months later. Though both the Nationality Law and immigration controls have since been revised several times, the key principles of the 1899 versions remain intact.

The 1899 System was powerfully shaped by the domestic and international circumstances of the late Meiji period. In the late 1890s, Japan had just defeated China in the Sino–Japanese War and acquired its first colony – Taiwan. The Japanese nation state was an emerging world power in an international system which (like the present day global order) was characterised both by high levels of international migration and by growing xenophobia. Rising levels of migration from China were a topic of particular debate in places like the United States and in Australia (which, on the eve of Federation, was already moving towards the creation of the White Australia policy). Against this background, the migration and citizenship policies introduced by the Meiji government aimed to prevent a feared influx of unskilled labour, particularly from China, and to restrict access to Japanese nationality for those whose loyalty to the state might be seen as in any way 'suspect'. So, for example, the Nationality Law of 1899 was considerably more restrictive than earlier drafts which had been drawn up and debated before the Sino–Japanese War (see Itô, 1935: 524–46; Haniwa, 1980).

The 1899 System defined Japanese citizenship as being based on *Ius Sanguinis* – the principle by which nationality is inherited, rather than being determined by the territory where an individual is born. The first Nationality Law also embedded in the system a still-surviving reluctance to allow Japanese citizens to possess dual nationality. The Immigration Ordinance, meanwhile, set the parameters for an exclusionary system in which only a few carefully specified categories of skilled foreign migrants would be allowed to live and work in Japan (see MacNair, 1933: 37–8; Hômushô Nyûkoku Kanrikyoku, 1964). It is worth noting that 1899 also saw the introduction of several other policies which were to have an enduring impact on definitions of 'Japaneseness', among them the 'Former Natives Protection Act' (*Kyû Dojin Hogo Hô*) which formed the mainstay of assimilationist policies towards the indigenous Ainu people of northern Japan for almost a century.

In the wake of Japan's defeat in the Pacific War, many of the political and social institutions created in the Meiji period were radically overhauled. Yet, as far as the definition of nationality was concerned, much of the 1899 System was left untouched. The revised Nationality Law of 1950 was closely modelled on the 1899 version (which had itself been the subject of minor revisions in 1916 and 1924), and postwar migration control policy continued essentially to follow the course charted by Imperial Ordinance 352. The one really important transformation was brought about by the loss of Japan's overseas empire.

In the prewar empire, Japan's colonial subjects had (with a small number of exceptions) been officially defined as 'Japanese nationals', though possession of Japanese nationality did not, of course, entail equality of rights. In some colonies (like Taiwan and Karafuto) locally modified versions of the 1899 Nationality Law were introduced, and throughout the empire the system of family registration (*koseki*) was used to discriminate between imperial subjects from the 'external territories' (*gaichi*) and metropolitan Japan (*naichi*). At the end of the Pacific War there were approximately 2 million colonial subjects, mainly from Korea, living in Japan, and although most returned home soon after the end of the war, about 700,000 remained. During the postwar Occupation period, the Japanese authorities adopted an ambivalent approach to ex-colonial subjects, on the one hand attempting to assert the right to jurisdiction over their lives, but on the other enacting measures which denied their status as Japanese nationals (Hirowatari, 1993: 102). The most obvious example of this denial was a clause appended to the new postwar election law, restricting voting rights to those with family registers in (pre-1945) *naichi* (before and during the war, male colonial subjects living in *naichi* had the right to vote provided they fulfilled certain residence criteria. In the 1932 general election twelve Korean candidates stood for the Japanese parliament, of whom one – Pak Chunkim, from the Tokyo constituency of Honjo-Fukagawa – was elected.) (Matsuda, 1995).

Former colonial subjects were also required to register under the newly introduced Alien Registration Ordinance of 1947 (although they were not at that stage officially 'aliens'). Then in 1952, after Japan recognised the independence of the former colonies under the Treaty of San Francisco, the government unilaterally abrogated the Japanese nationality of ex-colonial subjects, a move arguably in contravention of Article 15 of the 1948 UN Universal Declaration on Human Rights, which states that 'no one shall be arbitrarily deprived of his nationality'. So, while postwar political reforms extended the reach of *substantive* citizenship in Japan, particularly by giving women the right to vote, postwar changes to *formal* citizenship regulations intensified (rather than loosening) the restrictions of the 1899 System.

In the past two decades, however, this system has begun to face growing challenges from a variety of directions. For one thing, the extension of international human rights regimes and domestic campaigns for civic rights have brought about incremental changes to citizenship and migration policies. In 1985, as one of its official responses to the UN Women's Decade, the government revised the Nationality Law, removing its patriarchal assumption that Japanese nationality was inherited from fathers (but not from mothers).[1] With accession to the International Convention on Refugees in 1982, Japan also began to open the doors to a small number of asylum seekers, and the government was required to dismantle some of the social structures which had until then excluded foreign permanent residents from access to social security, pensions and public housing (Shin, 1995). Both international and domestic indigenous rights movements also forced the Japanese government to acknowledge the distinct traditions of Japan's Ainu population, and in 1997 the assimilationist 'Former Natives Protection Act' was, after almost a century, abolished and replaced by a law offering rather limited support for the preservation and transmission of Ainu culture.

By the early 1990s, a third generation of non-citizen permanent residents – descendants of prewar and wartime migrants from Korea and Taiwan – was coming of age, and the state attempted to resolve some of the anomalies of the situation by introducing a new category of 'special permanent resident', which allowed *zainichi* Koreans and Taiwanese greater rights of security and re-entry than they had previously possessed. In 1992, after a long and impassioned campaign, the much-hated system of compulsory fingerprinting of permanent residents was also abolished. (The use of fingerprints on the registration cards of all other foreigners was finally discontinued in 2000.) But other forms of structural discrimination against foreign permanent residents remain, including most significantly exclusion from voting rights and from many forms of public employment.

Crossing the demographic divide

While domestic and international human rights movements have begun to erode the foundations of the 1899 System, an even more powerful challenge to the system has come from profound shifts in the structure of the Japanese population. Here again, Japan's experience is just one example (though a rather extreme example) of a global trend. As Jeremy Harding points out, today the world is more than ever divided into two distinct demographic realms: 'whether you die young or old depends more clearly than at any time on where you were born'. Young migrants who move from poorer to richer countries thus seem to be 'crossing the forbidden boundary between two worlds that resemble enchanted worlds in a myth of primal sundering. In the first, there is only eternal youth, endlessly extinguished and replaced: here the young seem to have swallowed up the aged. In the second, crowds of mature adults and elderly extend the limits of longevity, deferring the moment of death, unwilling to cross the threshold but unable to return and regenerate the landscape over which they hastened: here the old have begun to devour the young' (Harding, 2000: 20). Japan, quintessentially, is a country where the old are devouring the young.

Over the past half century, Japan has experienced a drastic reshaping of its population pyramid. At the height of the postwar baby boom, about 2.7 million children were born each year; in 1997, the figure was less than 1.2 million. With the rapid ageing of the population, it is estimated that by 2050 there will be just 1.7 working persons for each person aged over 65, as compared with 4.8 in 1995 (Jung, 2001). Against this background, Japanese society has already begun to absorb a growing number of migrants into a wide range of areas of employment: share trading, textile production, restaurant work, language teaching, computer programming, prostitution, construction, machine making, entertainment, etc. In 1985 there were 850,612 registered foreign residents in Japan (0.7 per cent of the population); by 1999 the figure was 1,556,113 (1.2 per cent of the population) (Hômushô Shutsunyûkoku Kanrikyoku, 2000: 3). A large share of the inflow came from Latin America, and particularly from migration to Japan by descendants of former Japanese settlers in Brazil and Peru (who receive special treatment under Japanese immigration laws), but migration from countries like China and the Philippines also rose rapidly during the 1980s and 1990s (see Table 9.1).

Table 9.1 Registered foreigners in Japan by nationality 1980–99

Year	1980	1985	1990	1995	1999
Korea	664,536	683,313	687,940	666,376	636,548
China	52,896	74,924	150,339	222,991	294,201
Brazil	1,492	1,955	56,429	176,440	224,299
Philippines	5,547	12,261	49,092	74,297	115,685
USA	22,401	29,044	38,364	43,198	42,802
Peru	348	480	10,206	36,269	42,773
Thailand	1,276	2,642	6,724	16,035	25,253
Other	34,414	45,993	76,223	126,711	174,552
Total	782,910	850,612	1,075,317	1,362,317	1,556,113

Source: Sôrifu Tôkeikyoku, *Nihon tôkei nenkan 2001*. http://www.stat.go.jp/data/nenkan/zuhyou/y0215000

So far, this expansion has taken place without any fundamental reform of the restrictive migration control system set in place in the Meiji era. Rather than opening the doors to migrants, the government has made use of incremental changes around the edges to make narrow windows of opportunity for certain groups. The *nikkei* Peruvians and Brazilians form one such group. Another is made up of some 40,000–50,000 'trainees', mostly from other Asian countries, admitted to Japan for one year's 'on-the-job-training' followed by two years' 'work experience' in particular industries. Though the 'trainee' system is officially an aid programme intended to develop the skill base of the workers' home countries, there tends, in practice, to be a striking overlap between the industries where the programme is concentrated and those which are experiencing the greatest difficulty recruiting Japanese workers. For the past two decades, some sections of the Japanese economy have also depended quite heavily on the labour of visa overstayers and other 'illegal immigrants', of whom there were believed to be around 270,000 in 1998 (see Hômushô Shutsunyûkoku Kanrikyoku, 2000: 10).

The rapid greying of Japan may force the government to go beyond this incremental opening of loopholes. One recent UN report calculates that, to maintain its working-age population, Japan needs to accept more than 60,000 migrant workers a year over the next fifty years (Jung, 2001). Of course, estimates of future labour demand depend on complex sets of assumptions about economic growth, the structure of the economy, employment conditions and the availability of particular skills. A growing number of politicians, bureaucrats and academic researchers, however, now seem to acknowledge that a fundamentally new approach to immigration is becoming necessary.

For example, the Ministry of Justice's second Migration Plan (*shutsunyûkoku kanri kihon keikaku* – literally, 'Basic plan for the control of exit from and entry to the nation'), published in March 2000, speaks of the need to rethink migration policies in the light of globalisation, the declining birth rate and the ageing of the population (Hômushô Shutsunyûkoku Kanrikyoku, 2000: 1–2). A wide-ranging 'vision of Japanese society in the twenty-first century', produced by a government-commissioned discussion group and published early in the year 2000, goes further. The discussion group proposes that 'in order to adjust to globalisation and to maintain Japan's vitality, it will be essential in the twenty-first century to create a general environment in which many foreigners can live normally and comfortably in Japan.... Increasing ethnic diversity has the potential to expand the scope of Japan's intellectual creativity and to raise the level of social dynamism and international competitiveness' ('21-Seiki Nihon no Kôsô' Kondankai, 2000: 12). It, therefore, calls for the state to embark on a ' "migration policy" (*imin seisaku*) for foreigners who wish to live and work in Japan'. This notion of 'migration policy' as a radically new venture is significant. Current approaches are commonly referred to, not as 'migration policy' but as 'policy for the control of exit from and entry to the nation' (*shutsunyûkoku kanri seisaku*), a term which tellingly reveals the government's limited vision of its role as gatekeeper or security guard, keeping a stern watch over the movement of people as they step across the threshold of the national border.

But when it comes to specific proposals, official statements about policy reform suddenly become more cautious. So the 'twenty-first century vision' goes on to warn against an 'abrupt opening of the doors' to foreign migrants, and is very thin on specific suggestions for a new 'migration policy'. The Ministry of Justice's concrete proposals for expanding immigration, meanwhile, go little further than plans to extend the 'trainee' scheme to agriculture and the hospitality industry, and ultimately perhaps also to aged care (Hômushô Shutsunyûkoku Kanrikyoku, 2000: 13–15; *Asahi Shimbun*, 14 January 2000).

From 'ethnic homogeneity' to 'cosmetic multiculturalism'

In an age when commodities, money and information are globally mobile, it seems futile to imagine that human beings alone can be neatly contained by national boundaries. Mass migration is necessary to production and, indeed, we might say that throughout Japanese history, mass migrations have always been necessary. But whereas in the past these migrations brought workers from Japanese farm villages to factory towns, from the colonies to metropolitan Japan, or from the villages of metropolitan Japan to new colonial frontiers like Manchuria, now they predominantly bring foreigners into Japan (Iyotani, 1992). The issue is not really *whether* Japan will open its doors more widely to migration: rather, the question is – which doors will be opened, and to whom, and what sort of lives will they find waiting for them when they enter the door.

Efforts to maintain a semblance of strict migration controls while using systems like the 'training' scheme as a loophole for the admission of low cost labour risk replicating the problems of early phases of the German *Gastarbeiter* system: immigrants come to be viewed strictly as 'labour' – as working bodies who will leave the country when their labour is complete. This makes it easier for the host government to postpone addressing ultimately inescapable issues of the presence of non-citizens, not simply as 'workers' but as people with social aspirations, families, health problems, needs for housing, education, entertainment etc. The recruitment of migrants as a source of low cost labour for aged care is also likely to perpetuate entrenched gender stereotypes in which the work of care is seen as a task to be performed by women for minimal financial reward. In this sense, the current incremental approach to change in some ways serves to shore up existing structures of social inequity, instead of promoting a serious debate about the possibility of transformation to more diverse, mobile and equitable patterns of social existence.

But such debates are necessary, and need to go far beyond the bounds of narrowly defined problems of 'controlling entry'. Even the Ministry of Justice suggests as much, when it states that 'as social awareness of and interest in foreigners increases, and their numbers and areas of activity expand, it is becoming necessary for the migration control administration (*shitsunyûkoku kanri gyôsei*) to present a future image of the way in which Japanese and foreigners may coexist in our national society' (Hômushô Shutsunyûkoku Kanrikyoku, 2000: 1). In practice, contemporary developments in Japan suggest that a variety of divergent 'future images' of coexistence, diversity, inclusion and exclusion are already taking shape.

At the level of popular culture, a growing range of 'foreign faces' (and names and accents) are appearing in daily life and in the media. Official recognition of this diversity is evident in a number of contexts, of which the Ramos Rui tax advertisement is just one example. When Emperor Akihito celebrated the tenth anniversary of his accession in November 1999, the festivities included prominent appearances by sports stars of non-Japanese ethnic origin. Another dimension of diversity was also acknowledged in an interview marking the occasion, where the emperor spoke at particular length about the issue of Okinawa and about his interest in Okinawan history and culture (*Yomiuri Shimbun*, 12 November 1999). The distinctive culture of Okinawa was also showcased at the July 2000 Kyushu–Okinawa

Summit. The Ainu Cultural Promotion Law of 1997 too can be seen as a cautious step away from official ideologies of Japanese ethnic and cultural homogeneity.

Yet, so far at least, this shift in official presentations of national identity might best be interpreted as a move towards 'cosmetic multiculturalism'. This term is not meant to be wholly dismissive. Appearances matter, and, since Japan has never in fact been an ethnically homogeneous nation, it is better that its diversity should be acknowledged than that it should be denied. All the same, I use the term 'cosmetic multiculturalism' to suggest a vision of national identity in which diversity is celebrated, but only under certain tightly circumscribed conditions. First, desirable diversity is understood in terms of a narrowly defined vision of 'culture': culture as an aesthetic realm divorced from politics and from the mundane world of everyday existence. So for example, the Ainu Cultural Promotion Law supports the preservation and transmission of the Ainu language, song, dance and legends, but not of the memory of the Ainu struggle for social and civil rights. Second, this cultural diversity is to be displayed in particular, controllable forms and spaces. Okinawan music can be incorporated into the celebrations surrounding the Summit; Thai dance can become past of local multicultural festivals. But, for example, groups of Nigerian men performing rock music in an urban underpass are something else altogether.

Third, diversity is accepted on condition that it remains essentially a form of exterior decoration that does not demand major structural changes to existing institutions (a point I shall return to shortly), and fourth, growing acceptance of cultural difference is accompanied by increasing pressures for the visibly 'different' to *earn* acceptance by visible displays of their loyalty to the nation. So Ramos Rui may appear in a government-sponsored context as a representative Japanese citizen, but only on condition that he presents himself as the model law-abiding tax payer. More generally, the 'cosmetic multiculturalism' of the contemporary Japanese state seems to combine growing acceptance of certain forms of 'cultural diversity' with growing insistence on displays of loyalty to the unifying symbols of the nation state. It was, therefore, perhaps no coincidence that Emperor Akihito's tenth anniversary celebrations coincided with a campaign by the Ministry of Education to enforce the flying of the national flag and singing of the national anthem in Japanese schools and universities.

An emerging cosmetic multiculturalism, however, is only one strand in a complex set of responses to questions of migration, citizenship and national identity in Japan. It coexists with, and is challenged by a variety of other responses. The nature of Japan's society in the next few decades will depend crucially on the way in which these varied responses interact and are played out in the political realm. Before attempting an assessment of future directions, I should like to look briefly at two issues which help to illustrate some of this complexity of responses, and which expose some of the inherent problems of official approaches to cultural diversity.

Permanent residents and voting rights

Cosmetic multiculturalism meets relatively little resistance because it poses little threat to existing interests, and requires little fundamental rethinking of existing institutions. But efforts to take debates beyond the realms of a thinly defined cultural sphere soon encounter more deeply entrenched structural and ideological obstacles. These obstacles have been exposed, for example, in the ongoing debates over the extension of local voting rights to foreign permanent residents. Although Japan's resident foreign population, in percentage terms is still quite small (on a par with Spain's or Finland's, and far below the levels of countries like Switzerland or Germany), the Japanese state, like other nations, is beginning to have to come to terms with the presence of a group of long-term denizens who are not Japanese nationals. In Japan as elsewhere, the presence of foreign denizens poses fundamental challenges to conventional models of democracy, in which rights have commonly been seen as being inseparably connected to formal citizenship.

In the Japanese case, the issue is complicated by various historical factors. The abrogation of the Japanese nationality of former colonial subjects meant that, in the postwar period, some 700,000 *zainichi* Koreans and Taiwanese were classified as foreigners and lack the right to vote in Japanese elections (a right previously possessed by Korean and Taiwanese men who lived in Japan before and during the war). As a second and third *zainichi* generations have grown up, in many cases speaking Japanese as their first language and having lived all of their lives in Japan, this situation has become more and more obviously anomalous. So far the only way in which this section of Japan's population has been able to obtain the right to political participation is by becoming naturalised Japanese citizens.

This is an option which many have chosen: since the end of the Pacific War, about quarter of a million people, the majority of Korean origin, have acquired Japanese citizenship through naturalisation. In recent years, naturalisation procedures have gradually become less cumbersome, but the processing of a naturalisation application in Japan is still a relatively slow and intrusive process, involving character checks and interviews in which the applicant is likely to be asked fairly searching questions about his or her finances, job aspirations, friends and family etc. Most importantly, Japan's nationality laws require naturalised citizens to renounce their former nationality, and, given memories of the colonial past, many Korean residents in particular are reluctant to take this step.

One obvious way of addressing the continuing anomalies of disenfranchisement would be to extend at least some voting rights to foreign permanent residents: an approach adopted by a growing number of countries around the world. Today, for example, Sweden, Denmark, the Netherlands, Ireland and New Zealand allow all people with permanent residency to vote in local elections, and many other countries, including France, Germany and the UK, give this right to some groups of permanent residents. (New Zealand also allows permanent residents to vote in national elections) (*Japan Times*, 28 September 2000). In Japan, a movement to extend local voting rights to foreign permanent residents has been gathering momentum since the early 1990s, and by 1998 over 40 per cent of Japan's local authorities had adopted resolutions favouring this extension. In February 1995 the Japanese Supreme Court handed down a ruling confirming that it was constitutional to allow permanent resident foreigners to vote in local elections (Hirota, 2000: 58–60). However, national voting laws still need to be changed in order to put the change into effect.

Since 1999, the Japanese government has repeatedly expressed its intention to introduce the necessary legal changes, but parliamentary debates on the issue have again and again been cut short or postponed. The government's hesitant attitude reflects the fact that the Japanese political establishment is deeply divided on the question of local voting rights for foreign residents. Reform is strongly favoured by Kômeitô (a partner in the current coalition government) and by some LDP politicians, but it is equally vehemently opposed by others. Unlike the celebratory performances of cosmetic multiculturalism, the issue of permanent residents' voting rights has the potential to make a real, if small, impact on structures of power. As an overall percentage of Japanese voters, foreign permanent residents are a tiny minority, but there are one or two local government districts where their numbers might be large enough to have an impact in a closely contested local election.

More importantly, perhaps, the issue touches on deeply entrenched ideologies in which ethnicity, nationality and loyalty to the political order are seen as inextricably interconnected. The influence of this ideology is evident in some of the arguments put forward by opponents of local voting rights for foreigners. One of the more ingenious of these runs as follows. Recent changes to the regulations governing Japan's security agreement with the United States (the so-called 'Law for Situation in Surrounding Areas') allows for local authorities to play a role in times of military emergency. Voting in local elections therefore has national security implications, and should not be entrusted to foreigners (whose loyalty is assumed, according to this logic, to be always suspect). This implicit equation of foreign citizenship with political perfidy is expressed even more strongly by conservative commentators like Sakurai Yoshiko, who argues that giving permanent residents the right to vote in local elections would be 'the first step towards the ruination of the nation' (Sakurai, 1999).

Xenophobia and 'foreigner crime'

So cautious steps towards cosmetic multiculturalism coexist both with more far-reaching efforts to bring about substantive reforms to civic rights (e.g. by giving local voting rights to foreign residents) and with nationalist reactions against these efforts. It would be too simple, however, to see these varied reactions simply as alternative approaches to diversity which can be identified with clearly distinguishable opposing groups: 'liberals' versus 'conservatives', for example, or 'cosmopolitans' versus 'nationalists'. For in Japan, as in most other countries, the strands of tolerance and prejudice, xenophilia and xenophobia are intertwined in more complicated ways. The very people who may welcome the presence of foreigners in certain circumstances may fear and reject it in others.

It should not be entirely surprising, therefore, that a growing day-to-day acceptance of the presence of foreign residents in every day life, and (at times) an adulatory enthusiasm for foreign presences in the media should have gone hand in hand with rising levels of grass roots fear of the foreign, expressed (in the past year or so) particularly in media hysteria over 'foreigner crime'.

This hysteria came to a head in the wake of Tokyo Governor Ishihara Shintarô's notorious comments in a speech to the Self-Defence Forces in April 2000, in which he stated: 'If you look at Tokyo today you can see that very vicious crimes are repeatedly being committed by many *sangokujin* (third country people), foreigners, who enter the country illegally. The nature of crime in Tokyo is already different from in the past. In these circumstances, you can imagine that if there were a major natural disaster, there might be big, big riots. That's the current situation. There are severe limits on the power of the police to deal with that sort of thing. So you see I hope that in such times, in the pursuit of one of your major functions, it will be possible to request the mobilisation of all you (Self-Defence Force members), not just for disaster relief of citizens but also for maintaining public order.'

Ishihara's comments provoked outrage in many quarters for a variety of reasons, not least because of his use of the discriminatory word *sangokujin*, and because his statement evoked echoes of the massacre of Korean and Chinese residents in Tokyo in the wake of the 1923 earthquake. Here, however, I should like to comment on just two aspects of Ishihara's remarks. The first is the seemingly paradoxical fact that, despite his xenophobic comments to the Self-Defence Forces, Ishihara does not apparently advocate more restrictive immigration controls. On the contrary, in a magazine interview given in June 2000, he echoed the words of the government's 'twenty-first century vision', stating that 'Japan needs a proper "migration policy"... Japan has entered a new age. We need to create a proper policy to deal not just with the falling birth-rate but also with the difficulty of recruiting workers'. Ishihara went on to add that foreign workers would be particularly needed in areas like aged care and nursing, and that they should be encouraged to 'blend into Japanese society, marry and settle down to stable jobs' (*Newsweek Japan*, 7 June 2000: 29).

The second point to be made about Ishihara's comments is that they both echoed and amplified widespread grass roots fears of 'foreigner crime' (*gaikokujin hanzai*) These fears are sustained, less by the reality of a crime wave by immigrants (illegal or otherwise), than by sensationalist uses of crime statistics by the media and the police authorities. In particular, figures published by the Police Agency shortly before Ishihara's speech were widely presented as revealing a 'foreigner crime wave'. In fact, although arrests of foreigners for some types of crime have increased, a more careful look at the figures shows that the number of foreigners arrested for criminal offences in Japan was virtually the same in 1998 (10,248) as it was in 1980 (9,647) (Hômushô Hômu Sôgô Kenkyûjo, 1999: 513). Since the number of foreigners in Japan had roughly doubled between 1980 and 1998, this hardly seems to suggest a sudden outbreak of criminality amongst the non-citizen population. The 'foreigner crime wave', indeed, was largely a statistical artefact, created by the fact that arrested foreigners are now more likely than they were in the past to be charged with multiple offences (including visa offences and document fraud), and by the fact that the Police Agency divides the category of 'foreigner' into two groups depending on residence status. While arrests in one group have fallen, arrests in the other have risen. By looking only at the group whose arrest rate had risen, citing figures for numbers of offences rather than numbers of people arrested, and choosing as a starting point a year when 'foreigner crimes' had been unusually low, it was possible to come up with some rather impressive looking graphs of soaring alien criminality. The publicity given to these figures was, perhaps, not unconnected with the fact that the Police Agency had been rocked by a series of scandals in late 1999 and early 2000, and urgently needed to raise its public profile and win popular support for the maintenance of its budget.

Public fears of 'foreigner crime', however, are not simply a media artefact. They should also probably be seen as reflecting widespread popular anxieties over economic recession, uncertain employment prospects and the rapidity of social change. In this context, the unfamiliar faces of identifiable '*gaikokujin*' (and in this context *gaikokujin* implicitly suggests foreign migrants from other Asian countries, Africa or the Middle East rather than from North America or Western Europe) become a kind of focus for inchoate social anxieties, just as the faces of 'refugees' and 'migrants' do in many other parts of the world.

Towards a conclusion

What sense are we then to make of these complex currents, where demands for a more open 'migration policy' receive support from figures like Ishihara Shintarô, where growing celebration of cultural diversity goes hand in hand with rising fears of 'foreign crime', and where widespread local support for foreign resident's voting rights contends with impassioned resistance from sections of the political establishment?

In search of a tentative conclusion, I should like to suggest that in Japan today we are witnessing a profound, though often tacit, contest over the redrawing of the boundaries of national inclusion and exclusion. At one end of the spectrum, there are signs of a recognition in some quarters that in a new age of human mobility the definitions of nationality, citizenship and civic rights need to be rethought. Even cautious movements towards the rethinking of civic rights, however, evokes a reaction from the opposite end of the spectrum, where some commentators resist any attempt to change the boundaries of national belonging.

More complex and perhaps more significant, however, is the response which seeks to redefine these boundaries by means of an ambivalent and limited 'multiculturalism' – drawing an imagined line between the acceptable and unacceptable faces of 'foreignness'. The nature of this line is always implicit, always ambiguous. It separates the culturally acceptable from the politically threatening; the (assumedly) skilled western professional from the low paid third world 'foreign worker'; the settled, married migrant who 'blends into Japanese society' from the unruly 'illegal immigrant' liable at any moment to commit 'vicious crimes'. The power of this imagined line lies precisely in its uncertainty, its imaginary quality, its capacity to be redrawn. It makes possible the acceptance of diversity, and yet it renders the non-citizen always vulnerable because he or she knows that that acceptance may at any moment be withdrawn. The boundary may be shifted; those who are classified as 'good foreigner' may find themselves reclassified by media or populist politicians as 'bad foreigner'; the person who is in one context a sought after technician or professional may in another be seen as a Chinese or Indian immigrant, eyed with fear by neighbours or with suspicion by police. In this context Ishihara's stance is not paradoxical but entirely logical. It makes eminent economic sense to create a society in which immigrant workers are recruited to care for the sick and elderly, but where fears of 'foreigner crime' can be stirred up to keep such workers marginalised, vulnerable and low-paid.

In this context, I would argue that there is a particularly pressing need for a reform of the foundations of the '1899 System'. In an age of globalisation, Japan (like other countries) needs to address fundamental problems of the relationship between formal nationality and civic rights. It needs to create the basis for a society which goes beyond 'cosmetic multiculturalism': a society where people of many nationalities and identities can experience economic and social security, and can participate in the shaping of a new Japan. The current debate about foreigners' voting rights, and the impending debates on the postwar Japanese constitution, might perhaps provide starting points for a fresh approach to these issues.

Acknowledgement

The research on which this chapter is based was supported by the generosity of the Toyota Foundation.

Note

1 Before 1985, children born to married couples were presumed to inherit the nationality of their father, and only illegitimate children of Japanese women could, in some circumstances, inherit Japanese nationality from their mothers.

References

'21-Seiki Nihon no Kôsô' Kondankai (2000), *Nihon no furontia wa Nihon no naka ni aru*. http: //www.kantei.go.jp/jp/21century/houkokusyo/1s.html.

Haniwa, S. (1980), 'Meiji 32-nen no kokusekihô seiritsu ni itaru katei: nihon kokusekihô josetsu', in Haga Kôshirô Sensei Koki Kinenkai (ed.), *Nihon shakaishi kenkyû*, Kasama Shoin, Tokyo.

Harding, J. (2000), 'The uninvited', *London Review of Books*, 22(3), February.

Hardt, Michael and Negri, Antonio (2000) *Empire*. Cambridge MA.: Harvard University Press.

Hirowatari, S. (1993), 'Foreigners and the "foreigner question" under Japanese Law', *Annals of the Institute of Social Science,* University of Tokyo, vol. 35.

Hirota, Y. (2000), 'Gaikokujin shisei sanka no hôteki kentô', in Miyajima Takashi (ed.), *Gaikokujin shimin to seiji sanka*, Yushindô, Tokyo.

Hômushô Nyûkoku Kanrikyoku (1964), *Shustunyûkoku kanri to sono jitai*, Ôkurashô Insatsukyoku, Tokyo.

Hômushô Shutsunyûkoku Kanrikyoku (2000), *Shutsunyûkoku kanri kihon keikaku (dainiji)*, Hômushô, Tokyo, 24 March, http: //www.moj.go.jp/PRESS/000300–2/000300–2-2.htm.

Hômushô Hômu Sôgô Kenkyûjo (1999), *Hanzai hakusho 1999*, Ôkurashô Insatsukyoku, Tokyo.

Itô, H. (1935), *Hôsei kankei shiryô*, vol. 1. Tokyo: Hisho Ruisan Kankôkai (edited collection of Meiji period documents).

Iyotani, T. (1992), 'Sakerarenai kadai: Sengo Nihon keizai ni okeru gaikokujin rôdôsha', in Iyotani, T. and Kajita T. (eds), *Gaikokujin rôdôsha ron: genjô kara riron e*, Kôbundô, Tokyo.

Jung Yeong-Hae (2001), 'The politics of gender and nation-rebuilding', *Traces*, 2.

Jung Yeong-Hae (2001), 'Jendâ no seiji to kokumin no saikôsei Traces 2 (Special edition of Shisô, no. 928) August 139–153.

Kang, S. and Yoshimi Shunya (2001), *Gurôbaruka no enkinhô: Atarashii kôkyôkûkan o motomete*, Iwanami Shoten, Tokyo.

MacNair, H. F. (1933), *The Chinese Abroad*, Commercial Press, Shanghai.

Matsuda, T. (1995), *Senzenki no Zainichi Chôsenjin to senkyôken*, Akashi Shoten, Tokyo.

Sakurai, Y. (1999), '"Eijû gaikokujin no chihô sanseiken" wa bôkoku no dai-ippo de aru', *Shûkan Shinchô*, 18 November.

Shin, Yong-Hong (1995), 'Zainichi Chôsenjin to shakai hoshô', in *Zainichi Chôsenjin: Rekishi, genjô, tenbô*, Akashi Shoten, Tokyo.

10 The reformatting of Japan for the people

Science, technology and the new economy

Morris Low

As we enter the twenty-first century, Japan is being reformatted (see Morris-Suzuki, 1998: 162–7). First, Japanese government ministries and agencies are being reorganised as part of wide-ranging administrative reforms. Parts of the reforms are aimed at ensuring greater public participation and transparency in policy-making. The second major transformation is the technological shift from the 'old' economy to the new, where telecommunications, the service sector and e-commerce dominate and demand is consumer-driven. This change is being heralded by the government as Japan's 'rebirth'. More than ever before, Japan is setting its hopes on science, technology, and research and development (R&D) to guarantee its economic future. While the very structure of the economy is experiencing change, we may see a merging of the old with the new, rather than a repudiation of one for another. There is thus both continuity and change and it is important for us to understand the transformations. In this chapter, I examine these transformations, the policies that underlie them, and their impact on the Japanese people.

Administrative reforms

The power relationship or 'iron triangle' between big business, the bureaucracy and the Liberal Democratic Party has been seen by many as hindering Japan's ability to respond to the challenges of the twenty-first century (Kume, 2001). The Prime Minister's Office and twenty-two ministries and agencies have been reorganised into one Cabinet Office and twelve ministries and agencies. This is seen as helping to correct the sectionalism that has been rife in administration. The total number of national civil servants is to be reduced by 25 per cent over ten years beginning in FY 2000.

As part of the reforms, in early 2001, the Science and Technology Agency (STA) merged with the Ministry of Education, Science, Sports and Culture to create a new Ministry of Education, Science, Technology, Sports and Culture (Monbu Kagakushô). The new ministry controls about 75 per cent of the government's science and technology-related budget. The remainder will go to the Ministry of International Trade and Industry (MITI) now renamed the Ministry of Economy, Trade and Industry (METI), a testimony to its influence and success (National Science Foundation, 2000a).

These reforms were, at least partly, instigated by public concern and pressure to include civic participation in the political process. For example, the development of nuclear power and uranium processing at Tôkai-mura, and unsuccessful satellite launches by the H-II rocket (Lies, 2000: 61) had prompted concerns about technology management and the role of the STA. Japan's worst accident at a nuclear facility at Tôkai-mura in September 1999 also saw a dramatic increase in public concern about the safety of nuclear power. There were strong calls to abandon plans to construct a further twenty-two reactors and, in response, electric power companies decided to build a maximum of thirteen plants by 2010 (Medlock III, Soligo, 2000).

Also, the Atomic Energy Commission decided on 24 November 2000 to implement a new 'Long-Term Programme for Research, Development, and Utilization of Nuclear Energy'. The programme promotes further safety measures and disaster prevention, as well as more active information disclosure, specifically to allay public fears in the aftermath of a number of accidents. The creation of the new *Monbu Kagakushô* may benefit the troubled Japanese space programme, one part of which is located at the National Space Development Agency (NASDA) and overseen by the STA. Responsibility for the activities of the space programme at Institute of Space and Astronautical Sciences (ISAS) rests with the Ministry of Education. Against the background of accidents at nuclear facilities, STA's Atomic Energy Bureau and Nuclear Safety Bureau will be lost to MITI and renamed the Agency of Natural Resources and Energy.

As of 1 April 2001, a system of Independent Administrative Institutions (IAIs) came into existence in Japan. The introduction of the system was motivated by concerns with public welfare and transparency in policy-making, and a desire to maintain a degree of autonomy in activities. It effectively separated implementation, planning and drafting of policy by assigning aspects of implementation to IAIs.

In addition to administrative improvements and transparency, the Japanese government acknowledged the need to fund basic research. As part of the Second Science and Technology Basic Plan, effective from April 2001, about half of the government's research funds over the next five years will be devoted to supporting areas such as life sciences, information technology (IT), environmental science and materials science (National Science Foundation, 2000b).

The rise of the new economy

As Porter *et al.* (2000: 5–6) found, it was as if there were two Japans. In agriculture, chemicals, medical products, software and the service sectors, Japanese firms had often been protected to the detriment of their competitiveness. In terms of percentage of total employment, Japan had twice as many people employed in agriculture and construction as the US in 1999.

From late 1997, a surprising divergence emerged between the more established 'old economy' companies and new companies in Japan. The latter were often small, more flexible, and more likely to take risks. They posted returns of up to 177 per cent in 1999, whereas returns of the old economy' firms returns declined by 12 per cent (*Australian Financial Review*, 1999: 18). Sony, Matsushita and NTT DoCoMo are among the new technology leaders and Sony, for example, is exploring ways to link its games console PlayStation2 with NTT DoCoMo's cellular phone internet service.

The need for companies to reinvent themselves is more urgent than ever. Not all is well in the old-style economy. In fiscal year 1998, Toyota Motor Corp. reported its first drop in profit in five years and Toshiba Corp. reported its first losses in forty-eight years. The current technological shift has rendered old techniques of innovation such as Toyota's incremental improvement system less relevant, suited as they are for assembly-line production rather than high-tech industries that focus more on each item. The ability for blue-collar workers to contribute to product improvement is much more constrained, given the very specialised know-how required. The old economy also confronts challenges posed by over-capacity. Industries such as steel-making and shipbuilding have lost market share and there are concerns that the same will happen in automobiles and consumer electronics. The lead that Japan enjoyed in these industries has declined and the domestic market for these products largely satiated.

Instead, Japan now looks to IT, the internet, and next-generation technologies to ensure its future. Hitachi and Toshiba plan to develop more internet-related businesses and products. Innovative small and medium-sized high-tech enterprises have created internet-based networks that bypass traditional channels of information (Ibata-Arens, 2000). In the wake of public criticism of excessive spending on public works to shore up the economy, the Japanese government, too, belatedly turned to IT to strengthen economic competitiveness in the twenty-first century.

The rise of the internet

The number of internet users in Japan was estimated at over 5 million in 1997 and by February 1999 had trebled, exceeding 15 million. A survey of users in Japan (March 1997) found that 94.2 per cent were male; 51.9 per cent were engineers; and that 74.6 per cent used it for both work and pleasure. Almost half, 46.4 per cent used it at work or at an educational institution, and about a third, 34.3 per cent used it mainly at home (Toshio, 1997: 4). Among those who use the internet in Japan, around half of high-tech researchers use e-mail, with the highest percentage of such users being located in universities and colleges. Those aged up to thirty-nine years most often used e-mail, with usage declining with age.

There is, however, considerable scepticism that the rush to install computer networks is anything more than an attempt to keep up with the neighbours. 'Apart from electronic mail, few companies have a clear idea how to use their networks' says Kobayashi Toshinori, a planner in the machinery and information bureau of the former MITI (*The Australian*, 1997: 7). A cultural ramification of this growth in usage is the spread of 'Japlish', a hybrid language with a logic of its own, whereas handwriting and calligraphy provided a window to one's character, people look to other things now by which to evaluate the person whose fingers touch the keyboard.

Why did not the internet have the same effect in Japan as it had in the US? There are many reasons for this, but we can note that there is more Japanese language material available on the internet and it has become more user-friendly for the Japanese. While the internet may encourage an international outlook in terms of sourcing of products, use of Japanese script allows users to retain their sense of Japaneseness.

Access via cellular phones

The current enthusiasm for internet access is via cell phones rather than desktop computers. It is estimated that over ten million Japanese access the internet in this way. The use of cell phones now exceeds that of home phones. Cell phones bring together the Japanese penchant for electronic gadgets and the beginnings of a real embrace of new technology. NTT DoCoMo's i-mode system provides users with cheap and continuous wireless access to the internet, using cellular phones with a screen the size of a business card. By January 2001, there were 19 million subscribers to the service. As a result, it has been suggested that Japan might even surpass the US in terms of internet usage by 2002. Japan is already considered ahead in cell communications.

How do we account for the belated growth in the use of cell phones to access the internet? Cell telephone services started in Japan in 1979. In the late 1980s, they became popular in Europe, but in Japan, due to the monopolistic role of NTT in telecommunications, the spread of cell phones lagged that of Hong Kong and Taiwan. Cell phones became popular with the young Japanese only in 1994 and the level of ownership reached five million people. A system of having three or four carriers in each area was introduced and subscribers were able to actually purchase the cell phones (Nishimura, 1998). The number of subscribers doubled the following year and reached 2.6 million in 1996.

Why is access via cellular phone so popular? The i-mode system enables users to move from Tamagotchi-style electronic devices to using the internet without such a big leap. The Tamagotchi ('cute little egg') was manufactured by the Japanese company Bandai and released in the market in November 1996. This electronic pet chicken kept on the end of a key chain, became the toy of the moment the following year. By July 1997, shipments exceeded ten million, and the goal was to sell 50 million by March 1998. This egg-shaped toy with a small screen operated on the principle that it was the owner's responsibility to keep the pet alive.

The Tamagotchi came with three buttons, 'select', 'execute' and 'cancel' which were located below the screen and enabled the owner to feed it with a meal or snack, play with the Tamagotchi when it was in a bad mood, and provide treatment when it was sick. A bathroom icon had to be pressed after the Tamagotchi had 'used the bathroom', otherwise it would get sick. Pressing the health icon enabled the owner to monitor the Tamagotchi's age, weight, hunger, mood, and behaviour. The Tamagotchi beeped when it wanted attention, and owners were reminded to check the health icon when this occurred. A discipline could be used if the Tamagotchi refused to eat even when it was hungry, and if it beeped for no apparent reason. The more attention lavished on the device, the longer it lived.

Japan's biggest advertising company Dentsu saw the year 2000 as characterised by the release of a series of small devices with internet connectivity such as cellular phones, digital cameras, portable music players and wristwatches. For the first time, sales of these digital devices were better than for their more conventional counterparts. Cell phones outnumbered fixed telephone lines, digital cameras outdid ordinary cameras, and shipments of PCs surpassed that of television sets (Cornell, 2001: 8). This illustrates the very real shift to the new economy.

Research and development

The perceived link between the Tamagotchi and the i-mode system is not surprising. Japanese R&D is more market-driven than discovery-driven, and the desire for small, new gadgets which feature cute cartoon-like characters is strong. As Mowery and Rosenberg (1989: 219) have noted, it was the ability of Japanese firms to commercialise new products, some component of which may have been invented elsewhere that was their strength.

What part has government played? Many countries seek to encourage the growth of knowledge-based industries, but this requires major investment in R&D and public funding on education. In fiscal 1998, total R&D expenditure in Japan was 16,139.9 billion Yen, second only to the US. It had been steadily increasing for four years, despite the economic recession. That year, the ratio of gross domestic R&D expenditure to GDP (gross domestic product) reached the record high for Japan of 3.26 per cent. If we compare Japan to the US, Germany, France and the UK, this ratio has been consistently the highest since 1989 (Tomizawa, 2000: 7).

The METI was, like other government ministries, slow to embrace IT but realises that Japan must catch up again with other countries, not only the US. A report in 2000 accounted for the large gap in IT investment per worker between Japan and the US as arising from the bursting of the economic bubble in the 1990s. In a classic case of bad timing, Japan's recession coincided with an IT paradigm shift. While Japanese investments in IT have increased, there is considerable room for improvement (*Japan's IT Business and IT Policy*, 2000). This report noted also that there was a particularly wide gap in e-commerce market. Despite the relatively low penetration of personal computers in Japan, it is expected that various devices such as the next-generation, mobile phones, car navigation systems and next-generation games will surpass the number of PCs. Whether it be i-mode internet accessible telephone, Sony Play Station 2, or car navigation systems, it is expected that the devices will be more specific usage-focused.

What the report failed to acknowledge was that other Asian countries such as Singapore and Taiwan were leaving Japan behind as well. For example, in Singapore, higher value-added goods such as semiconductors and telecommunications equipment are expected to replace personal computers and disk drives as the main drivers of the country's output. In September 2000, Prime Minister Mori announced a new IT strategy called 'e-Japan' which involved bringing down online costs and subsidised education programmes. A special science and technology budgetary allocation has been proposed in Japan for 2001 to facilitate the transition to the new economy, a major component of which is the promotion of an IT revolution.

The internet and IT in themselves will not provide all the answers for Japan's problems. In meeting the challenges that they present, the economic system will be forced to become more global in nature. We are seeing the emergence of what has been described as 'the new *zaibatsu*' (financial conglomerate) or 'Net-*batsu*', led by Masayoshi Son's Softbank Corp., the world's largest conglomerate of internet-related firms. Son's basic strategy was to import American World Wide Web companies such as Yahoo and to establish them in Japan. While trying to transform Japan from an industrial to an information society, Son and others like him have been criticised for merely importing US technology and not contributing to domestic development of technology.

The existing strategy is not only to encourage growth of the 'new economy' but to also revitalise the old. To what extent government should have a role in this is a moot point, but Samuel Coleman (1999) recently stated in his book on Japanese science that governments could create research environments to facilitate individual creativity.

Rather than the result of wise government policy, the growth in popularity of the internet has been facilitated by the enthusiasm for mobile phones, a phenomena which has been largely consumer-led. The Japanese government has arguably been more of a hindrance. There have been calls for the government to deregulate and open up the telecommunication sector to competition. Indeed, Porter *et al.* (2000: x) suggest that it is when the Japanese government allows competition to flourish that industries flourish.

Science and technology workforce

In the 'new economy', a skilled workforce is more important than ever. It was estimated that in Japan in 1999 there were 733,000 researchers. This figure has steadily increased for the past thirty years, largely thanks to the increase of personnel in industry. These people may not necessarily have doctorates. Germany leads the world in terms of the number of doctoral degree holders per million of population, with 279 persons. The UK is next with 174, followed closely by US (170). The figure for Japan is 111 persons, about 40 per cent of the figure for Germany (Tomizawa, 2000: 7). This reflects the tendency for industry in Japan to recruit master degree holders in preference to those holding doctorates. The latter are sometimes considered too specialised.

While Japan can boast of academic R&D expenditure on a par with that of other leading industrialised nations and we can note that many researchers are based in universities, university–industry links are perceived as relatively weak, and outputs in terms of patents and spin-off firms are low. One conclusion would be that Japan needs to encourage closer ties and more market-oriented activity in universities. But is that what Japan needs? While we can point to the commercialisation of technology as one of Japan's strengths, it has arguably resulted in the relative material poverty of scientific research in universities (Coleman, 1999: 7). Another view is that links are not as weak as one might think. Kenneth Pechter (2000: 27–31) suggests that if we use co-authorship as an indicator of university–industry ties, they are comparable to that of the US.

Samuel Coleman takes a different approach and suggests that Japanese science would achieve more if an American-style 'credit cycle' which more fully rewarded researchers was allowed to operate in Japan. He attributed inflexibility to the *kôza* or 'chair' system in Japan where the full professor was all-powerful. Of course, a major constraint is to what extent the Japanese themselves want a Western research system in which the individual pursued self-interest and maximised his or her rewards. The situation in Japan has been shaped by social expectations of its education system. Companies seek future employees (especially male) who meet the admission standards of prestigious universities, rather than those with highly developed research skills.

The Japanese now realise that research organisations should be flexible and geared to promoting individual creativity and an innovative workforce. Researchers themselves are increasingly coming to understand the benefits of competition, the promotion of Coleman's credit cycle. Thus, one-third of respondents in a STA survey for fiscal 1999 replied that a competitive principle should be introduced for the distribution of research funds and positions (*STA Today*, 2000: 7). It was reported in September 2000 that the Prime Minister's Technology Advisory Council had recommended that national research laboratories abandon lifetime employment and offer fixed-term contracts instead to young scientists under the age of thirty-five years. Those who performed well would have the option of renewing their contracts beyond the initial five years (*Japan Washington Watch*, 2000).

Tsugawa and Kanomi (1996) have traced the careers of women scientists in fields such as medicine, botany, organic chemistry, mathematics and physics. The life stories of these women suggested that female university graduates had difficulty securing research positions in the public and private sectors. However, once in the workforce, another study by Endo *et al.* (1993) found that, in national laboratories there were no perceptible gender differences in work and educational opportunities. Research involved both men and women, often working overtime during the week and on Saturdays and Sundays. At one laboratory, there appeared to be a gender bias in favour of men when it came to overseas trips. In universities, women experienced difficulties in being considered for new positions. Family and home duties cut into their research productivity, and even if on a par with male candidates, it was thought that men would probably be chosen over women. In private laboratories, there was a perception that women tended to be assigned work, which was less urgent and less crucial to the company.

According to Coleman (1999) the 'credit cycle' that rewarded researchers in the US did not operate fully in Japan. This worked against women. He singled out the role of the *kôza* or 'chair' system whereby full professors were all-powerful and, needless to say, few professors in science and technology were women. A major obstacle to change was the way status and privilege was rewarded rather than ability and merit. Coleman examined female participation in the life sciences today, and their continuing career handicaps and suggested that the field of pharmacology served as a 'halfway house' for women interested in research. They could operate a shopfront pharmacy, aspire to do research, and at the same time attend to home duties.

Japan today confronts the challenge of opening its borders to foreign skilled workers to supplement a shrinking population and workforce. It is estimated that Japan requires an annual intake of 600,000 immigrants to offset the impact of an ageing population and a declining birth rate, but such ideas are not popular in a country experiencing high unemployment. A report prepared by an advisory panel to former Prime Minister Obuchi suggested that foreign students be allowed to stay in Japan after completing their studies (see Cornell, 2000: 11). This is certainly the situation in the US where the majority of foreign students stay behind after graduation. In Japan, however, an STA survey (*STA Today*, 1999: 9) of the research activities of private companies in fiscal 1998 found that while companies were prepared to employ mid-career researchers who had previously been employed elsewhere, they were reluctant to employ foreign researchers, and researchers with doctoral and post-doctoral qualifications.

However, foreigners are increasingly becoming players in the Japanese economy at the highest levels. Japanese auto manufacturers, apart from Toyota and Honda have aligned themselves with foreign partners and in 2000, Renault executive Carlos Ghosn became Nissan's first non-Japanese president. Such linkages provide Japanese firms with ways of taking advantage of technological knowledge and resources abroad. Previously, it had occurred through licensing agreements with foreign firms, or by sending Japanese personnel overseas. More recently Japanese firms have contracted research to foreign organisations, formed R&D consortia with them and established overseas R&D facilities. Overseas research facilities are not without problems and, according to Odagiri and Yasuda (1997) can make the management of innovation within a Japanese firm more difficult as well as making it harder to maintain links between sales, manufacturing and overseas R&D facilities. Another common problem is the maintenance of good communications between a parent laboratory in Japan and overseas facilities where non-Japanese researchers were employed.

Science, technology and gender

The need for companies to reinvent themselves and change their attitudes to the gender makeup of the workforce is more urgent than ever. With an ageing population and a declining birth rate, Japan needs to make more use of its female work force. The linkage between science, technology and gender has changed over time. Shunya (1999), for example, argued that after the 1980s, images of electrical appliances transgressed borders of nation, culture, gender and race. Users of technology increasingly move around the world and those driving cars, using fax machines, and holding cell phones can be either gender.

The use of computers in Japan and the emphasis on information processing has been portrayed as allowing women to compete equally with men for jobs (Ekusa, 1992: 33). In the same way that Japanese women mastered the large cumbersome typewriters, used to produce formal documents in Japanese offices, without any commensurate rise in status, the increased use of computers has seen a shift from manual work to routine 'information transfer' work for women.

There are, nevertheless, hopes that the new economy offered women opportunities to participate fully in the workforce at higher managerial levels. Just as it is possible to portray oneself as being of the opposite gender when chatting on the internet or participating in role-playing online games with fictional characters, the internet enables people to escape rigid gender categories and to go beyond normal rules of behaviour. In a way, the new economy enabled women to gender switch.

Two major features of the internet economy which make it attractive to women is its relative anonymity and newness. Although women comprised more than half of the total Japanese workforce, there were only 2.4 per cent of women in middle management positions in companies of thirty or more employees. In contrast, there were five to ten times as many women in senior positions in the new economy. While the world of IT is often associated with young men, it has been estimated that in 1999, 40 per cent of purchases of entry-level computers suitable for online use were by women. Whereas only a quarter of Japanese surfing the internet in 1999 were women, they now account for more than 40 per cent of those using it (Cornell, 2000: 32). At of the end of 1999, it was estimated that there were more than three million women who used the internet in Japan. This figure is likely to increase by five times by the end of 2003 as women have enthusiastically accessed the internet via mobile cell phones.

While lack of English language ability sometimes hinders Japanese from using the internet, the English language proficiency of young Japanese women and interest in foreign languages worked in their favour. In the same way that the resident Korean Masayoshi Son experienced difficulties obtaining loans from Japanese banks to fund his entrepreneurial activities, women too, have experienced discrimination, but theirs is based on gender. The advantage of internet businesses is the relatively small funding needed to start out and web sites such as womenjapan.com deliberately target women and help them to participate in the new economy. Given the difficulties that young Japanese women have experienced in finding employment in Japan during the recession of the 1990s, some women see the new economy as heralding not only a technological revolution, but a social revolution.

Social protest

While the internet is potentially a powerful source of economic opportunities, it also has subversive qualities as well. Before French nuclear tests recommenced in the Pacific in late 1995, students at the University of Tokyo circulated a petition via the Net, which attracted tens of thousands of signatures. The citizens of Hiroshima and Nagasaki called for a stop to the French testing via the World Wide Web, and another page listed French companies with the plea to boycott their products. In response to the rape of a Japanese schoolgirl by two American Marines and a sailor based in Okinawa on 4 September 1995, a home page was created nine days later which explained the problems of American bases, and on 18 September, a petition was circulated.

At the end of March 2001, South Koreans launched a cyber-attack on Japanese government web sites in protest at the publication of a history textbook that failed to mention 'comfort women', described Japan's annexation of Korea as legitimate, and portrayed Japan as liberating Southeast Asian nations from the West. The official web sites of the Ministry of Education, Culture, Sports, Science and Technology came under attack by millions of simultaneous hits, as did the web sites of the Liberal Democratic Party, the Hokkaido Prefectural Government, and the publisher.

Conclusion

More than ever before, science, technology and R&D look set to underwrite Japan's continued prosperity, but we must beware that certain groups are not excluded from this. While the very structure of the economy is experiencing change, we may see a merging of the old with the new, rather than a repudiation of one for another. The reorganisation of Japanese government has the potential to facilitate this transformation in a way which is more attuned to the public good. It remains to be seen whether the change in ministerial cultures will have a real impact, but it is clear that the internet and new technologies will.

Acknowledgement

This paper was completed while visiting the Centre for Critical and Cultural Studies at the University of Queensland as Faculty Fellow in the first half of 2001. I am grateful to Professor Graeme Turner and Ms Andrea Mitchell for facilitating my visit. I also thank my colleagues in the Department of Asian Languages and Studies for their assistance during my partial absence.

References

Australian Financial Review (1999), 'Japan's challenge: a budget beyond politics', 24–8 December.
Coleman, S. (1999), *Japanese Science: From the Inside*, Routledge, London.
Cornell, A. (2001), 'Summer memories a hot seller in Japan', *The Australian Financial Review*, 25–8 January.
Ekusa, A. (1992), 'The rise of women's power', *Journal of Japanese Trade and Industry*, 11(5), October.
Endo, H., Yoshiko Yokoo, Yukihiro Hirano, Y. and Ryuji Shimoda (1993), *Josei kenkyûsha no genjô ni kansuru kiso chôsa*, NISTEP. Report, no. 30, National Institute of Science and Technology Policy, Tokyo.
Ibata-Arens, K.C. (2000), 'The business of survival: small and medium-sized high-tech enterprises in Japan', *Asian Perspective*, 24(4).
Japan's IT Business and IT Policy (2000), Ministry of International Trade and Industry, Tokyo, electronic report, June.
Japan Press Center (2000), 'Japan's nuclear power construction plan shaken by decision to abandon Ashihama plant project', *Japan Brief*, 2 March.
Japan Washington Watch (2000), 4(29B), 18–24 September.
Kume, I. (2001), 'Japan's central government reorganization and its effects', *Policy Analysis Series*, no. 2, 21 March.
Lies, E. (2000), 'Rising sun eclipsed in space', *The Australian*, 4 April.
Medlock III, K. B. and Ronald Soligo (2000), 'Japanese energy demand to 2015', paper prepared in conjunction with an energy study by The Center for International Political Economy and The James A. Baker III Institute for Public Policy, Rice University, Houston, May.
Morris-Suzuki, T. (1998), *Reinventing Japan: Time, Space, Nation*, Armonk, NY, ME Sharpe
Mowery, D. C. and Nathan Rosenberg (1989), *Technology and the Pursuit of Economic Growth*, Cambridge University Press, Cambridge.
National Science Foundation (2000a), 'Reorganization of the Ministry of Industrial [sic] Trade and Industry (MITI) and its agency for Industrial Science and Technology', *Report Memorandum*, no. 00–05, Tokyo, February.

National Science Foundation (2000b), 'Preview of the second science and technology basic plan', *Report Memorandum*, no. 00–18, 4, Tokyo, December.

Nishimura, H. (1998), 'The second phase of telecommunications deregulation in Japan', *NRI Quarterly*, 7(3), Autumn.

Odagiri, H. and Hideto Yasuda (1997), 'Overseas R&D activities of Japanese firms', in Akira Goto and Hiroyuki Odagiri (ed.), *Innovation in Japan*, Clarendon Press, Oxford.

Pechter, K. (2000), 'Understanding and communicating needs and solutions: a case of comparative policy analysis', *Social Science Japan*, no. 18, April.

Porter, M. E., Hirotaka Takeuchi and Mariko Sakakibara (2000), *Can Japan Compete?*, Macmillan Press, Houndmills, Basingstoke.

Shunya, Y. (1999), '"Made in Japan": the cultural politics of "home electrification" in postwar Japan', *Media, Culture and Society*, 21(2).

STA Today (1999), 'FY1998 survery on research activities of private companies', 11(9).

The *Australian* (1997), 'Japan's desks wired at last', 20 May.

Tomizawa, H. (2000), 'Science and technology indicators announced by NISTEP', *STA Today*, 12(6), June.

Toshio, T. (1997), 'Japanese internet development since 1995', paper presented at the 10th Biennial Conference of the Japanese Studies Association of Australia, Melbourne, 6–10 July.

Tsugawa, A. and Satoko Kanomi (1996), *Hiraku: Nihon no josei kagakusha no kiseki*, Domesu Shuppan, Tokyo.

11 Japanese 'Education Reform'
The plan for the twenty-first century

Shoko Yoneyama

Introduction

At the end of the twentieth century, a crisis-ridden Japan faced up to the imperative of administrative, bureaucratic, political party, economic, constitutional and educational reforms. However, as the twenty-first century gets under way, educational reform is being given an unexpected priority.

In March 2000, Prime Minister Obuchi stated that education reform was a 'top-priority agenda' of his cabinet, and in order to advise him on the matter, established the National Commission on Education Reform (*Kyôiku kaikaku kokumin kaigi*, March–December 2000).[1] His successor Prime Minister Mori also referred to education reform as top-priority and stated that the ordinary session of the Diet in 2001 would be the 'Education Reform Diet'.[2] Indeed, based on the Final Report of the Commission, the Ministry of Education, Culture, Sports, Science and Technology (MEXT), prepared the Education Reform Plan for the twenty-first century, hereafter the Reform Plan 2001,[3] and announced that it would present six bills to the Diet with the view to implement the reform. The year 2001 was declared 'The First Year for Education Reform Initiative' (*Kyôiku shinsê gannen*) by the MEXT Minister, Machimura Nobutaka.

In this chapter, I will examine the significance of Reform Plan 2001 through an analysis of deliberations of the National Commission, which functioned as the vehicle to bring education reform back to the centre stage of political agenda, about thirteen years after the dissolution of the former Ad Hoc Council on Education (1984–7). I will also look at the Reform Plan 2001 against the background of education reform in Japan. I will argue that while reforms are being introduced within the framework of a national debate that follows closely an established conservative *discourse* of education reform (Schoppa, 1999; McVeigh, 2000: 76–92), in *practice*, reforms will bring major changes to education, equivalent in their overall effect to restructuring (*risutora*) in other sectors. In the process, I will clarify the relationship between what is and what is not new in the Reform Plan 2001.

The National Commission on Education Reform

The National Commission on Education Reform was established initially for Prime Minister Obuchi and consisted of twenty-six members headed by physics Nobel Prize winner Esaki Reona. It held nine general meetings and several subcommittee meetings, before producing its Interim Report in September 2000. Subsequently, consultative meetings with selected citizens were held in Fukuoka, Osaka, Tokyo and Niigata, followed by four meetings of the drafting committee. The Final Report was submitted to Prime Minister Mori on 22 December 2000.[4]

The deliberations of the National Commission were prompted, at least on the surface, by concerns of first, a sense of crisis in education and society at large and second, a perceived need for reforms to meet requirements of the new century. The preamble of the Final Report reads:

> The devastated state of education at the beginning of the twenty-first century should not be overlooked. As indicated by bullying, school non-attendance, the collapse of classroom order, the frequent occurrence of atrocious crimes committed by the young, the current state of education is grave. We are faced with the crisis that society will cease to function if these situations are left as they are ... .
>
> In the twenty-first century, the scientific technology, such as IT and biological science, will be advanced with an unprecedented speed; people in the world will be linked directly; information will be shared in seconds; and economic globalisation will be developed ... . The existing educational system has been left behind by such trends.

The current education reform was initiated in the same way as education reforms in the past. Speaking of earlier reforms, Schoppa (1991: 22), stated that, 'On the surface, the debate over education in Japan since 1967 has been about immediate concerns: the university protest of the late 1960s, the school violence of the 1980s and the growing need for a 'flexible' education system to meet the needs of the twenty-first century'.

Behind the seemingly current concerns of education reform lie long-established agendas of postwar education reform. One is the agenda of the Liberal Democratic Party (LDP) and its sympathisers of promoting nationalistic education. Businesses, on the other hand, seek to 'liberalise' and 'diversify' education, with the aim to produce individuals equipped with 'creativity', so that they can take the lead in cutting-edge science and technology. Schoppa (1991) argued that as a result of these divergent goals, the conservative camp was 'divided' and that this led to the immobility of education reform in Japan. These same divergent goals also characterised the deliberations of the National Commission and contributed to tension between members with different interests and orientations.

However, unlike earlier reforms efforts, Reform Plan 2001 appears to have 'resolved' the competing orientations, by undermining the very foundation on which postwar education in Japan has stood: the principle of equality of opportunity.[5] It appears that all sorts of preparations to bring about the stratification of education system are under way, with the view to separate elite and non-elite students early in their academic career and to stream them separately with differentiated education. In order to institutionalise this idea, the whole structure and the nature of Japanese education confronts major changes. This constitutes the third agenda of Reform Plan 2001.

Agenda 1: Promotion of nationalistic education

Proposals

Despite the fact that problems such as bullying, non-attendance, classroom discipline and juvenile crimes provided the grounds for initiating education reform, these were hardly discussed in the deliberations of the Commission. Instead, concern over the 'educational problems' was used to justify the promotion of nationalistic education, as had often been the case earlier. Thus the Final Report observed, in its preamble, that the current crisis stemmed from selfishness and lack of morals on the part of children and adults:

> The Japanese have enjoyed a long-term peace and materialistic prosperity which are rare in the world. On the other hand, the way education should be (*kyôiku no arikata*) is in question. Children are weak and unable to control their desires. Adults, who are to raise children, do not have their feet on the ground to reflect upon their lives, have fallen into selfish values and simplistic self-righteousness, and sometime are unable to distinguish fiction from reality.

As a 'remedy' to this 'moral collapse', the panel proposed to discuss how to prepare the youth 'into becoming open and warm-hearted Japanese'.[6] This task was delegated to the First Subcommittee, the 'Humanity' (*ningensei*) Subcommittee, the most influential and hawkish of the three subcommittees. Its members were also the oldest: six of the ten members were over 65 years of age, which meant that 60 per cent of the Commission members in this age group were members of the First Subcommittee. The subcommittee made three key proposals to achieve the objectives of Reform Plan 2001.

1   'For everybody to be engaged in community services', including:

- promotion of community service at school and in community: two weeks for primary and junior secondary school students and one month for senior secondary school students.
- creation of social structures which enable youth over 18 years of age to be engaged in community service for a certain period of time.

2   'For schools not to hesitate to teach morals', including:

- establishment of new subjects, that is, 'morals' in primary, 'subject on humanbeings' (*ningen-ka*) in junior secondary, and 'subject on human life' (*jinsei-ka*) in senior secondary schools.

3   'To review and modify the Fundamental Law of Education to make it suitable for the new century'.

These proposals were in line with LDP's pursuit of 'restoring national values', regularly affirmed throughout the postwar era. In fact, most of the LDP's postwar agenda for education was endorsed in the Final Report of the National Commission. Moreover, the proposals made by the Commission are likely to enhance the nationalistic aspect of Japanese education to a level above that of previous decades. For instance, in the case of moral education, the LDP has always emphasised the inculcation of strict Japanese values through 'moral education' (*dôtoku kyôiku*) (Schoppa, 1991: 54–60). The present proposals stipulate that new subjects be established to implement moral education not only in primary schools, but also in junior *and* senior high schools, even beyond the compulsory education. Satô (2001: 109), Professor at the Graduate School of Education, Tokyo University, pointed out that to establish moral education as a new subject would mean that, (1) its content would have to be prescribed in a national curriculum, (2) new officially approved moral education textbooks would have to be produced, (3) new teaching qualifications for this specific subject would have to be established, and (4) students would have to be numerically assessed. This, Satô regarded as nothing but the revival of the '*shûshin*' (moral training) of prewar Japan.

Another major education agenda of the LDP in postwar era has been the 'cleansing' of Japanese education to free it of the dross 'introduced by the

196 *Shoko Yoneyama*

Occupation' by revising the 1947 Fundamental Law of Education (Schoppa, 1991: 54–60). Reflecting this, some members of the Commission blamed the 1947 Fundamental Law of Education as the cause of current problems and advocated its revision. Katsuta Kichirô, the Vice-Chancellor of Suzuka International University and the winner of Sankei Shinbun's 'Great *Seiron* Prize' for the year 2000,[7] urged the revision of the Fundamental Law in the first general meeting. He supported Kajita Eiichi, the Vice-Chancellor of Notre Dame Women's College of Kyoto, who insisted at the third general meeting that the Fundamental Law was imposed on Japan by the American Occupation authorities. He claimed that changes brought about by the General Headquarter (GHQ) (including, in his view, the Fundamental Law) can be summarised as the shift from 'militarism to pacifism', from 'totalitarianism to individualism', 'Japanism (*nihon-shugi*) to internationalism', and 'state shintôism to a secular society'. 'After 50 years,' he concluded, these transformations had 'caused outrageous problems'.

The proposal for community service, however, was an entirely new development and did not derive from the menu of traditional conservatives. It is necessary, therefore, to enquire about its rationale and inclusion in the agenda of the National Commission. This proposal was introduced by Sono Ayako, a well-known novelist and Director of The Nippon Foundation (*Nippon zaidan*), formerly known as The Sasakawa Foundation.[8] In her introductory statement at the first general meeting, Sono stated that young Japanese today were like 'little rich kids' (*ojôchama*' and '*obocchama*). She continued:

> About two out of six billion people in the world live without electricity. For those with no electricity, there is no democracy. Democracy exists only where there is electricity … . I am going to propose in this Commission to create a system in which all Japanese of 18 years of age are to be engaged with community service for one year. Even those with physical handicap will have a lot to do … . I believe that the problem of the care of the aged will be almost solved with this system.

Clearly, the notion of community service was born as a means of training (or disciplining) young Japanese who, according to Sono, had become spoilt by prosperity and democracy. Her views on nationalism and education are clear from her '*Seiron*' column in the *Sankei* newspaper, where she wrote:

> The Great East Asia War deprived 3 million Japanese of their lives. But the post-war education resulted in the killing of 100 million people through abortion … . I recently came to understand that nationalism is

not a creed that one can choose. It is that which enables us to 'eat' and 'live a basic/fundamental life'.

(Sono, 2000)

Sono played a pivotal role in the National Commission, not only because her nationalistic ideas were well received by members of the First Subcommittee who tended to be more influential than others but also because she was engaged in drafting documents for the Commission. Sono was solely in charge of drafting a 'communiqué' entitled 'To the Japanese People' (*Nihonjin-e*), which was written on the basis of discussions held in the First Subcommittee. It appears that this moralistic and condemnatory document functioned as the concept paper behind the recommendations made by the Commission. Sono also served in the drafting committee of the Final Report of the Commission.[9]

The proposal of the National Commission to introduce (compulsory) community service in official school curriculum was enthusiastically welcomed by Nishio Kanji, Professor at the University of Electro-Communications and the founder of Japanese Society for History Textbook Reform (*Tsukuru-kai*). In October 2000, almost immediately after the release of the Interim Report of the National Commission, he published a book titled, '*Community Service' for All Over 18 Years of Age: Emergency Report of the 'Commission to Revise the Fundamental Law of Education*', which began by quoting the entire text of Sono's 'To the Japanese people'. Nishio (2000: 4) praised it for its 'elegant prose' and bold proposals, calling it 'epoch-making' in the history of all the commissions on education in postwar era.

Mori factor

Behind the 'successful' completion of the old nationalistic agendas of postwar education and the introduction of the new agenda, was the presence of Mori, a central figure in the education *zoku* of the LDP and Prime Minister at the start of the second meeting of the Commission. In contrast with Obuchi, who never clarified his position regarding the revision of the Fundamental Law of Education (Sakurai, 2001: 115–19),[10] for Mori, education reform meant the accomplishment of the pursuit of the nationalistic agenda of postwar education: the augmentation of 'moral education' and the 'cleansing' from Japanese education of influences from the 1947 Fundamental Law. This was clear from his first two speeches at the general meeting.

It is likely that Prime Minister Mori, famous for his 15 May 2000 speech declaring Japan to be 'a land of the gods centred on the emperor', pulled his weight during the deliberations of the National Commission in order to achieve his nationalistic goals. Some incidents, which occurred during the deliberations of the Commission, suggest that there might have been considerable behind-the-scene political manoeuvring by Mori.

First, the membership of the drafting committee was changed at the last minute. Originally, Esaki appointed five members, only one of whom was from the First Subcommittee. Before the deliberations on the Fundamental Law were held in the seventh general meeting, however, he announced that Sono Ayako and Kajita Eiichi were to be added to the drafting committee. It was also decided that drafting of the Interim Report would be done by the committee members alone, without the officials of the Education Ministry (Kawakami, 2000: 203). The Education Ministry was clearly against the idea of revision, and had long been of that view (Schoppa, 1991: 98–9). At the seventh general meeting, Secretary-General Kondô negated all the claims Kajita Eiichi had made about the Law, insisting that its preamble on 'the creation of universal and individual culture' included enrichment of Japanese culture (and thus implying that there was no need to change the Law in order to appreciate Japanese history and culture). He also stressed that the Law was not a product of the Occupation but of Japanese government. This point turned out to be most contentious of all in the Commission's deliberations.

Second, twice during the 10-month deliberation of the Commission, the Minister of Education was replaced. Each of these appointments amounted in some sense to a high-level intervention in the process. When the Commission was established, Nakasone Hirofumi was in office. At the fifth general meeting in August, however, Nakasone was replaced by Ohshima Tadamori of the former Kômoto faction, who in turn was replaced in December by Machimura Nobutaka, who was close to Prime Minister Mori. Machimura (*Mainichi Interactive*, 6 December 2000) expressed the opinion that it is a matter of course that there was no education that did not force children to do things, and that the community service, proposed by the panel, would naturally be required of all students.

It is also possible that the representative observer from the New Komeito was changed from Ohta Akihiro to Yamashita Eiichi for political reasons, in the context of the reshuffle of the Mori government in July. Ohta was at the time chair of Constitution Research Council (House of Representatives). Kanzaki Takenori, leader of New Komeito, said on 15 June 2000 (*Mainichi Interactive*) that the Fundamental Law was closely tied to the Constitution and should therefore be discussed with reference to the result of studies conducted in the Constitution Research Council. Ohta's successor Yamashita is said to have been 'asked to cooperate' by Prime Minister Mori on 17 July at the Prime Minister's Residence.[11]

The difference between the Interim Report and the Final Report also points to the likelihood of some behind-the-scenes political manoeuvring. In the Final Report, the section on the Fundamental Law was expanded considerably so that revision was presented as a core recommendation. Second, the position of the Commission shifted from 'neutral' to 'having approved change'. The crucial text dealing with revision of the Fundamental Law was revised as follows:

> Interim Report: The National Commission on Education Reform has deliberated on the Fundamental Law of Education as part of the examination of education in this country, from the viewpoint that it does not presuppose that the revision of the law is necessary, nor does it see it necessary to regard it as 'taboo' to mention it .... The future of the Fundamental Law of Education ... needs to be discussed by the people from a wide perspective, and without limiting the discussion only within the Commission on the Education Reform. We hope that the Interim Report will initiate such discussion in various fields.
>
> Final Report: It is necessary for the government to grapple with the revision of the Fundamental Law of Education. Needless to say, the discussion on the revision must not be based on nationalistic or totalitarian views.

It should be noted, however, that advocates of nationalistic education were not completely successful in securing commitment to the revision of the Law in a way that they wanted. In the end, the revision of the Law was left for further discussion in the Central Educational Council, under the jurisdiction of MEXT, instead of being submitted to the 2001 Diet. The proviso included in the Final Report, which cautioned against the move towards nationalistic education, also suggests resistance to the nationalistic agenda. The development of this issue will depend on a number of factors, including (1) the general trend towards reactionary nationalism of Japan as reflected in the moves towards revision of the Constitution, (2) the view adopted by business circles on this issue, (3) the position taken by MEXT, (4) the role of New Komeito in the party politics, and finally, (5) how the citizens of Japan respond to the ongoing reactionary agenda in general.

In terms of resurgent nationalism in Japan, it should be noted that three important aspects of the nationalistic reform agendas have already been accomplished. The *Hinomaru* and *Kimigayo* were adopted by a special law in 1999 as the national flag and anthem, respectively. Furthermore, the textbook censorship issue had reached an end, at least domestically and in legal terms, with the conclusion of Ienaga case in 1997. In 1996, The Japanese Society for History Textbook Reform was formed, and its textbook was officially approved by the MEXT in 2001 despite strong official protests from South Korea and China. Nikkyôso (Japan Teachers' Union), on the other hand, had made peace with the Education Ministry in 1995 and had ceased to be a real threat to the Ministry or the government.

Agenda 2: Stratification of education

Watanabe Osamu, Professor at Hitotsubashi University, pointed out that the economic globalisation had created new demands for Japan to become a conventional superpower in order to ensure the security and privilege of its capital especially in Asia. He (2001: 16–17) argued that at the time the new 'Defense Guideline' Law was passed in 1999, Japan had reached a new stage as a superpower, possessing independent military force. According to Watanabe, this had added to pressures to revise the Constitution, which in turn stirred the calls for nationalism to be nurtured through education.

In Watanabe's view, however, augmenting nationalistic education was just one aspect of Reform Plan 2001. What was outlined there was a new model of education, in which education had become stratified or rather, divided into two separate streams: one, enhancing academic aspect for the elite to maximise their creativity and individuality and another, emphasising moral and behavioural conformity for the non-elite.

Education for the elite – fostering creativity and individuality

Japanese business and industry have always been concerned about how to change education to serve their employment needs. The second concern expressed at the start of the National Commission, that education had failed to cater for the needs of the twenty-first century, reflected primarily the interest of such circles. More specifically, lack of 'creativity' was raised as one of the most pressing issues of the existing educational system. The word 'creativity' was repeated as many as seven times in the very short introductory speech by the Chair of the Commission, Esaki Reona. Subsequently, a 'Creativity' (*sôzôsei*) Subcommittee was formed in the Commission.

Business leaders were well represented in this subcommittee, including Ushio Jirô, Chief Secretary of the Japanese Committee for Economic Development (*Keizai dôyûkai*) between 1995 and 1999, Kôno Shunji, Chair of the Extraordinary Education Committee of the Japanese Federation of Employers' Association (*Nikkeiren*), and Hamada Hiroshi, Chair of the Personnel Education Committee of the Federation of Economic Organisations (*Keidanren*). All these business circles had presented proposals on education reform throughout the postwar period, but especially since the mid-1990s.

Japanese 'Education Reform' 201

As was the case with the nationalistic agenda, reforms proposed by business leaders in the Commission tended to combine long-standing and relatively new ideas. Since the late 1960s, business (the *zaikai*) has consistently called for (1) reduction of the uniformity of Japanese education (or liberalisation/ diversification), (2) education for disciplined workers, and (3) maximum privatisation of education (Schoppa, 1991: 120–35). The following proposals made by the Commission were largely in line with what business circles had proposed for over three decades.

1 Change the uniformism (*ichiritsu-shugi*) of education and introduce an education system which would foster individuality.
2 Enhance the educational and research functions of universities in order to train leaders.
3 Promote education to foster vocational perspective.

In order to understand what actually was meant by these proposals, it is necessary to clarify the specific meaning of terms used in the discourse on education reform. For instance, 'changing the uniformism' or 'liberalising' education is commonly construed in the discourse of education reform as deregulation, as part of the design to continue the current education system rather than to create a 'spiritually freer form of schooling'. Likewise, the term 'diversification' is commonly construed in the limited and specific sense of a multi-tracking system designed to 'segregate students into various academic streams (rather than the current single-track system in which students study the same curriculum)' (see McVeigh, 2000: 87). In the same vein, the Commission adopted a peculiar interpretation of the word 'creativity' as something to be pursued for the elite rather than for all children.

Saitô Takao, a freelance journalist who has interviewed key figures in education reform, points out that underlying the notion of 'education for creativity and individuality' lies a social Darwinist or eugenicist view of human beings. Saitô (2001) quoted Esaki Reona as saying:

> No matter how hard untalented students try, it's completely pointless. In the future, children will undergo gene tests when they are enrolled in elementary school. They will be educated accordingly to their genetic aptitude.[12]

According to Saitô, this is what Esaki meant by 'education which recognises the difference among individual students'. Esaki's views are also presented in a chapter he contributed to the book edited by Nishio (2000: 218–28).

Underlying the rhetorical use of language such as liberalisation, diversification, individuality and creativity is the agenda of elite education, or more broadly, the streaming of education (and labour) for the elite and non-elite. Stratification of education, with a view to maximising creativity and individuality for the elite, while maximising disciplinary training for the non-elite, is the new direction adopted in Reform Plan 2001 (Yotoriyama, 2001: 13). This explains why deliberations in the 'Creativity' Subcommittee focused on ways to help elite students advance their academic career as quickly and efficiently as possible. Under the proposal to 'change the uniformism of education and introduce an education system which fosters individuality' were the following: (1) to promote 6-year secondary schools (*chûkô ikkan*), a common form of elite private school; (2) to promote achievement-based learning and implement a national academic achievement test; and (3) to abolish the minimum age requirement for admission to universities (to allow bright students to skip grades and enter university before reaching 18 years of age). Various current proposals for university reform are in line with this aim of producing leaders.

Education for the non-elite – for cheap and obedient labour

The other side of the same coin was the notion that minimum academic and maximum moral and behavioural training be forced upon the non-elite. Mechanisms to sort students out into different tracks of academic and vocational career are already underway. Based on the notion of 'liberal, flexible and comfortable education'(*yutori no kyôiku*), the new Course of Study, a controversial national curriculum, is to be implemented from 2002, with the aim of achieving basic scholastic proficiency in 'easy to understand classes'.[13] Its contents have been reduced by about one-third from the previous curriculum and have been widely criticised as being 'anti-academic' (Ohmori, 2000: 14–17). For instance, in English for junior high schools, the number of essential words to be learned is reduced from the current 507 to 100, and such basic words as 'always', 'ask' and 'arrive' are excluded. In the National Commission, remarks by Fujita Hidenori, Professor at the Graduate School of Education, Tokyo University, that curriculum reduction was against the general trend of advanced industrialised countries was ignored. While in theory the new curriculum had both positive and negative aspects,[14] discarding the non-elite was the underlying agenda of those who drafted it. Miura Shumon,[15] former chairman of the Curriculum Council, the advisory body to the Education Ministry which drew up the blueprint of the 'liberal, flexible and comfortable education', said:

> I expected there would be a decline in scholarship. In fact, there will be no future for Japan if the average marks do not drop way down. Let dull students remain dull. We have exhausted our energies ever since

the war in striving to maintain and raise their academic standards. Now we have to focus our energies to develop the abilities of the gifted. One in every 100 students would be enough. They are going to be our country's future leaders. All we can do for the absolute no-hopers is to have them brought up to be simple and sincere.[16]

While the basic curriculum has been truncated to a bare minimum, the National Commission also proposed that education be designed to strengthen the commitment to one's vocation and work ethic. Underlying this was the notion that young people lacked these qualities and thus had weak foundations to lead a 'steady and sincere life'. It was suggested in the deliberations of the Creativity Subcommittee that lack of work ethic had contributed to numerous technical troubles in industry triggered by minor errors.

According to Satô (2001: 113), the Subcommittee failed to grasp the nature of the problem of youth. He argued that the problem was not youth's attitude to work but the lack of job opportunities caused by globalisation of the economy and the collapse of the labour market for the young in post-industrial Japan. He remarked that the number of job offers for graduates of senior high schools declined from 1.64 million in 1993 to 0.37 million in 1999, that is, by approximately 80 per cent in seven years. He concluded that what the youth required was not lectures on work ethic but opportunities to work and study.

Saitô (2001) explained that it was precisely the perceived change in the employment needs of corporations that had worked as the driving force towards the 'class-isation' of education. He quoted the 1995 speech given by Sakurai Osamu, who was then head of the Education Committee of the Japanese Committee for Economic Development (*Keizai dôyûkai*):

> What is the structure which allows large corporations to survive? The ability of the top is of course important, but corporations need brilliant executives, equivalent to the General Staff Office (*sanbôhonbu*). Only a few who have studied thoroughly will be needed for this cluster .... This is followed by professional managers and a mass of specialists, who are recruited when needed, at the rate requested by each. The custom of recruiting freshmen will become obsolete. The rest are robots and peripheral labour force. Due to a large gap in wages, though regrettable, we will be naturally using the cheap labour in South East Asia.[17]

The Japanese Federation of Employers' Associations (*Nikkeiren*) produced a report, 'Japanese Management in the New Age', at about the same time as this speech. Like the address by Sakurai, it called for the reduction of personnel costs as well as the introduction of an 'employment portfolio' to encourage the mobility of labour. The report has been used widely since then as a manual for corporate restructuring to survive in the economic recession of the post-bubble era. In fact, it was not only education for future employees that is to be rationalised. Reform Plan 2001 contained policies that would lead to a major restructuring of school as well.

Agenda 3: Restructuring schools

According to Terawaki Ken (Wada and Terawaki, 2000: 54–5), a senior official of MEXT:

> The new Course of Study is bound to fail if it is introduced without changing the school system and the teacher evaluation system. The Education Ministry envisages school reform, teacher reform and the curriculum reform as a set.

Although this statement was relatively low-key, there is no doubt that restructuring of school holds the key to implementing the educational reforms discussed above. Based on the Final Report of the National Commission, the Reform Plan 2001 included the following objectives.

1. To make restrictions on school zones more flexible.
2. To establish a new system of rewarding and assessing teachers.
3. To introduce the conceptions of organisational management to schools and board of education.

These policies, together with other related items, suggested that Reform Plan 2001 will launch major school restructuring in three main respects: (1) fostering privatisation of education by introducing market forces even to elementary education, (2) strengthening the linkage between school and industry at all levels and thus fostering corporatisation of public schools, and (3) implementing mechanisms to expel students and teachers who were seen as 'unfit'.

Rationalising public schools and promoting private schools

There is no question that Reform Plan 2001 is designed to expose public schools to the principle of free market competition. Wada Terawaki (2000: 54–64) emphasised that the new national curriculum indicated only the 'minimum requirement' of teaching and learning, and therefore that good teachers would naturally teach much more than what was contained in the new Course of Study and that this would distinguish good teachers from bad teachers. If one is to ensure the maximisation of the 'creativity' of elite students under this scheme, the school zone will also have to be 'freed up', so that parents and children can choose schools with the best academic reputation; or to put it differently, avoid being 'stuck' with 'bad' teachers, who might deprive children of educational opportunities by teaching only what was prescribed in the national curriculum.

School zoning was abandoned in 1999 in Shinagawa Ward, Tokyo, at the primary school level. Due to the declining number of children, it had become common that there was only one class per grade. Many parents who were concerned that small schools might be closed in near future chose large schools when the school zoning restriction was lifted. As a result, enrolments in small schools declined substantially and residents in the vicinity of small schools thus faced the threat of losing their neighbourhood school. The 'freeing up' of the school zone can be expected to lead to the rationalisation of public schools.[18]

It has been pointed out that this process is driven by the demand of the business sector (Watanabe, 2001: 16). The Japanese Committee for Economic Development (*Keizai dôyûkai*) in 1995 proposed the 'slimming down' of public education by introducing competition. This proposal was consistent with the long-standing 'fiscal conservatism' of the business community with regard to public education as well as its preference for the privatisation of education (Schoppa, 1991: 128).

It is not surprising then that the Second Subcommittee of the National Commission, which addressed the questions of 'School Education' was well represented by the private school sector. The Head and Deputy-Head of the Subcommittee were both from top-notch private schools: Keio Yochisha Elementary School and Shibuya Kyoiku Gakuen. In the Reform Plan 2001, private schools were positioned to become the main provider of elite education. This was apparent from the contradiction between (1) minimum national curriculum and heightened behavioural control in public schools, on the one hand, and (2) emphasis on creativity and individuality, on the other. The promotion of the 6-year secondary school system as well as the deregulation and the introduction of competition to public education suggest the same.

Thus the 'School Education' Subcommittee, which was supposed to be responsible for discussing such pressing issues as bullying and school non-attendance focused its deliberations, instead, on school evaluation and teacher evaluation. During its deliberations, Zeniya Masami, a senior official of the Education Ministry, who was not supposed to participate in the discussion at all, had to intervene to request the Subcommittee to deliberate 'more' on student-related issues such as bullying and school non-attendance. Even for this Ministry official, it seems to have been plain that the deliberations of the National Commission were far removed from the everyday-life concerns of students, teachers, parents and educational administrators.

Teacher evaluation and Japan School, Inc.

The second wedge driven into the school system to induce major restructuring is a new form of teacher evaluation. More specifically, the reform plan stipulates that excellent teachers should be commended and awarded with appropriate salary increments, whereas teachers who were 'not suitable to teach' be either dismissed or transferred to other vocations without their consent. If this were to be applied to teachers who harmed students with physical violence or sexual abuse, it would be a welcome change for students and parents. The full implication of the plan, however, must be understood within the broader trend towards corporatisation of public schools in the name of 'opening up' schools to the community.

The third reform mentioned above – the introduction of 'conceptions of organisational management to schools and boards of education' – seems designed to allow corporate managers to have increasing discretionary power over staffing matters in public schools, as well as to be directly involved in their administration.

For example, the School Education Law was changed in 2000 to make it possible for local governments to appoint a principal who did not hold a teaching qualification. Consequently, the Board of Education of Tokyo Metropolitan Government appointed two principals from the list of recommendations made by the Tokyo Chamber of Commerce and Industry (*Tôshô*): one a former Quality Control Manager from Nissan Motors, and the other a former director of a subsidiary company of Hitachi. The Board had also adopted the policy since 1997 of employing personnel section chiefs recommended by *Tôshô* to conduct new teacher recruitment interviews (Saitô, 2000: 35). This was not only the practice in Tokyo but, in March 2001, the Hiroshima Board of Education appointed three managers of Mazda Motors as principals of a primary, a junior and a senior secondary school. In Saitama, a former bank manager was appointed principal of a senior high school, and Osaka is set to follow these examples (*Mainichi Interactive*, 9 March 2001). Furthermore, it is important to note in this context that the Reform Plan 2001 was designed to increase the power of principals in a number of ways, especially his power to appoint staff members.

It is possible that public schools will become a new ground for '*amakudari*' of former company managers after being made redundant in the course of corporate restructuring. Ueshima Kazuyasu, President of Japan Junior Chamber Inc. (*Seinen kaigisho*), stated in the 'School Education' Subcommittee that: 'It is necessary to upgrade the power of a principal. If he had discretion on personnel and budget matters, he would be able to bring his own staff to school'. Two trends may be discerned regarding the matter of personnel. One is the enhancement of executives, that is, increase in the number of deputy principals. The other is the casualisation of teaching staff. The overall effect of such measures is to match the current recruitment strategy of corporations discussed earlier. Satô (2001: 111) takes the view that the ostensibly desirable plan to 'teach some classes in small groups of 20 students' is in fact a move in the direction of casualisation of teaching, as an alternative to the maintenance of costly full-time positions. He further points out that MEXT had promised to accept three victims of corporate restructuring from the private sector into every primary and junior secondary school in Japan.

Under the current reform plan, it seems likely that both teachers and students will be saturated with corporate values and culture in the public school environment. Apart from the foreseeable influence of ex-manager principals and their (possibly) private executives, the reform plan dictates that teachers should take long-term working experience at companies. This is not a new practice. In 1999 alone, 540 teachers from 40 local boards of education participated in training at 67 companies. What is different this time is that the training will be for a much longer term, and that it will involve many more teachers. Furthermore, according to Saitô (2000: 34), the Federation of Economic Organisations (*Keidanren*) has a plan to dispatch 'lecturers' to primary and secondary schools to teach 'Integrated Study' which is to begin as part of the new Course of Study in 2002.

The corporatisation of school does not simply mean that school will be used as the receptacle of surplus labour from the business sector. It seems also designed to instil the corporate way of thinking and behaving in the minds of children in the era of globalisation. The middle-class myth which had bound the masses to corporate values has collapsed. Neither academic credentials nor employment in a 'good' company can secure one's job in the post-bubble, post-industrial, globalised economy. It is possible that the business sector is trying to establish a new way of maintaining legitimacy, that is by teaching its values directly to students in public schools. In that sense, the hidden functions of school as envisaged both by the LDP and by the business sector have now come unprecedentedly close. If Reform Plan 2001 is implemented, public schools are likely to become grounds for ideological and behavioural training.

Conclusion

Education for nation building

Since the Meiji period, discourse on education reform has swung between 'traditionalists' and 'modernists' (Marshall, 1994: 51–62, 106–17). The opposition between traditionalist, state-oriented, discipline-centred formulas and 'liberal', internationalist, and individual-centred approaches has persisted throughout the modern history of education reform. Irrespective of differences, however, both parties have shared the same assumption, that education is for nation building. What has served as the underlying principle of Japanese education since the Meiji period is the notion that education is able to foster industrialisation and economic growth (Schoppa, 1991: 25), as well as to maintain the nation state amid changing domestic and global environment (McVeigh, 2000). What has always been excluded from mainstream discourse of education reform is the notion of children as active participants as well as the notion that their 'learning' might be the main agenda of education. This long-established 'custom' was followed in the deliberation in the Commission.

It appears that different elements from within the conservative camp have found a formula in Reform Plan 2001 which will – if the legislation passes the national Diet – undermine the most fundamental principle on which postwar education system has stood: equality of educational opportunity. The abandonment of this principle will lead to major changes in the education system in Japan. First, it will mean the division of education for the elite and non-elite, where academic training is maximised for the elite and disciplinary 'ethical' training for the non-elite. Second, schools in Japan will go through a major restructuring (*risutora*), which will change the way students, teachers, and parents relate to school. While on the one hand schools will be exposed to 'market forces' allowing greater flexibility for students and parents in selecting schools, various mechanisms will be introduced to allow the rejection and exclusion of students and teachers seen 'unfit'. It also seems likely to introduce aspects of business management into the schools. Public schools in Japan will be saturated with ideological and behavioural objectives: the promotion of nationalism and corporatism.

The missing agenda: children and learning

The group of people whose voices were least represented and almost completely ignored in the deliberations of the National Commission are children. To only a slightly lesser extent, this may also be said of teachers. Instead, these are the groups to which the Commission recommended fresh measures for control and discipline, by suspension or expulsion of 'problem students' and dismissal or transfer of 'problem teachers'.

Children (and perhaps teachers as well) are seen primarily as problems to be suppressed and controlled by force (Kadowaki and Mizushima, 2001: 101–2). Ironically, this idea was most directly expressed by Kawakami Ryôichi, the only teacher representative in the National Commission, who said that in order for school to be effective in managing students it had to be equipped with 'weapons' (*buki*), by which he meant measures to prevent 'problem children' from attending school. His choice of a military metaphor was characteristic of the educational thinking in the Commission.

When such concepts as human rights or needs of children, and their right to learn, become the central concern of education reform, totally different issues tend to be raised. For instance, the confidential teacher's report on each student (*naishinsho*) as well as the point evaluation system (*kantenbetsu hyôka*) might have to be discontinued in order to liberate junior high school students from comprehensive teacher control, and to enable them to focus more clearly on learning (Satô, 2000). Such issues as 'corporal punishment', and the physical, sexual and verbal abuse of children by teachers would have to be stopped completely. The meaning of school rules and regulations would need to be questioned seriously. It seems beyond question that the *naishinsho, kantenbetsu hyôka*, corporal punishment and verbal abuse are all incompatible with the human rights of children. Japan signed the UN Convention on the Rights of the Child in 1990. Yet none of these issues seems to have been raised in the Commission.

More fundamentally, true educational reform will most likely require change in the way teachers and students relate with each other. This will involve not only breaking the 'vertical', authoritarian and bureaucratic relationship between teachers and students, but also making organisation of knowledge less hierarchical, more learner-centred, and more interactive and cooperative (Yoneyama, 1999: 61–118, 133–54). Theoretically speaking, the planned 'Integrated Study' (*sôgôgakushû*) programme, designed to encourage hands-on and problem-solving learning, is designed to bring about such a new dimension. How successful this can be, however, will depend on how liberated the teacher–student relationship is in each class. The promotion of free thinking through a student-centred curriculum seems inherently contradictory to the 'straight jacket' structure enforced through textbook censorship, imposition of *Hinomaru* and *Kimigayo* at school ceremonies, and the ideological and behavioural control over students and teachers which seems to be foreshadowed in the Reform Plan 2001.

Ultimately, to achieve a student-centred education, it might be necessary to bring about a paradigmatic change, where the word 'education' would be replaced with 'learning' and the subjectivity of the student placed at the centre of the schooling process. This may sound radical, but the steady 'desertion' of Japanese schools by students in recent days suggests an alternative paradigm might be the only solution to many of the 'problems' related to the youth and to schools (Yamada, 2000: 24–9). Meanwhile, while not addressing any of the specific issues listed above (let alone fundamental issues), Reform Plan 2001 is unlikely to constitute an antidote to contemporary youth-related 'problems' such as bullying, school non-attendance and juvenile crimes. On the contrary, the enhancement of 'moral education', the augmented power of the school to suspend 'trouble makers', and the negative notion of children/youth embedded in the notion of 'social service', are likely to make schools even more alienating and suffocating, and to worsen the current situation.

The need for further assessment

This chapter analysed the hidden agendas of the Education Reform Plan for the twenty-first century by exploring the thinking of those involved with its making. How successful the Plan can be will depend on a number of factors, which it is too premature to assess at this stage. In order to assess the full implication of the Plan, it will be necessary to pay attention to the following. (1) the analysis of other 'push' factors such as the impact of Ishihara Shintaro's administration in the Tokyo Metropolitan Government and his possible shift into national politics; (2) the analysis of the 'pull' factor, or resistance to the Plan, including the response of Nikkyôso, the media, opposition parties, as well as citizens, especially those who are involved with alternative education movement (Yoneyama, 1999: 186–250); (3) the leadership factor, that is, the impact of the new Prime Minister Koizumi and the new Ministry for MEXT, Tôyama Atsuko; (4) the New Komeito factor, that is, how this ruling coalition party which has been cautious about the revision of the Fundamental Law of Education and the Constitution will respond to education reform in the power politics of the new coalition government; and most importantly, (5) the MEXT factor, that is, the factional politics within MEXT, the development in the Central Education Council, as well as the relationship between the MEXT and other major players of education reform, that is, politicians and business.

As Ohmori (2000: 12–18) pointed out, the discourse on education is highly rhetorical and thus can be read both as the 'scenario for hope' and 'scenario for danger'. With sufficient funding and strong leadership to promote genuinely community-based, student-centred education, it might be possible for public schools in Japan to become a place where creativity and individuality of students are nurtured. However, the future of Japanese education suggested by this study of the process of the Commission and its recommendations is bleak.

Acknowledgement

The author expresses her sincere thanks to Dr Katalin Ferber of Shizuoka University of Arts and Culture and Dr Hiroshi Noya of Hôsei University for their insight as well as for providing updated research materials.

Notes

1 The speech by Obuchi Keizo presented at the first general meeting of The National Commission on Education Reform on 27 March 2000.
2 The speech by Mori Yoshiro presented at the ninth general meeting of The National Commission of Education Reform on 22 September 2000.
3 '21 *seiki kyôiku shinsei puran*' available at http: //www.mext.go.jp/a_menu/ shougai/21plan (accessed on 30 April 2001).
4 All the documents and minutes of the National Commission referred to in this chapter can be found at http: //www.kantei.go.jp/jp/kyouiku (accessed on 13 December 2000 and 5 January 2001).
5 As Kariya Takehiko points out, equality of opportunity in Japanese education has not taken into consideration the inequality of opportunity stemming from the different socio-economic background of students, as seen in the lack of compensatory education. This caused significant inequality as described by Okano and Tsuchiya, and the inequality has been increasing in recent years as demonstrated by Kariya. However, the uniformity of education under the single-track system has ensured a certain level of equality of opportunity so far. This is about to be changed in the current education reform. For further details, see Kariya Takehiko, 'Confused Thinking about Equality of Education', *Japan Echo*, December 2000, pp. 8–13, as well as Kaori Okano and Motonori Tsuchiya, *Education in Contemporary Japan: Inequality and Diversity*, Cambridge, Cambridge University Press, 1999.
6 The Japanese version is '*Ningen-sei yutaka na nihonjin o ikusei suru*'. For the English translation, see 'The education reform plan for the 21st Century – The Rainbow Plan – The Seven Priority Strategies' available at http: //www. mext.go.jp/english/topics/21plan/01030.htm (accessed on 30 April 2001). It should be noted that the English version is far less detailed and less decisive than the Japanese version.
7 *Sankei shinbun* is the national newspaper with the fifth largest circulation in Japan and by far the most nationalistic of all the major newspapers in Japan.
8 Sasakawa Ryôichi, founder of the Foundation, was well-known as an ultra-nationalist and was held in Sugamo prison between 1945 and 1948 as an indicted 'A' class war criminal.
9 During the deliberations of the Commission, the ability to write and speak in 'beautiful Japanese' was rendered to be a big issue by the members of the First Subcommittee, who, apparently, tended to have very limited ability in English, in clear contrast with members of the Second and Third Subcommittees, who often had spent substantial time abroad. Sono's Japanese as professional writer was praised at various occasions by members of the First Subcommittee, which established legitimacy for her to be heavily involved with drafting and/or writing key reports. The power Sono held in the Commission was thus closely associated, among other factors, with the power politics developed concerning the 'elegance' of the national language.
10 See *Obuchi naikaku sôri daijin nentô kisha kaiken*, 1 January 2000. http: //www.kantei.go.jp/jp/souri/2000/2k0101kisha.html (accessed 5 January 2001).
11 New Komeito, 19 July 2000 update. http: //www.komei.or.jp/kensaku_files/ 2000/07/19/006.htm (accessed 5 January 2001).
12 Interview conducted by Saitô Takao in June 2000, quoted in Saitô (2001: 12). The English translation is quoted from the book review by Ogawa (2001).

13 'The Education Reform Plan for the twenty-first century'.
14 The positive aspect being that the 'integrated study' (*sôgôgakushû*) period to be used to promote hands-on and problem-solving learning. See Ohmori (2000: 12–18). It is also true that the national curriculum has been too condensed and taught too fast, with the result of producing many students who could not follow lessons.
15 Miura Shumon is also a well-known novelist and the husband of Sono Ayako.
16 Interview conducted by Saitô and quoted in Saitô (2001: 40–1). English translation follows Ogawa (2001), except for the last sentence. The original quote in Japanese is: '*Kagirinaku dekinai hisai, musai niwa, semete jicchoku-na seishin dake o yashinatte oite moraeba iin-desu*'.
17 Minutes of the training session (*kenshûkai*) for those in charge of student life guidance at private universities, held at Shigaku kaikan on 14 July 1995. Quoted in Saitô (2001: 26–7).
18 NHK ETV2001 'Kyôikuchô no chôsen 1: gakkô sentaku', Series *Nippon no shukudai: gakkô*, broadcast on 11 April 2001.

References

Kadowaki, A. and Mizushima H. (2001), 'Hansei subeki nanowa otana-tachi da', *Sekai*, April.
Kawakami, R. (2000), *Kyôiku kaikaku kokumin kaigi de nani ga ronji saretaka*, Sôshisha, Tokyo.
Mainichi Interactive (2000), http://www.mainichi.co.jp, 6 December.
Marshall, B. (1994), *Learning to be Modern: Japanese Political Discourse on Education*, Westview Press, Oxford, 1994.
McVeigh, B. (2000), 'Educational reform in Japan: fixing education or fostering economic nation-statism', in Eades, J. S., Gill T. and Befu H. (eds), *Globalization and Social Change in Contemporary Japan*, Trans Pacific Press, Melbourne.
Nishio, K. (ed.) (2000), *Subete no 18-sai ni 'hôshigimu' o*, Sôgakkan, Tokyo.
Ogawa, A. (2001), 'Dumbed-down curriculum for a 'smarter' elite society', *Asahi Evening News*, 21 January.
Ohmori, F. (2000), 'The flawed consensus on education reform', *Japan Echo*, December.
Saitô, T. (2000), *Kikai fubyôdô*, Bungei shunjû, Tokyo.
Sakurai, S. (2001), 'Seiji rikigaku de susumu 'kyôiku kihonhô' rongi', *Sekai*, April.
Satô, M. (2000), *Kyôiku kaikaku o dezain suru*, Iwanami Shoten, Tokyo.
Satô, M. (2001), ' "Kyôiku kaikaku kokumin kaigi hôkoku – kyôiku o kaeru 17 no teigen" o hihan suru', *Sekai*, April.
Schoppa, L. (1991), *Education Reform in Japan: A Case of Immobilist Politics*, Routledge, London.
Sono, A. (2000), 'Kyôiku ni hôshi o toriireyo: ataeru koto no yorokobi o shiru tame ni', *Sankei shinbun*, 12 July.
Wada, H. and Terawaki, K. (2000), *Dôsuru gakuryoku teika*, PHP, Tokyo.

Watanabe, O. (2001), 'Kaiken no ugoki to rendô shite kyôiku kaikaku nerau', *Shûkan kinyôbi*, 9 February.

Yamada, J. (2000), 'Dare no tame no, nan no tame no 'kyôiku' ka: tachidomaru kodomo no koe o kikou', *Gunshuku*, no. 242, December.

Yoneyama, S. (1999), *The Japanese High School: Silence and Resistance*, Routledge, London and New York.

Yotoriyama, Y. (2001), '17 teian ga egaku risô no kodomo-zô', *Shûkan kinyôbi*, 9 February.

12 Conclusion

Jeffrey Graham

Japan is a country that has achieved a great deal in a relatively short period of time. Since the latter part of the nineteenth century Japan has undergone tremendous transformation, and much of this has been the result of purposeful reforms planned and implemented by the Japanese government in relation to a broad array of political, economic and social issues. Foreign intervention during the post-Second World War Occupation also played a major role in reforming the legislative and institutional framework of Japanese society. Since the mid-nineteenth century Japan has been constantly changing, however, only at certain times has this change been transformative, or clearly the result of intervention.

Until recently, Japan exhibited an uncanny ability to adjust to, and successfully meet the challenges of a rapidly changing world, but at the same time maintained, and successfully integrated many characteristics of its traditional culture and social practices. Furthermore, in the course of its modernisation Japan set high standards in terms of industrial and energy efficiency, product quality, export competitiveness, education, technological development and social harmony. To a large extent, the achievements of the Japanese have added weight to expectations that the country will respond to existing problems, especially within its own policy and institutional foundations; and implement necessary reforms.

This book examined key areas of Japan's political economy or socioeconomic institutions which in recent years have been either central to the reform debate or experienced significant pressure for transformation – namely the political system, financial regulation, business management, science and technology, environmental protection, immigration and citizenship. The preceding chapters show that in recent decades, and particularly the 1990s, Japanese policy makers and business leaders have been forced to reassess existing policies, managerial practices and inter-organisational arrangements. While these policies, practices and arrangements had operated successfully in the past, and continue to provide elite groups and other interested parties with direct benefits, reform had become imperative in the context of changing domestic and international political economy. In many instances, however, vested interests have stalled reforms, despite the potential for longer term damage to broader societal interests.

This is not unique to Japan but the result has been to preserve many inappropriate elements of existing systems, especially in the political arena. Fears of diminished political power and the potential backlash of key support groups have frustrated efforts to transform the political system into one focused on policy, rather than one driven by money and riddled with corruption. Similarly, in regard to regulatory reform of the financial sector, the government's handling of the bad loan problem has involved one of delayed intervention for the sake of protecting short-term self-interest. This was illustrated in the way Ministry of Finance officials and politicians prevented the prompt implementation of structural reform for the sake of protecting *amakudari* opportunities and solvency of poorly run businesses in key constituencies.

Clearly, obstacles to reform continue to exist but we can not overlook the many important changes to facilitate adjustment to changing domestic and international circumstances. These reforms have been largely driven by persisting economic, financial and administrative crises. In the area of science and technology, for example, reforms have been a result of public concerns about the safety of an accident prone nuclear power plant industry, the troubled Japanese space programme, and the lack of transparency associated with the regulation and administration of these issues.

Calls for greater transparency and civic participation have also been a central factor behind changes to the way in which environmental policy is developed and administered in Japan. In recent years, pressure from citizens, the media, and other non-government groups led to the introduction of legislation in 1998 to promote the role of non-profit organisations. Furthermore, uncharacteristically for Japan's central bureaucracy, the drafting of the legislation itself involved a process of consultation with citizen groups, as well as parliamentary members.

In addition to internal drivers, external factors also stimulated the debate about reform. In relation to immigration and citizenship, international human rights campaigns, and regimes such as the UN Decade for Women and the International Convention for Refugees, played a role in bringing about policy change in Japan. In the area of international environmental diplomacy, criticism from abroad played a key role in triggering the development and introduction of a broader and more significant policy structure from the late 1980s onwards. Additionally, Japan has been under pressure from the United States since the 1970s to transform its economic and trade policies in order to provide a more open market and fairer trading environment.

In the sphere of political reform, change thus far has been largely superficial and the business of money politics continues as before. In the 1990s, the frequency with which different politicians passed through cabinet positions, and the short-term nature of prime ministerial appointments did little to change the real face of politics in Japan, and only perpetuated the notion of a political system out of touch with its broader electorate and driven by the interests of economically inefficient but politically powerful industrial groups. However, the recent appointment of Koizumi Junichiro to the office of Prime Minister, the unconventional makeup of his cabinet team, along with the broad parameters he established for resolving various political, economic and social ills, provides some hope for the near future. Clearly bold and politically sacrificial decisions will need to be made by current and future administrations in order to carry Japan beyond its current troubled state. The government, and in particular political leaders, must show that they can identify what is necessary in terms of reform, and act with focused intent on addressing those needs. What is of particular concern, though, is that some form of crisis, beyond what many would identify as the current economic and financial crisis, might be needed to drive the transformation of the political system into one which is flexible and efficient enough to address current and future challenges.

Likewise, in regard to financial sector reform, while changes can be observed in terms of the dynamics of financial information flows, Japan has only just begun to effectively deal with regulatory issues. It is necessary for Japan to establish a much more prudent banking system with acceptable levels of transparency in terms of the process of regulation. It is unlikely that the dizzy heights of Japan's banking prowess during 1980s will be revisited for some time. However, the process of integration with overseas financial institutions which began in the 1990s, either through mergers and acquisitions, or other cooperative arrangements, will continue, and that the momentum towards institutions providing a broader and more flexible array of financial services to their clients will add strength and competitiveness to the sector.

In the field of business management, there is speculation that competitive pressures will force Japanese firms to converge on Western models but evidence suggests that the traditional characteristics of the so-called 'J-type' remain largely intact. At the same time, there are indications that increasingly the appraisal of corporate governance and the frequency of senior executives appointments is being determined by Western-style performance criteria. Similarly, in considering the development of human capital, while there is an acute need for reform in the area of Japan's dependence on the established system of universal schooling followed by on-the-job training, there is an emerging focus on the implementation of performance-based remuneration and promotion systems within Japanese firms, as opposed to the traditional life-time employment and seniority-based promotion systems. While the forces of continuity remain dominant within business management and human resource development circles, the combination of weak economic conditions and the onslaught of globalisation pressures have provided added weight to the need for reform within the structure and operation of Japan's private sector organisations, and a large part of this change involves the convergence of Japanese and Western models.

In the postwar period, technological development was a key element of not only Japan's economic achievements, but also its ability to overcome serious environmental problems. To a certain extent this gave the Japanese a sense of confidence in their ability to solve the majority of problems through technocratic policy, and through their established research and development systems. For example, technology was central to Japan's recovery from the devastation of the Second World War, as well as its responses to pollution-related diseases during the 1960s, the energy crises of the 1970s, and the emergence of global-scale environmental problems during the 1980s and 1990s; and more generally Japan's ability to reach the highest levels of international competitiveness in industries such as automobiles and consumer electronics. It is expected that Japan will continue to excel in its application of technology towards meeting economic and environmental challenges. However, we should also expect that in the field of science and technology policy, reform will broaden the extent to which the population embraces new technology not only for the sake of consumer satisfaction but also for the sake of improving labour efficiency, the level of creativity, and the ability of Japan to operate more effectively in an increasingly globalised economy. In the case of environmental issues, the focus of recent policy changes indicates that while money will continue to flow into technological solutions, there will be an increasing and more balanced focus on the role of non-government organisations.

Japan's approach to the issues of immigration and citizenship in recent years is yet to involve wholesale reform of the relevant legislative systems and the positive trends that have emerged have been a result of incremental policy shifts. In terms of enabling the development of greater domestic cultural diversity, and in terms of dealing with the reality of an ageing population and shrinking workforce, it is obvious that reform of Japan's century-old legislative system is critical. Until now, there was only anecdotal evidence to suggest that the Japanese were gradually becoming more accepting and less discriminatory towards the permanent existence of foreign cultures. Furthermore, the Japanese government still appears uncomfortable with the idea of inducing the development of a permanently and increasingly diversified population in terms of race and culture. However, we can expect that the sheer weight of economic necessity and the seemingly unstoppable and accelerating demographic trends of the Japanese population will give Japanese authorities little choice but to significantly increase the inflow of foreign workers and the number of approved permanent residents. If that happens, there might be significant improvements to the rights of ethnic groups and their ability to become fully fledged Japanese citizens. However, it is unlikely that these reforms will be achieved as a result of the same factors, or that they will be implemented concurrently. It is probable that economic pragmatism will drive the former, whereas other international pressures such as stricter international regimes or Japan's aspirations within the UN institutional framework will be the primary factors behind the realisation of the latter.

The process of reform in Japan, and the extent of resultant change, can only be assessed on the basis that better alternatives to the existing features of the political economy are possible and that through the realisation of those alternatives the Japanese population will benefit over the longer term. Most will accept that this is the case, and that during the 1990s the Japanese government started to address perceived systemic and structural problems. This process of reform, however, is only just beginning to produce any real change and we expect that under existing economic and social pressures the momentum towards progressive change will continue to build. It would appear, however, that in relation to many aspects of Japan's current political economy or broader social institutions, most observers are yet to be convinced that the necessary turning point has been reached.

Index

1899 System 164–7
1955 System 164
1999 System 164
401 k-style mutual funds 66
401 k-style portable pension system 66

academic R&D expenditure 185
access via cellular phones 182–3
accounting index 73
Acid Deposition Monitoring Network 143
Action Plan to Arrest Global Warming 134
Ad Hoc Council on Education 192
Ad Hoc Group on Global Environment Problems 129–31
adaptive change 31
administrative reform 179–81; committee 42
administrative structure 20
Africa 176
ageing of the population 169
agency-assigned functions 23
Agency of Natural Resources and Energy 180
aid administration 142
Ainu people, indigenous 165–6; 1997 Cultural Promotion Law 171; struggle for social and civil rights 171
Alien Registration Ordinance of 1947 166
Allen, F. 86

amakudari: of former company managers 206; options for retired bureaucrats 50; practice of 5
America 34, 112
American occupation forces 35
American-style credit cycle 186
American World Wide Web companies 185
Anglo-American-style market-based system 100
anti-graft law 18
anti-monopoly legislation 34
anti-pollution laws and regulations 149
Aoki, M. 80
Arikawa, Y. 78
Asahi Shimbun 20, 152
Asian countries 176; investment relationships 141
Asian financial crisis 1997 31, 38–40
Asian region cooperation initiatives 145
Asia-Pacific Seminar on Climate Change 143
asymmetric information problem 78
Atomic Energy Commission 180
Aum Shinrikyo subway gas attack 20
Australia 150, 160, 164
Australian Conservation Foundation (ACF) 150
Australian Freedom of Information Act 159

baby boomer cohort, ageing of 109
baby boom, postwar 167

'backdoor' entry 16
bad debts 63; definitions of 60; disposal, direct 64, 66; sale of 64, 66
bad loans 64, 77
Bandai 183
bank-based financial system 78
bank-centred governance 72; structures 75
bank–firm relationship 92
bank-guaranteed warrant bonds 74
Banking Bureau 61
banking crisis 6, 30
Bank of Japan (BOJ) 54; Law 62
bankruptcy procedures, invocation of 66; use of 67
banks: accounting standards 61; borrowing 73–4; regulation 68; shareholders 57; shares, price of 57
Basic Environmental Law (BEL) 136–7, 145, 148
Basic Environment Plan (BEP) 148
Basic Law for Environmental Pollution Control 1967 126, 135
Basic Law for Reform of Central Government and Ministries and Agencies 20
Bibi River wetland 156
Big Bang Reformation Plan 39, 41–3; financial reforms 60; objectives of 40
Big Six Corporate Groups 84
birth rate, declining 169
Board of Education of Tokyo Metropolitan Government 206
Bond Issuance Committee 73
bond: issue criteria 73; market 74
bribery, cases of 20
Britain 33–4, 37, 150
Broadbent, J. 152
bubble economy 37, 63, 77
Budget Bureau 58
bullying 205
bureaucrats: adjustment of roles 10; shifting power to politicians 19–25
business: management 216; restructuring 88–92

Canada 142
capital markets 96, 101
career-long employment systems 58
Carlile, L.C. 38, 42
cell telephone services 182
Central Council for Environmental Pollution Control 135
Central Educational Council 199
central financial control 23–4
centre–local conflict of policy interests 25
centre–local relationship, reforming 20
cheque-book diplomacy reputation 132
children: concepts of human rights of 209; and learning 208; problem 209
China 167, 200; migration from 164
Chinese scripts 34
Chitose River Diversion Channel Plan 156
CITES 158
citizen science (*shimin no kagaku*) 156, 160
Citizens Forum on Education Reform 117
citizenship 215; migration policies, changes to 166
civic rights, domestic campaigns 166
Civil Code 153
Civil Rehabilitation Law 66
climate change 139
Cold War 35
Coleman, S. 185–7
collective advancement obsession 118
Committee to Promote Decentralisation 22
communication and information technology (IT), advances in 30
community service 195–6
competitive two-party system 16
computers, use of 188
Conference of the Parties to the UN Framework Convention on Climate Change (COP3) 133
constitutional reform 36
Constitution Research Council 198
contract labour 115
controlling entry, problems of 170

conventional industrial structure 72
Convention on Biological Diversity 133
convoy approach (*goso sendan hoshiki*) 57
corporal punishment 209
corporate borrower 65
corporate contributions 152
corporate finance, changing structure 73–5
corporate governance: Anglo-American models of 5; changing patterns of 75–9; devices 100; effect of insiders' commitment 97–100; reform of 102; structure, emerging 5
corporate linkages 152
corporate rehabilitation 67
corporate restructuring 106; plans 68
Corporation Laws 151
cosmetic multiculturalism 169–74
Council of Ministers for Global Environmental Conservation 130
creativity 117, 186; fostering 200–2
Creativity (*sôzôsei*) Subcommittee 200, 202–3
credit cycle 187
cross-shareholdings among firms 100
Curriculum Council 202

Dai-Ichi Kangyo Bank 78
debt: to equity ratio 80; waivers 67–8; with implicit rescue-insurances (RI) 74; without implicit rescue-insurances (NRI) 74
decentralisation advisory committee 23
Defense Guideline Law 200
delinquent borrowers 55, 63–8
Democratic Party of Japan (DPJ) 19, 45, 47
Democratic Socialist Party (DSP) 48
demographic divide, crossing 167–9
Denmark 173
Dentsu 183
deregulation (*kisei kanwa*) 42
developmental state model 1
Diet 62; behaviour in financial regulation 55; financial policy-making process 68; and local assembly members 19; passive 56–7
diversification 201; trend 88
diversification-oriented firms (DV firms) 89; performance and insider succession in 92
divine wind *(kamikaze)* 40
doctoral degree holders 185
Dore, R. 38
driftnet fishing operations 131
dual candidacy arrangement 16

East Asia 33; role of governments 1
Eastern Europe 33
e-commerce 179; development of 5
economic bubble, bursting of 184
economic downturn 61
economic globalisation 33
economic performance (ROA) 81, 88
Economic Planning Agency (EPA) 62
economic recession 9, 175
economic resurgence 36
Eda Kenji 20
education 2, 208; elite 200–2, 205; nation building 207; non-elite 202–4; reform and human capital formation 116–21; reform initiatives 117; and training systems 106
Education Ministry 198
Education Reform Diet 192
Education Reform Plan 192, 210
Eighth Election System Council 12, 15
e-Japan 184
elder party politicians 15
electoral changes in 1994 15–16
electoral districts, rural and urban 12
electoral reform 10–19
Elliot, L. 149
Emperor Akihito 170, 171
employees: average tenure of 97; commitment to firm 97, 100; stock ownership 97
employment portfolio 203
endangered species, trade in 131
Endo, H. 186
English language: ability 188; corporate training needs 119

entrepreneurialism in students 118
entrepreneurial spirit 41
enterprise unionism 37
entropy index of sample firms 81, 88
entrusted functions (*hotei jutaku jimu*) 23
Environment Agency (EA) 127, 130–2, 135–8; Planning and Coordination Bureau 131
Environmental Congress for Asia and the Pacific 143
environmental diplomacy, policy foundations of 126–33
Environmental Impact Assessment (EIA) 156; law 6, 137, 159
environmental management 6
environmental non-governmental organisations (NGOs) 148; constraints faced by 157–9; cross-national membership of 150; and government 148; Japanese 149–52
environmental policy: agendas, changing 125; evolution of 6; making 2; reforms 139
environmental politics, history 149
environmental pollution 136
environmental projects 142
environmental protection: activities, 144; approach 139; developing countries, funding 129; initiatives 143; North–South tensions 132
Environment Ministry (EM) 138, 143, 145, 152–3, 159
equality of opportunity 194
Esaki Reona 193, 198, 201
ethical standards 17
ethnic homogeneity 169–74
ethnicity 173
Europe 132, 183
European Union nations 134
exceptional promotion 83

Fair Trade Commission 34
fair trade practices 35
Fakuoka 193
family registration, system of (*koseki*) 165

Federation of Economic Organisations *see* Keidanren
female entrants to labour market 116
female work force 188
financial and technological support 144
Financial Reconstruction Commission (FRC) 54
Financial Revitalisation Law (FRL) 60
financial sector: consolidation and restructuring of 61; problems 63; reform 216
Financial Services Agency (FSA) 54, 62–3
Financial Supervisory Agency (FSA) 40, 54, 60
financial system reform 54; Act 75
Finger, M. 149
fingerprinting of permanent residents 166
firm performance (OPR) 86
firm-specific management 112–14
the First Year for Education Reform Initiative 192
foreign aid programme 139
foreigners, registered 168
foreign permanent residents 173
foreign populations, resident 172
foreign pressure, *gaiatsu* 36
foreign skilled workers 187
former colonial subjects 166, 172
Former Natives Protection Act 165–6
Framework Convention on Climate Change 1992 133–4
France 173, 184
Freedom of Information (FOI) Law 159
freeter phenomenon of young people 114
French nuclear tests 189
Fuji Bank 78
Fujimae tidal flat 155
Fundamental Law of Education 1947 196–9
future skills base 114–16

Gale, D. 86
gender stereotypes 170

General Federation of Labour Unions
  (*Rengô*) 149, 155
German *Gastarbeiter* system 170
Germany 112, 150, 173, 184–5
Gifu 25
global environmental issues,
  importance of Japan's role 138
global environmental management,
  politics of 148
Global Environment Information
  Centre (GEIC) 157–8
Global Environment Protection Board
  131
Global Environment Research 134
globalisation 30, 169
Glova 119
Gotoda Masaharu 15
governance structure, effect of 94–5
government–NGO relationships 152
grass roots fears of foreigner crime 175
Grassroots Grant Assistance 150
Great Hanshin earthquake 20
Great Stagnation 35
Green Aid 142
Green Day 151
Green Donation programme 151
greenhouse gases (GHGs) 134
Greenpeace Japan 149, 153
green political parties 2
greenwashing 152
Green Week 151
greying of Japan 168
gross domestic R&D expenditure to
  GDP, ratio of 184
Group of Seven industrialised
  countries 65
gyosei kaikaku (administrative
  reform) 10

Hamanaka Hideichiro 63–4
Harding, J. 167
Hashimoto Ryûtaro 135; government
  49; Prime Minister 39, 41
Hata Tsutomu 44; cabinet 22
Hatoyama Ichiro 12
Hatoyama Yukio 19
H-II rocket 180
Hinomaru 199

Hino Motors 83
Hiroshima 189
Hirota, S. 77, 86
Hitachi 181, 206
Hitotsubashi University 200
Hokkaido 156
Honda 41, 187
Hong Kong 183
Hoshi Takeo 40, 49
Hosokawa Morihiro 14; cabinet 22;
  leadership of 15
Hrebener, R.J. 26
human: capital formation 107–9;
  mobility 176; movement 164
Humanity (*ningensei*) Subcommittee
  194
human resource management (HRM):
  practices 106; strategies 2

Ikuta, T. 19
illegal immigrants 164, 168
immigration 7, 215; and citizenship
  163, 217; controls 164; new
  approach to 168; policies 2
Immigration Ordinance 165
i-mode system 183
Imperial Ordinance No. 352 164
imperial subjects: from external
  territories (*gaichi*) 165; from
  metropolitan Japan (*naichi*) 165
implicit rescue-insurance 75
Independent Administrative Institutions
  (IAIs) 180
Industrial Bank of Japan 78
industrial waste: disposal facilities 25;
  dumping operations 131
Information Disclosure Act
  (IDA) 159
information disclosure: new legal
  requirements for 62; pressures on
  private sector actors 60–2
information dynamics, shift in 59–63
information technology (IT) based
  economy 2
initial public offer (IPO) firms 84
innovation 41; barriers to 121
innovative workforce 186
Inoguchi, T. 118

insider succession 82, 86, 92; effect of employees 98–9; probability of 100; seniority rule for 97
Institute of Labour 112, 119
Institute of Space and Astronautical Sciences (ISAS) 180
institutional inertia 19
Integrated Study programme 209
inter-governmental relations and financial regulation 55–9
Interim Report of the National Commission 22, 197, 199
internal governance mechanism 96, 101
international competitiveness 41
International Convention for Refugees 166, 215
international environmental diplomacy 132, 144
international environmental issues, fundamental legislative and administrative change 135–9
international environmental policies 125–6, 145
international human rights 166
internationalisation 118
International Monetary Fund (IMF), structural adjustment programmes 33
International Whaling Commission (IWC) 128
internet: businesses, advantage of 189; rise of 182
Ireland 173
iron triangle 179
Isahaya Bay 156
Ito Masayoshi 15
IT: revolution 34; society 40; Strategy Council 116

Japan Agenda 21 148
Japan Bankers' Federation 63
Japan branch of Friends of the Earth (FOEJ) 149, 153
Japan branch of the World Wide Fund for Nature (WWFJ) 149, 153
Japanese auto manufacturers 187
Japanese banks 55; reform of 54, 68
Japanese Big Bang 75
Japanese bubble economy 31

Japanese business and industry 200
Japanese Committee for Economic Development (*Keizai dôyûkai*) 42, 116, 200, 203, 205
Japanese Constitution 36
Japanese economy 37–8, 75
Japanese educational institutions 117
Japanese education: cleansing of 195; reform 192; and training 121; underlying principle of 208
Japanese electoral system 56
Japanese Federation of Employers Association (*Nikkeiren*) 200, 203
Japanese finance: policy breakdown 54; regulation 68; sector 58, 62
Japanese firms: bank-centred corporate governance structure of 73; incentive system of 80; institutional characteristics of 72; presidential turnover in 79–84, 97
Japanese history 34
Japanese HR: negative social consequences of 115; practice 108
Japanese human capital formation 106, 120; model 107
Japanese industries 37–9, 62; long-term competitiveness of 49
Japanese investments in IT 184
Japanese *keiretsu* groups 78
Japanese large firms 78
Japanese manufacturing firms, financial instruments issued 74
Japanese mass media 106
Japaneseness, definitions of 165
Japanese political economy 3, 37; continuity 31–5; positive features of 31; reform 31–5
Japanese settlers in Brazil and Peru, descendants of 167
Japanese society 2; multi-cultural character of 163
Japanese Society for History Textbook Reform 197, 199
Japanese space programme 180
Japanese Supreme Court 173
Japanese voters 173

Japan Fund for the Global Environment (KFGE) 151
Japan Institute of Labour 114
Japan New Party (JNP) 14
Japan Socialist Party (JSP) 44, 48
Japan Syndication and Loan-trading Association (JSLA) 65
Japan Vocational Ability Development Association 111
J-firms converging on Anglo-American system 72
job: opportunities, lack of 203; rotation system 108, 112
Johnson, C. 19
J-type corporate system 79, 101
J-type firm, change in 72
Jus Sanguinis 165
juvenile delinquency 117

Kaifu Toshiki 14, 135; government 12
Kajita Eiichi 198
Kanemaru Shin 13
kan kan settai (local officials entertaining central bureaucrats) 20, 24
Kanomi, S. 186
kara shutcho (paper business trips by local officials) 20, 24
kasumigaseki bureaucrats 20, 26
Kato, A. 78
Kato Koichi 43, 45, 49
Katsuta Kichirô 196
Kawamura, K. 86
Keidanren (Federation of Economic Organisations) 38, 42, 47, 149, 155, 158–60, 207; Personnel Education Committee 200
Keidanren Nature Conservation Fund (KNCF) 151
Keynesian liberalism 33
Kimigayo 199
Kôeki Hôjin (public service corporations) 151
Koike, K. 108, 113
Koizumi 46, 49, 117; Prime Minister 3
Kômeitô 48, 173

Korea 165
Korean peninsula crisis 20
kôza or chair system 186–7
Krauss, E.S. 19
Krugman, 49
KSD foundation 17
Kyoto Conference on Climate Change 126, 133–5, 145
Kyoto Initiative 134
Kyoto Protocol 134
Kyushu–Okinawa Summit 170

labour cost flexibility 115
labour market: collapse of 203; liquidity in 100
Lake Utonai 156
landfill site 155
Latin America 33
Laws for Financial System Reformation (LFSR) 40
Law to Promote Decentralisation 22
Liberal Democratic Party (LDP) 2, 10, 13, 43, 48, 55, 67–8, 152, 164, 193; education *zoku* 197; Environment Committee 129; fall from government 24, 26; leaders 56; policy abnegation 44; politicians 173; support base 68
liquidation of the borrower 66–7
loan forgiveness 67–8
local functions (*jichijimu*) 23
local governments, role of 136
local voting rights 173
Lockheed scandal 13
logit model, concept of 85
Long-term Credit Bank of Japan (LTCB) 64
long-term employment 88, 113
long-term market share 37
low cost labour 170
Lower House (House of Representatives) 11; Budget Committee 136; election 14; reform package 15
loyalty to the political order 173

MacAvoy, P. 50
Machimura Nobutaka 198

main bank: monitoring 80; and portfolio investors 92; relationship 76, 93, 96; role in corporate governance 78; system 78, 100
Maki Town 25
management system 111
managerial turnovers 84–8
Manchuria 170
market-based and arms length system 78
market-based structures 75
markets, liberalisation of 118
mass migration 169
material industry 88
Matsushita 181
media hysteria 174
Meiji period 34; nation-building 164
meritocracy 116
metropolitan areas 16
Middle East 176
migrants: crime 164; from Korea and Taiwan 166; recruitment of 170
migration control 168, 170
migratory birds, protection of 128
Mikiso, Hane 41
Miki, Takeo 13
Ministry of Construction 136
Ministry of Economy, Trade and Industry (METI) 180, 184
Ministry of Education, Culture, Sports, Science and Technology (MEXT) (*Monbu Kagakushô*) 121, 171, 180, 192, 199, 207, 210; web sites of 189
Ministry of Finance (MOF) 20, 40, 56–7, 61–2, 68, 154, 215; Banking Bureau 58–9; discrediting of 62; Financial System Planning Bureau 54; implicit guarantee of banks 65; jurisdictional monopoly on financial regulation 59; policy failures 62; renamed Treasury Ministry 42; Securities Bureau 58
Ministry of Foreign Affairs (MFA) 136, 138, 151
Ministry of Health, Labour and Welfare (MHLW) 155
Ministry of International Trade and Industry (MITI) 136, 159, 182
Ministry of International Trade and Industry (MITT) 62
Ministry of Justice 170; second Migration Plan 169
Ministry of Land, Infrastructure and Transport (MLIT) 155–6
Ministry of Posts and Telecommunications 151
Ministry of Transport (MOT) 156
minke whales, harvesting of 131
Mitake Town 25
Mitsubishi Sogo Kenjyujo 84
Mitsui 78
Miyauchi Yoshihiko 42
Miyazawa Kiichi: government 14; Prime Minister 136
Mizuho Holdings 78
money-for-favours corruption 11
money-politics problem 18
moral and behavioural training 202
moral education 195
Mori, Yoshiro 15, 197–200; cabinet 117; government, reshuffle of 198; Prime Minister 17, 39, 43, 184, 193
Morris-Suzuki, T. 149
Mowery, D.C. 184
multiculturalism 176
multi-member constituencies (MMCs) 11
multi-member districts (MMDs) 11; system 18
multi-member electoral system 44
multivariate logit model analysis 84
municipalities 24
Muramatsu, M. 19

Nagasaki 189
Nagoya 155
Nakatani Iwao 37–8
national anthem 16
national civil servants 179
National Commission on Education Reform 192–4, 203; Final Report of 199, 204
National Diet, joint resolution on decentralisation 22

national education system 107
national employers federation (Nikkeiren) 112
national flag 16
national inclusion and exclusion 176
National Institute for Environmental Studies 134
nationalism and corporatism 208
nationalistic education 193
Nationality Law 7, 166; of 1899 165; of 1950, revised 165; first 164
nationality laws 172
National Space Development Agency (NASDA) 180
national universities 121
national values 195
National Wildlife Federation 150
Natural Resources Defense Council 150, 152
Nature Conservancy 150, 152
Nature Conservation Bureau 153
Nature Conservation Council 135
nature conservation, legislation 127
Nature Conservation Society of Japan (NCSJ) 149, 153
Net-*batsu* 184
Netherlands, the 173
New Deal economic policies 33
new economy 181, 185, 188
New Komeito 49, 198–9
New Liberal Club 13
new postwar election law 166
new *zaibatsu* 184
New Zealand 173
NGO Forum Japan 151
Niigata 25, 193
nikkei Peruvians and Brazilians 168
Nikkei Shimbun 152
Nikkei Stock Index 54, 63–4
Nikkyôso (Japan Teachers Union) 200
Nippon Credit Bank (NCB) 64
the Nippon Foundation 196
Nishio Kanji 197
Nissan Motors 187, 206
non-citizen permanent residents 166
non-governmental organisations (NGOs) 2, 131; corporate legal status 158; as disseminators of information 160; field projects in developing countries 151; formation, barriers to 159; international community 143; policy advisory roles for 157; smaller 153
non-performing debt, sale of 64–6
non-performing loans 31, 55–6
non-profit organisations (NPO): legislation 154; support measures 154
Northeast Asian Conference on Environmental Protection 143
Notre Dame Women's College of Kyoto 196
Nova English conversation school group 119
NPO Law 152, 155, 158–9
NPO/NGO Tax 151
NTT DoCoMo 181; i-mode system 182; monopolistic role in telecommunications 183

Obuchi 197; administration 63; cabinet 117; coalition government 18; government 40; Prime minister 43, 192–3
Odagiri, H. 187
Official Development Assistance (ODA) programme 126, 136; environmental 138; environmental policy and administrative reform 140–1; expansion of 130; pledge 133; reform and Japan's regional role 139–44
Ohmori, F. 210
Okinawa 170, 189; prefectural government 25
Okinawan history and culture 170
on-the-job training (OJT) 106, 217; for blue-collar workers 108
open migration policy 176
ordinary profit ratio (OPR) 85
ORIX Corporation 42
Osaka 193
Otake Hideo 15, 17
outsider succession 86
overseas research facilities 187

ownership structure 78, 92–3; main-bank relationship and 76
Ozawa Ichiro 14–15, 18, 44, 46–7

Pacific: Century 1–2; War 165, 172
parasite singles 114
Patrick, H. 40, 49
Pekkanen, R. 155
Pempel, T.J. 47
pension funds 63
permanent residents and voting rights 172–4
Persian Gulf crisis 132
personnel costs, reduction of 203
Peru hostage crisis 20
Petcher, K. 185
pharmacology 187
Philippines 167
Police Agency 175
policy reforms, opposition to 56
Policy Research Committee 48
political dictatorships 33
political economy 160, 214
political reform 3, 9, 216
politicians/bureaucrats power distribution 19–20
politics of regulatory reform 42–9
pollution control standards 127
pollution-related disease victims 126
population pyramid, reshaping 167
Porter, M.E. 119, 181, 185
portfolio investors 79, 96, 102
Postal Savings system 151
post-bubble period 67
post-Second World War Occupation 214
postwar Occupation period 165
price keeping operations 63
Prime Minister's Technology Advisory Council 186
Princen, T. 149
private bureaucratic information 57
private schools, promotion 204
private sector financial institutions 57
profitability index 73
promotional competition 88
proportional representation (PR) 12, 30
protectionism 32
public schools, rationalising 204

public service corporations (*Kôeki Hôjin*) 153–4

radioactive wastes, low-level 131
Ramos Rui 163
Ramsar Convention 158; 5th Conference of Parties (CoP) 156
Ramseyer, J.M. 19
real estate investment trusts (REIT) 65
real estate market 65
recession and employment scarcity 109–10
Recruit Cosmos scandal 14, 17
reform: agenda 39; to civic rights 174; debate 35–42, 215; momentum for 13–14; movement features of 27; obstacles to 215; process of 218
reformists, ex-LDP 14–15
Reform Plan 2001 205, 209; promotion of nationalistic education 194–200; restructuring schools 204; stratification of education 200–4
regulatory reform 3, 30, 43; committee 37, 40, 42; government White Paper 50
Renault 187
rescue merger (*kyusai gappei*) 57
research and development (R&D) 183–5; consortia 187
Resolution and Collection Corporation (RCC) 65
Ricoh 82
Rio de Janeiro 132, 148
Rosenberg, N. 184
Rosenbluth, F.M. 19
ruling triad 152
rural–urban imbalance 17

Sagawa Kyubin scandal 13, 17
Saitô Takao 201, 203, 207
Sakigake (Harbinger Party) 14
Sakura Bank 78
Sankei Shinbun 196
the Sasakawa Foundation 196
Satô, M. 195, 203
Save Fujimae Association 156
School Education Law 206
School Education Subcommittee 205

school: hidden functions of 207; non-attendance 205; zoning 205
Schoppa, L. 193–4
Science and Technology Agency (STA) 180; Atomic Energy Bureau and Nuclear Safety Bureau 180; survey 187
science: technology and gender 188–9; technology and R&D 189; technology and the new economy 179; and technology workforce 185–7
Second Science and Technology Basic Plan 180
Second World War 35
seiji kaikaku (political reform) 9–10, 20, 26
seiji kenkin 26
Self-Defence Forces 174
Seligmann, A.L. 18
seniority-based insider: succession 96; turnover 80
seniority-based wages 108–9, 111; structure 37
service sector 179
Shinseito (Renewal Party) 14
Shinshinto (New Frontier Party, NFP) 44, 46–7
Shogun 43
Shunya, Y. 188
shûshin (moral training) of prewar Japan 195
Sierra Club 150, 152
Singapore 184
single-member districts (SMD) 11, 30; proportional representation system 18
single non-transferable votes (SNTV) 11
Sino-Japanese citizenship 165
Sino-Japanese War 164
skill: attainment of graduates 119; formation thesis 113
Sklair, L. 152
small-and medium-sized enterprises (SMEs) 40
social inequity, structures of 170
social learning 149
social protest 189
socio-economic institutions 214
Softbank Corporation 184

Sogo Department Store 66
Sohyo 48
Sono Ayako 196–8
Sony 41, 83, 181
Sony Play Station 2 181, 184
South Korea 200
South Koreans 189
specialisation-oriented firms (SP firms) 89, 92
specialisation trends 88
Specified Nonprofit Activities (NPO Law) 154
speculative asset bubble 54
Statement of Forest Principles 133
state subsidy system 16
stock market, plunge in 2001 62
stock prices 64
Stockwin, J.A.A. 18
streaming of education 202
student-centred education 209
students, problem 208
succession pattern 83–4
Sumitomo Bank 78
supply-side economics 33
sustainable growth trajectory 40
Suzuka International University 196
Sweden 173

Taiwan 164, 183–4
Takemura Masahisa 135
Takemura Masayoshi 14
Takeshita Noboru 129, 135–6
Tamagotchi 183
Tanaka Kakuei 12–13
tax benefits 154
Tax Bureau 58
teachers: evaluation 206; problem 208
technological development 217
technological innovation 88
technology transfer 135
telecommunications 179
temporary labour 115
tenancy laws, amendments to 65
tenure of former president 93; effect of 86; prolonged 92
territorial redistribution of power 10
Tôkai-mura 180
Tokugawa period 43

Tokushima 25
Tokyo 25, 193, 195; Chamber of Commerce and Industry 206; Conference on the Global Environment and Human Response Towards Sustainable Development 129; Governor Ishihara Shintarô 174–6; Metropolitan Government 210; Stock Exchange 63; third airport for 25; University 117, 202
Toshiba 82–3, 181
Toyota 187; Foundation 151; Motor Corporation 38, 112, 181
trade: liberalisation, Kennedy Round of talks 32; policies 216; restrictive practices 32
trade-related structural adjustment programmes 32
trainee system 168
transboundary environmental problems, issues of 127
Treaty of San Francisco 166
tropical deforestation 129, 131
Trust Fund Bureau 63
Tsugawa, A. 186
turnover performance 93

Unequal Treaties, dismantling of 164
unincorporated organisations (*Jinkaku naki Shadan*) 153
United Kingdom (UK) 142, 150, 173, 184–5
United Nations (UN) 126; Convention on the Rights of the Child 209; Decade for Women 166, 215; Environment Programme 127; Universal Declaration on Human Rights 166
United Nations Conference on Environment and Development (UNCED) 132–3, 142, 145, 148
United Nations Conference on the Human Environment (UNCHE) 1972 127–8
United States (US) 33, 37, 50, 150, 128, 160, 164, 184–5, 215; Air Base in Yokota 25; Freedom of Information Act 159; military, land leases 25; new economy dynamism of 106; regulatory reforms 30; Savings and Loan crisis 65
universal schooling, system of 217
universities, role in HR development 120
the University Council 118–19; 1997 report 120
University of Tokyo 189
unsecured bond 74–5
Upper House elections 59
urban consumers 47
Utopia Politics Study Group 12, 14

voluntary informal groups 153

Wada Terawaki 204
Watanabe Osamu 200
West Germany 142
Wetlands Action Network (JAWAN) 149, 153, 156
whaling, moratorium on commercial 128
white-collar skills: Business-Career system for appraising 111; formation and performance 108, 110–11
Wild Bird Society of Japan (WBSJ) 149, 153, 156
Wilderness Society in Australia 150
women: in research 187; scientists 186; in senior positions 188
WWF 152

xenophilia 7
xenophobia 7; and foreigner crime 174–6

Yamada, M. 114
Yamaguchi Jiro 17
Yanagisawa Hakuo 65
Yasuda, H. 187
Young Diet Members for Political Reform 14
young *nisei* 14
youth, problem of 203

zainichi Koreans and Taiwanese 172